John Senior

NETWORKS
for the 1990s

edited by Ray Reardon

Publications

1987 London

British Library Cataloguing in Publication Data

Networks for the 1990s.
  1. Computer networks
  I. Reardon, Ray
  004.6 TK5105.5
  ISBN 0–86353–131–8

Library of Congress Cataloging in Publication Data

ISBN: 0–470–21026–5

Distributed in the United States of America by John Wiley & Sons Inc. 605 Third Avenue, New York, NY 10158–0012.

Typeset and printed in the United Kingdom by H Charlesworth & Co Ltd, Huddersfield.

Online Publications
Pinner Green House, Ash Hill Drive, Pinner, Middlesex HA5 2AE, UK
The Publishing Division of Online International Ltd, London

Contents

1
Introduction

Online International has organised scores of international conferences concerned with telecommunications and networking at which many of the world's most authoritative and experienced specialists have presented papers. The library of published proceedings now comprises many hundreds of such papers.

From this large repertoire, 25 papers have been selected from 12 recent conferences, written by more than 30 authors from 10 different countries.

The papers were selected for their particular relevance to the overall theme of *Networks for the 1990s* and the authors are all among the leaders in their field. As such this book provides a unique collection of leading-edge thought, prediction and experience. The facts and opinions expressed are those of the individual authors themselves and not those of the editor or the publisher.

The compilation is organised in four main sections:

> Transmission Technology
> Architecture & Protocols
> Application & Implementation
> Management & Operation

each preceded by an additional introductory paper by the editor setting the scene for the papers that follow.

Transmission Technology

Major Directions in Networking Technology

The introductory paper by Ray Reardon, examines the technological outlook for the 1990s and some of the major implications facing the corporate network planner.

ISDN Evolution in France: The Will to Innovate

Jean-Louis Pernin and Arthur J Schwartz present the operating concepts of the French network in several key areas of ISDN implementation: multiservice offerings, ubiquitous communication resources, and universal user access. The status and outlook for the RENAN pilot project is also described.

The ISDN Concept of the Deutsche Bundespost

Peter Kahl outlines the likely evolution of ISDN in the Federal Republic of Germany from today's non-integrated and experimental services, through the pilot services of the late 1980s, to the integrated and broadband services envisaged in the 1990s.

The UK ISDN: Interworking Features

Keith Gleen presents the UK ISDN, from the user's viewpoint. He examines the pilot ISDN access mechanisms, how the pilot network interworks with existing networks and services, and how the pilot services will gradually be replaced with access mechanisms corresponding to the I-series of CCITT recommendations.

ISDN in the USA: The Opportunity Begins

Thomas J Herr and Thomas J Plevyak write from an AT&T viewpoint. The thesis is that ISDN is a rapidly approaching reality. It brings with it numerous opportunities for end-users, network providers, and equipment and systems suppliers. The evolutionary plan towards Universal Information Services is described in addition to focussing on end-user research and field trials. Realising the full opportunity will require industry-wide commitment and studies of cost-effective network applications.

Integrated Broadband Communications: The Programme RACE

Dr Roland P O Hueber outlines and discusses the European Community's programme intended to encourage and develop very high speed advanced telecommunications in Europe. The action is the result of intensive collaboration of telecommunication operators and industry in defining future requirements and opportunities for cooperation in developing advanced telecommunications technology at a Community level.

Satellites: The Evolution of the VSAT

T Michael Kelley discusses the reasons why Very Small Apperture Terminals (VSATs) represent an area of rapid growth in satellite communications. The technical and operational features of VSAT networks that make them an attractive alternative to traditional terrestrial transmissions are outlined and some typical applications described.

Wavelength Division Multiplexing in Optical Fibre LANs

John M Senior, Stewart D Cusworth and Alan Ryley review techniques by which several optical wavelengths can be multiplexed and transmitted in parallel on a single fibre channel. Wavelength Division Multiplexing and its possible application within optical fibre LANs is discussed and consideration given to a novel token-passing multichannel access protocol.

Architecture and Protocols

Open Systems: Will The Future Ever Arrive?

The introductory paper by Ray Reardon raises the paradox that the 'nice thing about standards is that there are so many to choose from'. He goes on to identify some of the more positive trends that will determine the practicalities of open and interconnected systems in the 1990s.

Message Handling Systems as the Basis for Tele-Information Services

Dr Peter H M Vervest discusses the role of message handling as a basis for a wide range of tele-information services. At its most basic, electronic mail can be little more than a person-to-person correspondence system. However it can also be used as a means of offering access to remote information and to perform information transactions such as financial funds transfer, ordering, logistics and decision support. This paper (based on Vervest's book 'Innovation in Electronic Mail': North Holland, Elsevier Science Publishers,

Amsterdam 1987) describes the OSI/MHS model, why it is important and how it can serve as the guideline for the interworking between existing and new tele-information services.

FTAM: OSI File Transfer Access & Management

S Joe Hielscher, discusses the FTAM Draft International Standard and reviews the current status of implementation profiles of FTAM defined jointly by Manufacturing Automation Protocol (MAP), Technical and Office Protocol (TOP) and the US National Bureau of Standards. Protocols for the transfer and manipulation of file data between open systems have been under definition in ISO for several years. FTAM is one of the first expected international standards for the OSI Presentation Layer.

SNA Trends

Anton Meijer reviews the past, present and future of IBM's Systems Network Architecture, the most widely used data networking architecture in the world, and a *de facto* industry standard used by many other manufacturers for interfacing their products. He also discusses how IBM is moving SNA towards coexistence with OSI.

Interworking with LU Type 6.2

Chris Mairs introduces the key concepts of LU 6.2 and reviews the possible provision of an LU 6.2 services boundary to the OSI Application Layer. He also discusses LU 6.2 to OSI gateways and considers application access to OSI and SNA networks from a single system.

The MAP/TOP Initiative

Nicholas C L Beale discusses General Motors' MAP and Boeing's TOP which are becoming widely accepted as pragmatic user specified subsets selected from the wide range of Open Systems standards confronting the practising network manager. He describes their current status and the work of the European MAP Users Group.

The Emergence of TCP/IP

Steve Spanier discusses the history and recent emergence of Transmission Control Protocol/Internet Protocol (TCP/IP). Its features are described and reasons for its success with respect to other current protocols are presented. TCP/IP's flexibility is illustrated with the description of a method that provides an easy migration path from TCP/IP to future protocols. Finally TCP/IP's relation to OSI is addressed.

Standards & Compatibility in LAN Integration

Dr Gee Swee Poo, considers the problems associated with interconnecting LANs. Even though it may be possible to interconnect a wide range of devices to a LAN, it is not certain that the devices will be able to communicate cooperatively. This is due to the fact that there is, as yet, no widely accepted standard for higher level communication protocols. The problems of network integration are addressed in relation to the standards and compatibility issues currently facing CSMA/CD baseband LANs.

Application and Implementation

Corporate Networks

The introductory paper by Ray Reardon considers the corporate network both as a corporate utility and as a fundamental corporate asset. He describes the major drivers of corporate networking and identifies some of the issues for the future.

ISDN Basic Access Terminal Adaptors

Paul Freuck and John Kutney address both the technical and marketing issues and trade-offs which have to be considered in defining the terminal adaptor products needed for the application and implementation of ISDN. During the introduction of ISDN and for a number of years afterwards, it will be necessary to adapt existing devices to ISDN. Terminal adaptors will permit existing terminal and data network devices to interface to ISDN at the Basic Access S/T reference point.

EDI & Inter-Enterprise Systems

This a composite paper based on three separate presentations given by Dr Karol Szlichcinski, Nigel Fenton, and Bob Holmes. Firstly it assesses the benefits of electronic data interchange between organisations in theory and in practice. It then reviews the progress towards the data formatting standards that are necessary to make EDI a reality. Finally it describes a case study of paperless trading in the shipping industry.

X.400 Implementation for International Communications

Hiroshi Kurihara and Katsushi Sato describe the message communication system developed by KDD, the international telecommunication carrier of Japan, according to the CCITT X.400 series recommendations. The paper presents the features of the new system, and the possible applications to international commercial telecommunication services, including media conversion between telex, teletex, and facsimile.

Applications for Facsimile

Lester Davis discusses the rapidly growing area of image transmission. A high data rate digital transmission medium, such as ISDN, is a natural network for the transmission of facsimile data. The raster method of scanning produces data normally unrecognisable for information content and generated in large quantities. New transmission facilities will enable higher quality messages and shorter transmission times, plus new applications and features. The nature of facsimile equipment and the characteristics of Group 4 are described.

An IBM Token Ring Backbone Facility

Norman Housley offers a case study of experience in implementing and operating an inter-building, campus-wide token ring backbone supporting a wide range of different vendor equipment at the University of Toronto. A number of significant planning, technical and managerial factors are highlighted.

Primary Rate LAN Interconnection for Office Applications

Peter Clark describes an Alvey-sponsored collaborative project conducting research into the use of local area networks interconnected by a prototype primary rate integrated services digital network for office applications. He outlines the 'Unison' project, its objectives, how the LANs will be interfaced to the network, and how the facilities provided relate to the needs of the modern office.

Management and Operation

Management & Organisational Issues

The introductory paper by Ray Reardon, addresses the general management and organisational issues in running networks. The increasing move towards establishing a single organisational focus responsible for all areas of an organisation's communications and networking needs is discussed together with the role and activities of such a group.

Creating a Communications Strategy

David Honey starts with the premise that modern communication services are no longer simply a means of reducing costs or improving efficiency; for many businesses, communications are about survival in an increasingly competitive environment. The need to consider communications as part of an overall corporate strategy is presented, together with what are seen as the key ingredients of a communications strategy relevant to corporate networking.

Network Management with NetView

David Foster considers the tools necessary for managing an operational network. To supply the high quality of service needed by the users of corporate information networks requires that the network manager be provided with the necessary skilled people and managers. They in turn need applications to enable them to control the network service and to obtain the information they need for controlling and reviewing the design of the network. The paper describes how IBM's NetView helps meet that requirement, and relates NetView to the IBM Open Network Management Architecture.

Security in Open Systems

Michael Harrop discusses the very important topic of security. The development of a security architecture specification for open systems has been under consideration for some time in the relevant ISO study groups. The paper reviews the background and progress of the work and also looks at some of the more general issues relating to the provision of security services in an open environment.

Justification of E-Mail & Conference Systems

Bengt A Olsen raises the issue of justification. Electronic communication increases the speed of information flow but also contributes to information overload. One of the main features of computer conference systems is the ability to cope with information overload. Electronic communication is playing an increasingly important role in society. Many different areas of application exist and new ones will appear – but how cost effective is this new technology in organisations? Are the benefits worth the cost? These problems are addressed through a number of examples.

The Seven Rules for Success

Neil Farmer, in the final paper in this compilation, offers guidance for successful implementation and acceptance. Experience of office systems over the last five years has too often been disappointing, with electronic messaging developing much more slowly that was often predicted. By examining the experiences of more than 400 organisations, seven key rules for achieving both user acceptance and justification for major investment in office systems have been identified. These rules sometimes run counter to the often naive assumptions made during the early to mid-1980s. The failures of the past need not be repeated.

TRANSMISSION
TECHNOLOGY

2

Major Directions in Networking Technology

RAY REARDON

Technology and speed

During the 1960s and 1970s we tended to be constrained by the limits of telecommunciations technology. Certainly dramatic progress was made, but the transmission speeds available to the corporate network planner were always more of a constraint than data processing speeds and capacity. This changed dramatically in the early 1980s as modem-less transmission facilities in the kilobit and megabit ranges became available. The further good news is that the ability of technology to deliver more speed is not likely to slow down in the 1990s.

> Silicon based processors have been giving a year-on-year price performance benefit of 25% per annum for two decades and this trend will continue, leading to multi-gigabyte/gigaflop machines in the 1990s.

> Typical digital transmission speeds, previously increasing more slowly than processors, are accelerating rapidly:
> | | | |
> |---|---|---|
> | 1960–1980 | Speeds increased | × 10 |
> | 1970–1990 | Speeds increasing | × 100 |
> | 1980–2000 | Speeds projection | × 1000 |

> Techniques for optically amplifying and regenerating signals along fibres are advancing rapidly, as are electrical arc techniques for producing high quality termination of fibre ends to facilitate high performance jointing.

> Higher frequency Ku-band (14 GHz up and 11/12 GHz down) transmission on satellites, enabling much smaller and cheaper dishes on user premises is leading to a resurgence of interest in satellites for business use.

> A new generation of ceramic superconductors is being developed that can operate at the temperature of liquid nitrogen (or higher) rather than the more difficult and expensive-to-achieve temperatures asociated with liquid helium. As well as increasing the speed of mainframe processors, superconductivity could lead, for instance, to very high efficiency antennae.

> Laser beams are being used for 'contactless' measurement of trillionth-second electrical pulses in circuits no wider than one micron.

> Multiplexers are being developed that work at the wavelength of light itself. These enable several optical sources operating at different wavelengths to be

combined into a composite signal for transmission down a single optical fibre and subsequently demultiplexed into the original constituent wavelengths.

Prototype gallium arsenide based opto–electronic receiver chips are being developed which allow optical laser signals to be recognised and translated into electronic computing/switching signals *on the same chip*.

What this all indicates is that while transmission speeds were lagging behind processing speeds, both are now advancing synergistically in parallel. Corporate network planners can confidently expect a decade of unprecedented opportunity limited solely by human imagination or, more seriously perhaps, by protectionist tariffing and/or political limitations in various countries.

ISDN and beyond

One of the most significant trends is the evolution of Integrated Services Digital Networks (ISDN: Integration Subscribers DO Want). Each major PTT has well–defined plans for implementing such services, initially as limited area pilots but extending in geographic scope and technical function into and through the 1990s.

British Telecom are offering switchable integrated digital access (IDA) in single or 30 units of 64 Kbits/s directly into the BT network in many areas of the country.

In eight cities in North–west France, the French RENAN project is intended to provide comprehensive ISDN user access and is expected to reach Paris in 1988/9.

In Germany the Deutsche Bundespost is building its ISDN project initially on Mannheim and Stuttgart and then plans to extend the service to another eight large cities throughout the country.

In the United States, operating companies such as Illinois Bell are carrying out field trials together with large users like McDonalds.

Quite apart from publicly provided ISDN offerings, large users of telecommunications are increasingly bringing together their own critical mass into privately leased, integrated digital megaspeed 'highways' (1.54 Mbits/s T1 circuits in the USA, and 2.048 Mbits/s in Europe) carrying both data and voice traffic.

To date not all users have fully exploited the kilospeed and megaspeed facilities already available to them. Many have not even started. However, as we progress into the 1990s, broadband communications as envisaged by the EEC programme, Research into Advanced Communications Europe (RACE), are predicted into the hundreds of megabits range. Not only will these offer the possibility of moving–image and very high–resolution graphics, but even more fundamentally they could change the whole structure of computing as it is currently known. Once multi–megabit channel speeds are no longer restricted to the confines of the machine room, wide-area mainframes and centralised corporate 'data warehouses' can become reality.

ISDN is not only about integrating different types of traffic over the same digital transmission path. Equally importantly, the new generation of PABX-based Business Communications Systems have interfaces to mainframe processors and to local area networks. These capabilities make possible fundamentally new approaches to combining voice, data and other types of traffic *at the application level*. If end-user applications are designed from the outset to accommodate person-to-person as well as person-to-mainframe communication, whole new areas of functionality become possible. The application development process itself could also be dramatically improved.

Managing the bandwidth

A prime concern of the telecommunications manager responsible for a corporate network is the optimisation of the basic transmission resource, to maximise function and performance while minimising cost. The increasing availability and tariff economics of 1.5/2.0 Mbits/s circuits offer obvious attraction and a major step function in capacity over previously available offerings. The fundamental question is how best to manage this increased bandwidth?

One simple, effective way is to use a modern, digital Private Automatic Branch Exchange (PABX) to provide end-to-end switching of 64 Kbits/s circuits which can be used either for data or for digitised voice. 'Smart' PABXs will have the ability to make dynamic decisions on routing calls and data over leased circuits or over public ISDN via primary rate access. They are becoming more and more sophisticated and conceptually could be designed to provide any level of multiplexing within the digital bitstream. Alternatively (and perhaps more likely) the job of manipulating and multiplexing the basic bit-stream can be carried out with more specialised multiplexing equipment.

The era of truly dynamically managed bandwidth is rapidly approaching as megaspeed multiplexers (often called T1 multiplexers) are becoming available with ever more powerful function. In their simplest form they are basically high speed, point-to-point, Time Division Multiplexers (TDM) which take a megaspeed circuit and chop it up into a number of individual kilospeed circuits. In this configuration they are usually known as 'channel banks' in that they literally provide a bank of up to 30 kilospeed channels from a single megaspeed circuit.

Rapidly they evolved into more complex Digital Access and Cross-connect Systems (DACS) which can operate in multi-level configurations and provide 'bundles' of timeslots to provide interconnected circuits at a variety of speeds between a number of different locations.

Currently they are entering the third generation of their short existence: Transmission Resource Management Systems (TRMS) which provide the extra facilities required to manage and configure the bandwidth to reflect changing traffic patterns and to react to and recover from individual path outages.

Certainly, megaspeed multiplexers will continue to evolve into the 1990s. In terms of their basic 'muscle-power' they will be able to handle ever faster speeds and multiple backbone circuits. In terms of their multiplexing ability, faster microprocessors will also enable them to move towards very high speed statistical multiplexing. In terms of their network management intelligence, they will be able to make very powerful operational decisions to optimise cost/performance across private leased and public switched facilities on a second-by-second or time-of-day/week basis.

As a general trend, the PABX will make inroads into the traditional multiplexing area, the multiplexers will make inroads into the traditional computer controlled packet-switched area, while the computer controlled packet-oriented architectures will take advantage of the basic transmission capabilities provided by the other two.

Developments in local area networking

A high proportion of today's installed local area networks are relatively manpower-intensive for often very low numbers of users.

In addition to providing connectivity between devices, a LAN should provide a solution to the general problem of wiring the workplace in a flexible, easily maintainable fashion and also address the question of bridging between the hierarchy of LANs that will undoubtedly be required in a building or campus of any complexity and size.

In this respect, probably the most significant recent development has been in the area of token passing ring architecture and the cabling systems that support it.

The standards for the token passing ring are defined in IEEE 802.2/802.5 and ECMA 82/89 and are draft ISO standards DIS 8802.2/8802.5. It is an 'open' architecture in that technical specifications are published and available to manufacturers generally and component chips are becoming available for implementation in a variety of devices and adaptors.

In the past, the inherent simplicity and predictable performance of ring topographies tended to be overshadowed by concern that, if one of the devices on the ring failed, it could break the continuity of the ring and interrupt the whole community supported. This problem has been overcome by providing implicit detection of a failing or inoperative device, plus 'self healing' capabilities that automatically remove the device from the ring and by-pass it leaving the rest intact. By these techniques devices can be added or removed from an active operating ring without disrupting other users.

Bridges are becoming available so that individual rings can be interconnected into a hierarchy of networks allowing connectivity between devices across different rings. This is particularly important for large buildings where individual floors can be wired and managed as separate entities, but also be integrated into a total location-wide network of considerable complexity (via one or more higher-level rings, for instance in the risers of the building) ensuring a high degree of resilience and practical manageability.

The physical cabling medium normally uses screened twisted pairs or optical fibre, the choice being primarily one of cost. Speeds for twisted pair technology will typically be in the range of 4 Mbits/s to 16 Mbits/s, which should provide sufficient capacity for most office applications. For applications that require capacity and speeds in the hundreds of megabits per second range, optical fibre can be used.

In addition to the basic medium itself, modern cabling systems have a range of standard adaptors and racking facilities that dramatically reduce the work involved in adding and moving users and devices and reconfiguring networks.

There is probably enough existing telephone twisted-pair wiring already installed to girdle the equator a thousand times. Unfortunately it is installed in a myriad of intra-building ducts and cavities, and lacks flexibility.

Re-wiring the workplace totally will probably take 30 years, well into the next century. Nevertheless, leading-edge users are already devising their location cabling strategies to take advantage of the advanced function and operational flexibility of modern cabling techniques.

Outlook for the 1990s

It is projected that by the mid-1990s there will be over 100 million intelligent workstations (IWs) installed throughout the world. The ratio per 'information worker' will vary according to the type of job, but many areas will be approaching a 1:1 ratio similar to the penetration of telephones in the workplace today.

These IWs will generate very high data volumes for the networks supporting them, albeit in bursts. In addition the end-user will come to expect sub-second response time at the workstation regardless of whether the application being accessed is local or remote. The user's own productivity will demand it.

At the same time the profile of usage will change dramatically. The modularity of IWs and advances in high resolution 'all points addressable' displays will provide the base for the integration of image, which in turn will drive the need for megabit network capacity.

The availability of multi-megabit capacity will itself change the architecture of corporate databases and where they are stored. The high degree of data and software duplication seen in today's distributed systems is a direct result of the performance and capacity limitations of today's wide area networks. Similarly the speed and power of the wide area network has an inverse influence on the degree of systems support manpower and distributed processing capability necessary in remote locations.

Whatever the eventual balance between centralised and distributed systems, whatever the comparative role of the PABX and the LAN, or the degree to which packet-switched networking will be impacted by cheap, switchable ISDN bandwidth, one thing is certain: the coming decade will not be dull!

Transmission technology will no longer be the constraint it was in previous years. The challenges and demands of users will be ever higher. And the telecommunications manager's toolbox will change more fundamentally in the next five years than it has in the previous 25, giving an unprecedented range of opportunities in supporting corporate needs and goals.

3

ISDN Evolution in France: the Will to Innovate

JEAN–LOUIS PERNIN &
ARTHUR J SCHWARTZ

Introduction

In France, by 1985, one-half of the Public Switched Telephone Network (PSTN) was already digital, made so by the combined efforts of the National Center for Telecommunications Research (CNET) and ALCATEL: geographical coverage was already nationwide, making it possible for 90% of all users to access a broad range of services, in line with the Series-I Recommendations. Since 1983, the vigorous, innovative Minitel Bearer Service has been measuring customer acceptance of service provider offerings. These capabilities represent two milestones along the road to ISDN.

The journey from PSTN to ISDN will be presented in three phases. The first will retrace the 'planning map' to show: the route chosen, the milestones for each leg of the journey and the means of attaining them. From the present standpoint, within the territory of ISDN, the near- and mid-term plans for completing the migration will be presented. The final phase will demonstrate how the concepts and architecture of the ALCATEL E10 digital switching system helped to clarify the route and simplify the journey, enabling the use of existing plant.

The planning map: ISDN tools and elements as milestones

A set of ISDN tools was adopted in the early 1980s. These tools assumed natural groupings, along three coequal evolutionary stems, or ISDN Elements. The convergence or integration of these elements would yield a digital network offering a broad range of services, including voice, data and image information, that is the ISDN. (*Figure 3.1*)

By 1986, at least two-thirds of the ISDN tools were available. By the end of the decade ALCATEL expect to complete the migration, by offering the full set of ISDN Tools to any user.

Based on the ALCATEL DMOST scheme[1] first presented in 1983, the parallel stems and branches of Figure 3.1 developed naturally. But the migration itself had to be accomplished serially, with cutover of each ISDN tool as a milestone. The overall movement cannot be coherently represented as a single stem, because it occurs as the convergence, that is integration, of the ISDN tools.

By 1985, the milestones of the migration had assumed a coherent sequence: digital connectivity; bearer services; synchronisation; the mechanism of service offerings; teleservices, especially via videotex; and the RENAN program (RENAN is a French

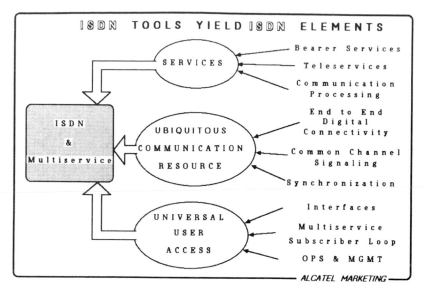

Figure 3.1

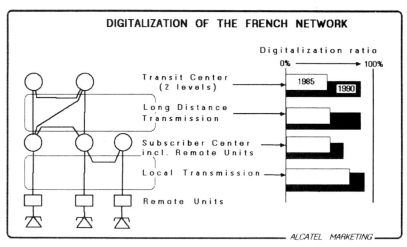

Figure 3.2

acronym for Digital Network Connecting Analogue and Digital Subscribers, but it is also the name of a well known French philosopher born in the area where the program implementation is starting). The RENAN program includes the ISDN tools of CCITT N° 7 signalling and universal user access, via a unified T interface. Network architecture will continue to be based on the switching system, which performs communications processing and includes operation/maintenance facilities.

Digital connectivity

The primary support of an ISDN is the standardised 64 Kbits/s Bearer channel, conceived to support digital voice, freeze-frame images and any kind of data. With all of these forms of information configured identically, a single set of network facilities can switch and transmit any information-bearing signal. 64 Kbits/s capability is integrated into both areas of the PSTN: the switching centres and the transmission links.

Switching centres

As indicated in Figure 3.2, the four levels of switching in the French network have reaching a 50% digitalisation ratio. Remote units are counted as part of the first level of the switching hierarchy.

Transmission links

The whole of continental France is served by all-digital electronic highways, at backbone rates of 140 and 565 Mbits/s, equipped with Automatic Protection Systems (APS) and alternate routing facilities. *See Figure 3.3.*

Bearer services

A set of digital bearer services is already available:

> packet switching is used on the Transpac network. Transpac, cut over in 1978, is probably the world's largest X.25 network. At the end of 1985, Transpac served 35,000 subscribers of its own, and supported 22 million Minitel connections per month.

> a non-switched network for leased lines, Transfix, supports digital access. Transfix, cut over in 1979, offers a variety of data interfaces. Transmission can occur via the Telecom 1 domestic satellite network for remote areas.

> via the existing PSTN, Transcom offers X.21, V.35 and digital PBX interfaces.

> for circuit-switched traffic, Transdyn supports data rates from 2.4 to 2048 Kbits/s. The existing service was cut over in 1985; it uses Telecom 1 and includes common-channel signalling facilities. The full articulation of Transdyn will be based on 120 ALCATEL E10 exchanges.

Service offering mechanism

In terms of demand, traditional PSTN service (based on Plain Old Telephone Service) is largely characterised by two straight-line relations: between the network provider and the user, a limited variety of voice-channel based services and facilities are exchanged for use charges, plus line and equipment rentals; between the network provider and the system provider, equipment orders and service contracts are exchanged for the material means of extending and upgrading the network and the quality of service.

Over the past decade the new forces affecting telecommunications have been technology, economics and law. As shown in Figure 3.4, telecommunication services now

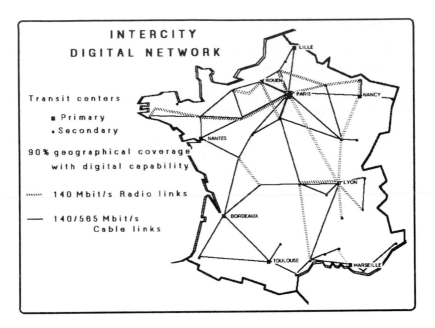

Figure 3.3

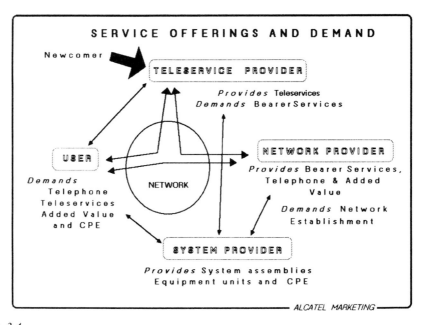

Figure 3.4

involve a complex set of relations and some vital new roles. Two specific reasons have propelled telecommunications towards ISDN.

The relation between system providers and users of special-purpose CPE used to be minimal. To meet user demands for new services, CPE has grown into a major industry (the consideration of which is beyond the scope of this paper).

The second reason concerns the new set of offerings, the Teleservices, which have been developed in the new telecommunications establishment, the teleservice provider seems to have a double nature, appearing as both provider and customer. Teleservices and their providers will therefore be major forces in the development of telecommunications in the future.

Teleservices

On the French network, most teleservice providers operate utilising videotex. The outstanding performance record of French videotex operations has already yielded a great deal of information for ISDN planners.

The French PTT serves 10 times as many videotex subscribers as the combined worldwide total for all other networks. In December 1985, a typical month, the PTT reported 8 million electronic directory service calls (including yellow pages) and 14.5 million videotex communications. The teleservices offered by more than 1,200 providers include: banking; entertainment and travel reservations; mail-order merchandising and professional information exchanges, for example biomedical laboratories and luxury caterers. During 1985, a major mail-order house reported that 5% of its business came in via Minitel. The TV networks provide for viewer response in certain cases, including off-screen participation in quiz shows. TELETEL, cut over in 1982, is the PTT videotex access service: it operates on existing plant, with Network Termination (NT) functions performed by the modem included in each Minitel. The electronic directory service replaces the annual printed directory: its customers receive basic Minitel sets free of charge. These sets support most teleservice offerings; enhanced capabilities are available, via rented Minitels.

Into ISDN territory: the RENAN Project

The advanced status of the French network is the direct result of PTT policy: to integrate service capabilities without waiting for complete digitalisation of the loop plant.

The next milestone of network migration is universal user access. This term implies making the network transparent to user demands at every level: from economical POTS to the farthest reaches and widest scope of ISDN capabilities. Over the past few years, the technical and economic aspects of this undertaking have been closely examined[2,3].

In 1986, the PTT started operating RENAN, an experimental ISDN including universal user access[4]. RENAN, based on existing ALCATEL E10 plant and a developing set of user services available to analogue and digital users, serves eight cities in northwestern France (*Figure 3.5*). RENAN will reach Paris in 1988 and one million subscribers are expected by 1992. The project's development will be phased as indicated below.

> The bearer facilities at the 1988 level provide circuit switching at 64 Kbits/s and user-user signalling. In future phases virtual data circuit facilities are

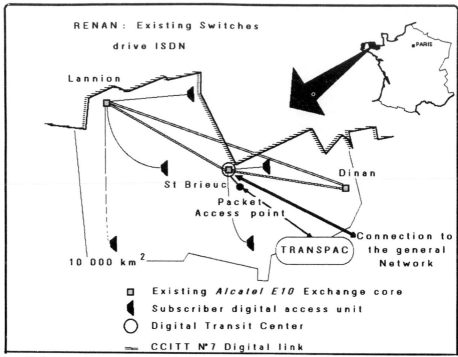

Figure 3.5

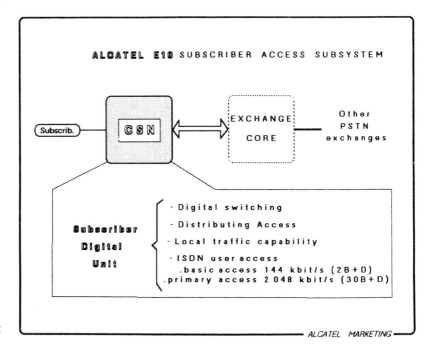

Figure 3.6

envisaged together with circuit switching at 384 Kbits/s and multiples of 64 Kbits/s.

Teleservices include POTS, videotex, teletex and audiographics, extending to 128 Kbits/s videotelephone, telealarm, and videotex/teletex in the D channel.

Supplementary service facilities include portability, calling number identification, sub-addressing, direct inward dial, priority access, and enhanced billing with evolution to new services as they are identified.

The prime mover of the French network's evolution, and its migration to ISDN, is the ALCATEL E10 digital switching system. This system's basic conception enables the integration of new capabilities on a per-subsystem basis, and service upgrades in per-subscriber increments.

The ALCATEL E10 scheme integrates four mutually independent subsystems (*Figure 3.6*). In each subsystem, the functional units are linked through standard interfaces; each unit can develop independently of all others, and new units can be added as necessary, to benefit from technological progress or incorporate new functions. This applies, for example, to CCITT N° 7 signalling, videotex gateway operation and ISDN software[5,6].

In the specific case of the subscriber access subsystem analogue and digital subscribers, in any mix, enter the digital PSTN via CSN access facilities. CSN units can be installed in the exchange or at remote sites. In turn, each of the digital concentrator modules of a CSN can be collocated with the control and switching module (UCN) or be independently remoted, bringing the attachment point even closer to subscribers. Thus all ranges of

Conclusion

The French network has entered ISDN territory, by providing a virtually-ubiquitous communication resource and a wide range of bearer services and teleservices. Nevertheless, to both network and system providers, the key problem of ISDN migration is still based on the relative unpredictability of subscriber acceptance: will the users validate the full migration, by making integrated services part of their lifestyles? There is no single answer to this question; it is not possible to predict confidently the rate at which subscribers will respond favourably to the offerings. Therefore, it remains for the suppliers to leave open all possible options, avoid needlessly tying down network financing, and match the scope and pace of ISDN advancement to the demands of its users.

With respect to the original planning map (*Figure 3.1*) two of the three ISDN elements are serving customers, and the third is being actively tested. As each element is cut over, its capabilities are absorbed into the network and the migration advances. By the early 1990s this journey will be complete.

4

The ISDN Concept of the Deutsche Bundespost

PETER KAHL

Introduction

The Deutsche Bundespost (DBP), today, operates a broad range of different telecommunication networks. Among these are the telephone network with approximately 26 million subscribers, the circuit-switched DATEX-L network with around 30,000 subscribers, the packet-switched DATEX-P network with up to 13,000 subscribers, the telex network with approaching 165,000 subscribers and the cable TV network with some 1.6 million subscribers. Customers wishing to use the services provided in these dedicated networks are supplied with a separate subscriber line for each service. Since investments in the subscriber line area make up 60 to 70 per cent of the total costs of a network, expanding the provision of subscriber lines is obviously uneconomical. Alternatively, the cost-effectiveness of networks could be increased considerably, if all services offered to a subscriber were to be made available via a single subscriber line.

Such a concept leads also to an economically optimised telecommunication service, since the investments in the overall network infrastructure are spread over a large number of subscribers. At present, the telephone network boasts the largest number of subscribers and this will continue to be the case for some time to come. All new developments must therefore be based on the further development of this network.

In view of the basic principles for optimising development of the telecommunications infrastructure, the DBP has drawn up a medium and long-term network development plan. This is generally referred to as the 'ISDN network development strategy' (*Figure 4.1*).

The 64 Kbits/s ISDN

The digitisation of the telephone network (that is the replacement of space division by time division switching systems capable of handling 64 Kbits/s signals), the substitution of FDM transmission systems by digital transmission systems between the exchanges and, finally, the implementation of digital subscriber lines (on the symmetrical copper pairs of the telephone network) will eventually result in a 64 Kbits/s ISDN. This represents the first phase of the ISDN network development strategy. Its key feature is the use of the 64 Kbits/s capacity.

The DBP's involvement will end at a network termination located on subscriber premises at internationally standardised user-network interfaces (S_O, S_{2M}), thus permitting the connection of compatible terminal equipment of the subscriber's choice. The conception of the 64 Kbits/s ISDN is based on three major principles: a clear delimitation of the scope of responsibility of the DBP and that of the subscriber; creation of the prerequisites for terminal portability; and establishment of the basic requirements for open communication for the mass applications of ISDN.

The ISDN pilot project was initiated in 1986/87 at Mannheim and Stuttgart to be followed by the introduction of series-produced equipment in 1988. With this in mind, a ISDN-backbone network is being implemented, consisting of eight ISDN-mode local exchanges in Hamburg, Hanover, Berlin, Düsseldorf, Frankfurt, Stuttgart, Nuremberg and Munich. Each of these will be connected to an ISDN transit exchange. The transit exchange will be fully intermeshed from a routing point of view. Signalling between the exchanges will be based on Signalling System No. 7 and will include an 'ISDN User Part' tailored to the needs of the ISDN. The local exchanges (which will obviously handle analogue telephone accesses as well) will initially be designed for 1,000 ISDN-subscribers each. Thus, by 1988, this backbone network will have a maximum capacity of 8,000 ISDN-subscribers. Access to the ISDN-mode exchanges will be restricted to subscribers in the eight aforementioned local networks.

From 1989 onwards, the DBP will only purchase switching systems with ISDN capabilities. In accordance with current plans for the expansion of the switching sector, about 100 new local exchanges will be installed in 1989. Since the development trends in the demand for ISDN accesses are not clear, a certain number must be assumed for planning purposes, at least for the years 1988/89. In accordance with this principle, all local exchanges newly installed in a local network and incorporating ISDN capabilities will be capable of catering for 1,000 subscribers; later exchanges will have the means to cope with 500 ISDN subscribers. So the ISDN implementation plans for the end of 1989 envisage a capacity totalling some 60,000 to 70,000 ISDN accesses. At this point it should be mentioned that the above plans are not final. If the DBP's implementation plans or demand diverge considerably from the figures given above, the technical concept is flexible enough to allow for a short-term adaptation.

The ISDN implementation plan is largely dependent on the development plan for the digitisation of the telephone network. The latter presupposes the coordinated introduction of digital transmission and switching systems, with all digital switching systems, in principle, being interconnected by digital transmission systems. This calls for considerable investment in digital transmission systems. If today's digital switching and transmission plans are taken as a basis, it may well be assumed that an ISDN with nationwide coverage will be available by 1993.

However, the introduction of the ISDN remains far from certain as it is dependent on the services and associated terminal equipment being available at the same time. To make sure that no delay is incurred, the DBP has drawn up an 'ISDN services concept' (*Figure 4.2*), according to which, the following services should be provided in 1988, the year in which the ISDN is to be launched:

telephony (3.1 KHz bandwidth)

facsimile Group 4 (64 Kbits/s)

teletex (64 Kbits/s)

data transmission at 64 Kbits/s (circuit-switched)

access to the DATEX-P network (via the 64 Kbits/s channel)

Bildschirmtext (interactive videotex) at 64 Kbits/s

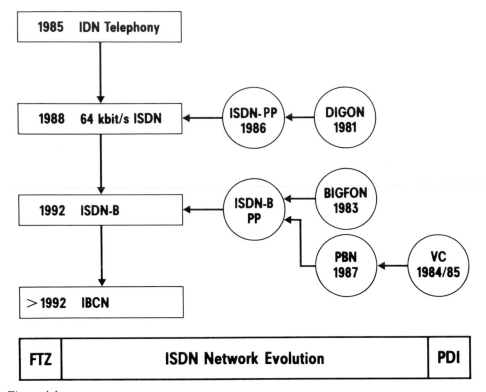

Figure 4.1

Apart from the above services, which will all rely on the capacity of the 64 Kbits/s user-information channel, it will be possible to connect terminal equipment used in conjunction with the analogue telephone network to the ISDN by means of a terminal adapter. The same applies to terminal equipment with an X.21 interface for which a terminal adapter TA X.21 has been developed. Network/service interworking will be provided for the teletex service so that teletex subscribers for the ISDN will be able to communicate with teletex subscribers in the DBP's Integrated Text and Data Network. For facsimile subscribers, service interworking will make sure that Group 4 users can communicate with Group 3 users.

The strategy described here for the introduction of the 64 Kbits/s ISDN covers a large number of applications. However, it must not be overlooked that a growing number of services are gradually taking shape for which the 64 Kbits/s capacity is inadequate. The provision of such broadband services, in addition to the 64 Kbits/s services, will lead to the later stage of the ISDN, namely Broadband ISDN. One of the main features of Broadband ISDN is that it will no longer be possible to use the symmetrical copper pairs of the telephone network on the subscriber line, and that the necessary steps will have to be taken for the implementation of optical-fibre subscriber lines.

The provision of optical fibres on the subscriber line will have to be accompanied by an exponential increase in the transmission capacity of the regional and supraregional trunk network, if intolerable traffic congestions are to be avoided.

The provision of the Broadband ISDN will be based on the principle of upward compatibility. This term implies that all services (64 Kbits/s + broadband) will be made available to subscribers over a single subscriber line. A single control channel (D-channel) will be provided for call set-up and release, and for the utilisation of the supplementary services such as call diversion and conference calls.

The local exchange will act as a subscriber reference point for all services; it will perform all subscriber-related network functions such as charge metering, handling of the D-channel and error location on the subscriber line.

The final technical details for the Broadband ISDN have yet to be finalised. Whereas the DBP has more or less completed its work on a concept for the Broadband ISDN, corresponding international recommendations still have to be drawn up before such a network can be introduced. However, to respond to the growing demand for broadband communication facilities in the Federal Republic of Germany until the work on international standards has been completed, the DBP has initiated several interim measures. These measures are described below.

Installation of optical fibre lines

For some years, the DBP has been introducing optical fibre lines in its trunk network on a regular basis. Today, the implementation of these lines, operating with 140 Mbits/s transmission systems, has reached a considerable scale. Furthermore, the DBP intends to install 565 Mbits/s systems on monomode fibres from 1987 onwards.

In addition to the trunk network, the DBP has started to implement optical fibres in the subscriber network. Hence 14 local networks were equipped with optical fibres in 1986, and another 15 local networks were retrofitted with optical fibres in 1987. The DBP is thus creating the necessary prerequisites for the eventual provision of broadband cable systems permitting broadband communication over the subscriber line.

The experimental videoconference network

In 1985, the DBP took the first steps towards the establishment of an experimental videoconference network. This network was initially used in conjunction with public videoconference studios installed by the DBP in Hamburg, Berlin, Bremen, Hanover, Dortmund, Düsseldorf, Cologne, Bonn, Frankfurt, Stuttgart, Nuremberg, Munich and Kiel. In addition the DBP is now promoting the provision of private videoconference

The network, as its name implies, is intended to provide visual communication between conference rooms, allowing groups of participants at two different locations to communicate. Videoconferences at which three or more groups can participate, are not envisaged for the time being. Data and facsimile communication complement the speech and visual communication facilities provided by the experimental videoconference network.

A typical feature of the network is that videoconference connections have to be applied for at the central reservation office in Cologne. The connections are then set up at the requested time. (The network does not allow connections to be set up by the subscriber dialling).

Videoconference studios are always connected via optical fibre lines, using a 140 Mbits/s connecting unit. For switching the lines within the network, switching matrices located in

ISDN Service concept

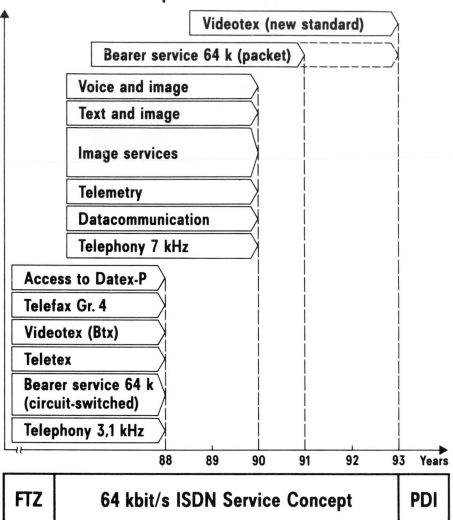

Figure 4.2

Hamburg, Hanover, Bremen, Berlin, Dortmund, Düsseldorf, Cologne, Bonn, Frankfurt, Karlsruhe, Stuttgart, Nuremberg and Munich are used. These matrices are activated by the central reservation office at the request of the videoconference user. The switching matrices will also be interconnected by means of 140 Mbits/s trunks. However, in many cases, especially for international connections, 2 Mbits/s trunks are used. This calls for the conversion of the 140 Mbits/s signal to a 2 Mbits/s signal by means of a network codec. The utilisation of the network codec depends on the availability of digital transmission systems operating at 140 Mbits/s. Videoconference users cannot exercise any influence over the use of such facilities. The network only supports the videoconference service and not, for example, transparent data transmission at 140 Mbits/s.

The experimental videophone network (BIGFON)

In the period 1983/84, the DBP established 'BIGFON islands' in Berlin, Hanover, Munich, Stuttgart, Hamburg, Düsseldorf and Nuremberg within the framework of the Technical Communication Programme. These islands allowed the use of optical fibres for the various broadband communication and distribution services to be tested in the local area of these cities. In accordance with the concept developed for these trials, bi-directional broadband communication was only possible within the BIGFON islands and subscribers were able to set up the videophone calls within each island themselves.

In an attempt to expand the original concept, the DBP is now taking the necessary steps to allow videophone communication between the BIGFON islands. For this purpose, transit exchanges with a capacity of 140 Mbits/s are being established in the Berlin, Hanover and Schwäbisch Hall local networks and 140 Mbits/s trunks are being installed between these transit exchanges and the exchanges of the BIGFON islands. The transit exchanges will be controlled by subscriber dialling. There is consequently a marked difference beween the experimental videophone network and the experimental videoconference network.

It should be noted that only those subscribers who have participated in earlier BIGFON activities can make use of the experimental videophone network. An expansion of the experimental videophone network to include other subscribers is not envisaged.

The provisional broadband network

Both the experimental videoconference and the experimental videophone networks have been designed for a limited number of subscribers and for a limited range of visual communication applications only. However, there are signs that a communication requirement combining videoconferencing, videophony and high-speed data communication is emerging. A key feature is the subscriber dialling capability. The DBP therefore decided to initiate the introduction of a provisional broadband network at the end of 1987. This network is eventually intended to replace the experimental videophone and videoconference networks, and should therefore allow both subscriber dialling and the establishment of reserved connections. It is consequently necessary to change the switching networks of the experimental videoconference network into independent, self-reliant exchanges. Also, the capacity of this network will be increased to cater for a greater number of subscribers (approximately 1,000 subscribers by 1990).

This provisional broadband network (*Figure 4.3*) will also make use of 140 Mbits/s information channels. Charge metering will therfore be based on the switching of channels with such a capacity. A network termination will be provided on subscriber premises, which, compared with that for the 64 Kbits/s ISDN, will perform a broader range of functions. As such, the network termination will comprise both the video codec for the conversion of the analogue video signals, and the sound codec for the conversion of the analogue speech signals. The dialling facilities for the activation and establishment of connections will also be incorporated in the network termination. Two groups of user-

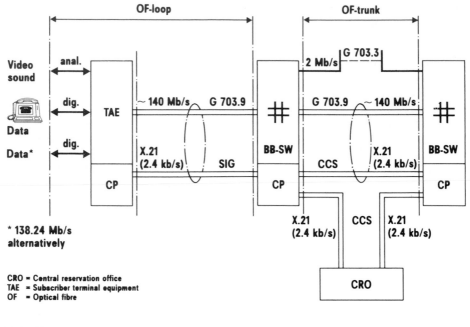

Figure 4.3

network interfaces may be made available to subscribers: the analogue video interface with the composite colour video signal for video communication, and the analogue sound interface for accompanying speech. Speech and video communication may be supplemented by data communication, for which a 2048 Kbits/s channel and two 64 Kbits/s channels will be provided. All these signals will be multiplexed in a 140 Mbits/s user channel and be made available by the network as a multi media connection. As an alternative to the above procedure, it will also be possible to use the 140 Mbits/s information channel exclusively for transparent data transmission. To this end, the subscriber will be able to use a digital interface with an overall bit rate of 139 264 Kbits/s and an information-carrying capacity of 137.216 Kbits/s. Both applications can be used for switched and reserved connections. The central reservation office will continue to set up reserved connections.

The provisional broadband network will have a two-level hierarchical structure consisting of the subscriber exchanges and the transit exchanges. Subscriber exchanges will be established in 13 local networks (Hamburg, Bremen, Berlin, Hanover, Dortmund, Düsseldorf, Cologne, Bonn, Frankfurt, Mannheim, Stuttgart, Munich and Nuremberg), and transit exchanges will be made available in Frankfurt, Düsseldorf and Hanover. The switching facilities will have a capacity of 256 connections per switching system. In view of the dimensioning of the switching facilities it will be possible to expand the capacity of the provisional broadband network beyond the 1,000 subscribers mentioned earlier.

It ought to be pointed out, however, that this will be an independent network, that its technical configuration is of a provisional nature, and in particular, that it will not provide access to other existing networks such as the telephone network, the 64 Kbits/s ISDN, and the circuit-switched DATEX-L and packet switched DATEX-P networks.

The Broadband ISDN

As mentioned earlier, the Broadband ISDN will be the logical consequence of the enhancement of the 64 Kbits/s ISDN in terms of the principle of upward compatibility already described. Depending on the progress made with regard to the international and national standardisation of this network, the introduction of series-produced equipment should be possible from 1991, the concept of which will conform to the basic principles of the 64 Kbits/s ISDN. This means that digital user-network interfaces will be placed at the disposal of subscribers at network terminations providing primarily transmission-related functions.

Apart from the already standardised user-network interfaces for the 64 Kbits/s ISDN (S_O and S_{2M}), another user-network interface (S_{BB}) is being defined for the broadband dialogue services. Ongoing discussions in international study groups are concentrating first and foremost on the structure and design of this interface, the user-information channels to be made available and the multiplexing of the various information channels. One of the possible S_{BB} interface structures proposed is $H4 + 4 \times H1 + 2\ B + D$, where $H4 = \leqslant 140$ Mbit/s, $H1 = 1920$ Kbits/s, $B = 64$ Kbit/s and $D_{16} = 16$ Kbits/s. Furthermore, discussions are also centering on the splitting up of an H4-channel into subchannels for which a basic block of approximately 32 Mbits/s is envisaged which, if used four times, would supply the capacity of the H4-channel.

Since the Broadband ISDN conforms to the basic principles of the 64 Kbits/s ISDN, its definition differs considerably from that of the provisional broadband network. One of the differences, for example, is that the coding equipment required for video communication will no longer be integrated in the network termination but in the terminal equipment. Furthermore, the dialling facilities needed for call set-up and for utilisation of the supplementary services will also form part of the terminal equipment. Initially, the Broadband ISDN will be a circuit-switched network. Packet-switching functions which are now being discussed by international bodies under the generic term 'asynchronous time division technique' must be considered as enhancement of the Broadband ISDN to be undertaken at a later date. From this perspective, too, the Broadband ISDN is modelled on the 64 Kbits/s ISDN in that the latter will also start out as a circuit-switched network to be supplemented by packet-switching functions at a later stage.

One of the key features of the Broadband ISDN is that it will allow both narrowband and broadband two-way communication. The exchanges yet to be developed are considered to be 64 Kbits/s ISDN exchanges whose range of capabilities is to be extended by the ability to switch broadband dialogue channels. The ensuing local exchanges will have suitable access units for analogue telephone subscribers, for subscribers using exclusively 64 Kbits/s applications and for subscribers using 64 Kbits/s and broadband applications.

Although the conceptual aspects of a Broadband ISDN have already been defined by the DBP, no corresponding international standards have as yet been drawn up. In cooperation with the German telecommunications industry, the DBP will attempt to expedite the adoption of concept-related specifications by CEPT and CCITT. Only when this has been achieved will it be possible to give a detailed description of the Broadband ISDN by way of DBP Technical Standards and DBP Equipment Specifications. Such delays are the reason for the relatively late introduction of the Broadband ISDN on a commercial basis and also for the intermediate solutions adopted by the DBP in the form of the experimental videoconference service, experimental videophone service and provisional broadband network.

The Integrated Broadband Communication Network (IBCN)

Whereas the Broadband ISDN will be configured for the provision of narrowband and broadband dialogue services, one of the later stages of expansion anticipates the provision of broadband distribution services, in addition to the dialogue services, over a single subscriber line. As far as can be foreseen now, it will be possible to integrate all broadband services (here, the term integrated is used in the sense of integration from a transmission point of view) on a single optical fibre subscriber line.

Any distribution exchanges required will be installed – according to present opinion – as separate units next to the exchanges of the Broadband ISDN. The configuration of the corresponding customer area has not yet been specified in detail. In particular, whether special broadband distribution interfaces will be needed in addition to the broadband dialogue user/network interfaces (S_{BB}) will require extensive studies and discussion.

Conclusion

With the network development concept presented here the DBP has created the prerequisites for a reliable and future-oriented strategy for the future development of the telecommunications network. In particular, this network development concept allows customers both in the private and business sector to the communication facilities that will be offered by the public network.

Furthermore, the early adoption of this network development strategy will permit appropriate service concepts to be developed, which in turn will pave the way for the technical development of terminal equipment and subscriber installations.

5

The UK ISDN: Interworking Features

KEITH GLEEN

Integrated digital access – the UK pilot ISDN

British Telecom (BT) is rapidly replacing its electro-mechanical exchanges by modern stored-program controlled digital exchanges, interconnected by digital circuits and using fast common-channel signalling. This Integrated Digital Network (IDN) will improve the quality of service and greatly extend the range of voice services available to the customer.

The Integrated Services Digital Network (ISDN) is a natural extension of this IDN, in which the digital nature of the network is extended to include the local circuit between the customer and his serving local exchange. Since the binary digit, or bit, is universal currency for information transmission, the ISDN can support both voice and non-voice (ie data) services without further contrivance.

BT is currently introducing an ISDN Pilot Service based on System X exchanges now entering service. To emphasise the unified access which the Pilot Service gives to both voice and non-voice services it is being marketed as Integrated Digital Access (IDA). Two forms of IDA have been developed; single-line IDA and multi-line IDA. This paper will concentrate on single-line IDA since the majority of interworking and access mechanisms are the same for both forms of single- and multi-line access.

Single-line IDA provides two exchange connections, each with a different directory number. One connection can carry voice or up to 64 Kbits/s data, the other connection can carry up to 8 Kbits/s data.

At the customer's premises a Network Termination Equipment (NTE) provides the customer with standard, existing CCITT interfaces for his terminal equipment. These include X.21, X.21 bis, V.24 and X.25. However, the main customer data interface used on single-line IDA is the existing CCITT X.21 recommendation. The NTE also provides protocol and rate adaption as required, multiplexes the two traffic channels together with an 8 Kbits/s signalling channel, leading to a customer data rate of 80 Kbits/s. This is arranged as a 64 Kbits/s voice/data channel (the B channel), an 8 Kbits/s data only channel (the B' channel) and the 8 Kbits/s signalling channel (the D channel). This structure is carried on a full duplex digital transmission system which operates over the normal two-wire local line to the exchange.

For single-line IDA the burst mode transmission technique has been developed to provide a simultaneous bothway line transmission information rate of 80 Kbits/s employing the WAL2 modulation technique. In the burst-mode technique 20 bits of data are transmitted alternately by each end of the link. The 20 data bits are comprised of two sets, each set being made up of eight bits of B channel plus one bit of B' channel plus one bit of D channel. These two sets are sent in a burst at an instantaneous rate of 256 Kbits/s to the far end. The transmitting end then listens for the return burst, sent in the opposite direction by the distant end after receiving a burst. (This send then listen method gives rise to the popular name for the technique – ping-pong)

As can be seen from the above, the transmission rate of the customer access offered by the pilot single-line IDA differs (80 Kbits/s) from that now agreed for the I-series service (144 Kbits/s). At the time that the pilot service was proposed in the late 1970s the designers had a number of criteria to guide them on the transmission rate of the connection between the customer's premises and the local exchange. These were:

the need to support PCM encoded speech which requires a 64 Kbits/s channel.

the need to provide extensive and flexible signalling capability; outband signalling has significant advantages over inband signalling and thus outband signalling was chosen requiring its own channel between the user and the network.

to provide significant advantages to the user over existing dedicated networks by offering enhanced facilities and services. Thus it was seen necessary that the customer's access should support more than one simultaneous call to different destinations. If both calls were PCM encoded speech this second channel must also be 64 Kbits/s.

the transmission system to be used in the local network must be capable of operating over the existing distribution cables and must have a sufficient reach to enable the majority of customers to be connected to their local exchange without the use of repeaters. In the UK, the transmission system is required to operate over lines with up to 43 dB loss in order to reach 98% of customers; in distance, this equates to a minimum acceptable reach of four to five km.

power feeding of the transmission system and a minimum portion of the user's equipment must be possible, without increase of the exchange battery voltage, to provide an emergency telephone service in the event of failure of the domestic power supply.

It can be seen that the first three points require a high bit transmission rate (144 Kbits/s user data plus additional framing structure) With the techniques available at the time the latter outweighed the requirements in the former and BT decided to adopt the 80 Kbits/s burst mode system for single-line IDA.

To meet the requirements of the CCITT I-Series Basic Rate (144 Kbits/s) access, BT has also developed an echo cancellation transmission technique. This is likely to become the standard local access transmission method in the future.

Multi-line IDA provides up to 30–64 Kbits/s exchange connections carried on a 2048 Kbits/s digital path. Separate 64 Kbits/s channels are allocated within the 2048 Kbits/s for signalling and synchronisation. The principal initial use of multi-line IDA is expected to be the connection of digital PBXs to the ISDN. Such a PBX is known as an Integrated Services PBX (ISPBX).

The 2048 Kbits/s data stream presented to the customer is in accordance with CCITT Recommendations G703 and G704[1]. In these recommendations the 2048 Kbits/s stream comprises 32 timeslots (numbered from 0–31) with signalling in timeslot 16 and synchronisation and alarms in timeslot 0.

In the absence of firm standards for user–network signalling a Digital Access Signalling System (DASS) was designed for the purpose. This is suitable for both single- and multi-line IDA and the many services they may support. DASS is a message-based, common-channel signalling system using variable length frames, which can be transferred over the 8 Kbits/s signalling channel provided in each single-line IDA, as well as the 64 Kbits/s signalling channel (timeslot 16) provided in each multi-line IDA.

The features and facilities offered by DASS for user–network signalling, led to its development into an advanced PABX signalling system. This signalling system, Digital Private Network Signalling System (DPNSS), extends DASS to include user–user (PABX-PABX) signalling. DASS itself has been further developed; DASS2 is compatible with DPNSS allowing existing modern PABXs to exploit fully the features and facilities offered by multi-line IDA.

Interworking requirements of an ISDN

With the structure described above, a single-line IDA customer may make two simultaneous calls to two independent destinations; for multi-line IDA, up to 30 simultaneous calls to 30 independent destinations. Often those destinations will be terminals on existing non-ISDN networks. IDA must therefore offer interworking (digital and/or analogue) to these existing networks and the services available over them.

The requirements of interworking can involve the following:

signalling conversion

call validation

speed, code and format translations

number translations

routeing

charging and tariffing

management procedures

Interworking IDA to other networks and services

The interworking requirements listed above can be satisfied in two ways: as an integral part of the IDA/ISDN network or via separate interworking equipment. For various reasons, not least costs, complexity and timescales, BT has chosen to employ the second method of providing the majority of ISDN interworking capabilities for the IDA Pilot Service. Interworking with the Public Switched Telephone Network (PSTN) for telephony is an inherent feature of IDA. No special arrangements or interworking equipment is required. The ISDN numbering scheme forms part of the UK PSTN numbering scheme and no translation or prefix is necessary. KiloStream is BT's 64 Kbits/s private digital circuit network. It is possible to provide interworking between IDA and KiloStream to extend and enhance a customer's private digital circuit network.

Interworking between the Pilot ISDN and BT's Packet SwitchStream (PSS), a circuit switched network and a packet switched network respectively, requires a two-stage call set-up. First a call must be made across ISDN, using ISDN call control procedures, to an

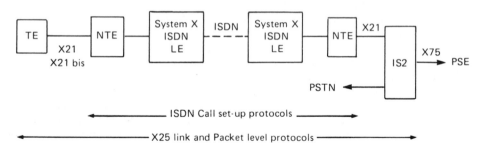

interstream 2

Key: IS2 InterStream 2
     TE   X25 Dial-up terminal
     NTE Network Terminating Equipment

Packetswitchstream interworking

Figure 5.1a

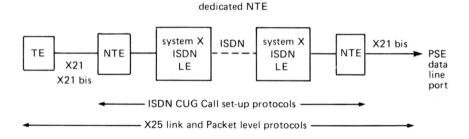

dedicated NTE

Key: TE X25 Dial-up terminal
       NTE Network Terminating Equipment

Packetswitchstream interworking

Figure 5.1b

ISDN interworking port on PSS. Second a call is set-up across PSS, using PSS call control procedures, to the destination address. Two methods of access are available both of which allow access with full X.25 protocols between terminal points, shared access (*Figure 5.1a*) and dedicated access (*Figure 5.1b*).

Shared access (Figure 5.1a)

InterStream Two (also called the Packet Network Adaptor or PNA) has been installed to act as a PSTN/PSS Gateway primarily for the Teletex service (*Figure*

5.1a). However, it can also be used to interwork between ISDN and PSS for non-Teletex applications.

Calls from ISDN-based packet terminals to PSS terminals are made by a two stage set-up procedure with initial set-up being a digital data call from the customers' NTE to InterStream Two using X.21 procedures from the customer terminal. Once this has been established the call is completed using X.25 Call Request procedures between the customers X.25 terminal connected to the NTE and InterStream Two.

Calls to ISDN-based packet terminals are completed by InterStream Two which performs an ISDN call set up across the ISDN to the called NTE. Once the link across the ISDN has been successfully established InterStream Two forwards the X.25 Incoming Call packet to the X.25 terminal connected to the called NTE.

The connection across ISDN, originated from the NTE, can be provided by either the fixed destination call feature of the NTE or by normal dial-up procedures appropriate to that NTE and terminal.

This method of interworking may employ either the 64 Kbits/s B channel or the 8 Kbits/s B' channel as a bearer but InterStream Two currently only supports a data rate of 2.4 Kbits/s.

Dedicated Access (Figure 5.1b)

For high usage access to PSS an NTE dedicated to the customer is provided at the Packet Switching Exchange (PSE). Calls may be originated across the ISDN only in the direction towards the PSS network and, unless this connection is already established, no incoming virtual calls may be set up between PSS and the ISDN customer. Connection to the PSE from the ISDN customer is either by leased line access or by utilising the closed user group facility on dial-up access. (Both methods form part of the X.21 protocol and prevent unauthorised use of this facility by other customers). With the ISDN connection established, normal PSS X.25 protocols complete the connection across PSS (*Figure 5.1b*).

All PSS data line rates up to and including 48 Kbits/s are available using the 64 Kbits/s B channel. PSS data line rates up to 2.4 Kbits/s are supported on the 8 Kbits/s B' channel.

Access to PSS allows interworking with packet switched services in more than 40 other countries, by means of BT's International Packet Switched Service (IPSS).

Methods of providing access between the ISDN and International Circuit Switched Data Networks (CSDNs) are currently being investigated by BT International. An International Circuit Switched Data Network Gateway employing CCITT Recommendation X.71 will become available during the IDA Pilot Service. It is likely that first connections will be to the German Datex-L CSDN.

ISDN-based terminals may interwork with the telex network via PSS, with access to PSS by one of the methods described above (*Figure 5.2*). Two interworking units are provided between PSS and telex. InterStream One, or the Telex Network Adaptor (TNA), provides interworking between the telex network and PSS for character (asynchronous) or X.25 terminals. InterStream Three allows ISDN (and PSTN or PSS) based teletex terminals to interwork with the telex network.

Whilst teletex is not in itself a network, being a multi-network service, it is of sufficient

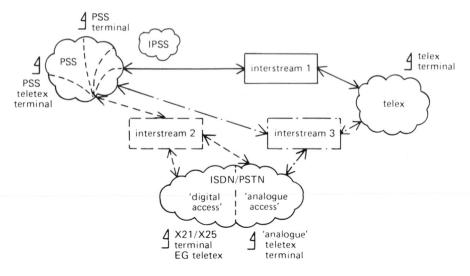

Interstream 1, 2 & 3

Figure 5.2

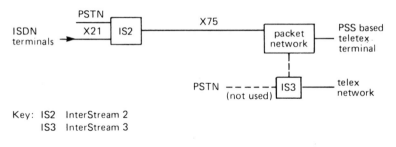

Key: IS2   InterStream 2
     IS3   InterStream 3

Teletex interworking

Figure 5.3

interest to merit special interworking arrangements. Three types of teletex terminal, operating to three different networks, are currently envisaged as using the teletex service; PSTN-based terminals, PSS-based terminals and ISDN-based terminals. It is also a requirement of the teletex service to interwork with the telex network.

ISDN teletex terminals are supported on IDA via the X.21/X.21 bis ports of an NTE and may use either channel (*Figure 5.3*). Two types of terminals are supported by this interface arrangement:

> ISDN (X.21/X.25) teletex terminals provide call set–up in the X.21 mode, followed by X.25 in the data transfer mode. Connection to customers' NTE is by the X.21 port.

> PSS–type teletex terminals use the X.21 bis port on the NTE.

Connection between either terminal across the ISDN will be possible using normal ISDN digital call procedures. Interworking with other terminals, including analogue-based teletex terminals connected to ISDN, require the use of InterStream Two. If interworking is required with the telex network use of InterStream Three (the Teletex Conversion Facility or CF) in tandem with InterStream Two will be necessary.

ISDN interworking in the future

The channel structure and signalling system employed in the ISDN Pilot Service were developed by BT in the absence of firm international standards. However, energetic activity by the CCITT has resulted in the agreement and publication of new standards[2]. Future ISDN customer access is described in the CCITT I-series of recommendations. This series of recommendations includes sections for support of existing user-network interfaces (I460–I469) and a complete section reserved for Internetwork Interfaces (I500-series). However, the only recommendations currently available are those for support of existing user-network interfaces. The most important and far reaching of these is recommendation I462(X.31) for 'Support of Packet Mode Terminal Equipment by an ISDN'. This recommendation recognises that the two networks may not in fact merge to become a true ISDN but may remain complementary networks, each suited to different services and facilities. It does, however, address the problems of integrated access procedures between the two networks.

At the customer end of the digital connection, I420 is the base CCITT recommendation for customer access. This recommendation (and the associated series of recommendations) encompass both circuit switch access and packet switch access. An integrated set of procedures is described that allow packet switched terminals and circuit switched terminals to use the same basic access mechanism to the exchange. At the exchange end the different types of call are separated into circuit switch and packet switch information by recognition of the different Layer 3 used in the signalling (D) channel. Hence each Layer 3 (packet or circuit) at the customer has a separate Layer 3 associated with it at the exchange end. For example one Layer 3 may be a circuit switch call control layer three, another a packet layer for an X.25 call. A customer may connect either type of terminal to the local Network Termination (NT) via the I-series passive bus. It is the terminal and network in combination that connect the customer end to the appropriate service/network.

The I-series of CCITT recommendations for customers basic rate access to ISDN are based on a 144 Kbits/s transmission system with two times 64 Kbits/s B channels and a 16 Kbits/s D channel. The 16 Kbits/s D channel operates the LAP D protocol allowing both signalling and data packets to be statistically multiplexed between the ISDN local exchange and customer terminal(s). High speed packet access is provided on the two B channels; low speed access via the D channel.

Two scenarios are described in CCITT recommendation I462 for the network handling of packet communications from I-series terminals.

The minimum integration (*Figure 5.4a*) scenario closely matches the methods of interworking adopted for the Pilot Service. This scenario refers to a transparent handling of packet calls through the ISDN. Only access via the B channel is possible. Support is given, as in the Pilot Service, to packet calls on a physical 64 Kbits/s semi-permanent or switched B channel. Two stage set-up procedures are still required to set-up calls both to

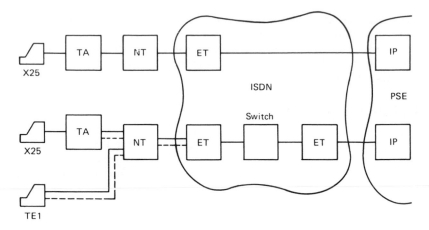

Minimum integration scenario

Figure 5.4a

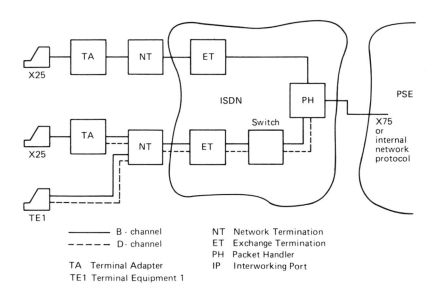

——— B - channel	NT	Network Termination
- - - - D - channel	ET	Exchange Termination
	PH	Packet Handler
TA Terminal Adapter	IP	Interworking Port
TE1 Terminal Equipment 1		

Maximum integration scenario

Figure 5.4b

and from the packet network using a special Interworking Port provided by the packet network itself.

The maximum integration scenario (*Figure 5.4b*) is the subject of active study and development within BT, UK industry and internationally. It refers to the provision of a packet handling function within the ISDN. Both B and D channel access is supported, with the Packet Handler (PH) performing the necessary processing for packet calls, standard X.25 functions for X.25, as well as path-setting functions and possibly rate adaption.

Generally, the B channel will support a single link access procedure with multiple packet calls (virtual circuits) achieved by Layer 3 multiplex procedures. The D channel will support multiple links (from separate terminals), via the Layer 2 multiplex procedures inherent in LAP D. Additionally, each link may have multiple virtual calls using the standard Layer 3 logical channel mechanism.

The procedures for B channel access (*Figure 5.5a*) are still separated into a similar two stage set up procedure as that described above. That is, the establishment of the ISDN access circuit using LAP D signalling procedures on the D channel followed by the control phase of the virtual circuit(s) using X.25 procedures on the B channel.

D channel access (*Figure 5.5b*) is on a 'permanent' access basis with no establishment phase being required across the ISDN. Although the link establishment beween the terminal and the exchange may require an exchange of link information concerned with activation, TEI assignment and verification, packet access is always available on the D channel. This D channel access requires only X.25 procedures to establish a call into and across the packet network.

The exact nature and position of the Packet Handler has yet to be determined, the CCITT recommendation allows a number of possible options and configurations. The options range from using existing interfaces between the PH and the packet network (for example X.75) to new protocols that more fully integrate the ISDN and PSS. The latter may require major changes to the packet network, in both its structure and interfaces. All options are being closely studied within BT to evaluate their impact on the customer and his requirements for existing and future networks and services

Two scenarios, minimum integration and maximum integration, are described in recommendation I461. These two scenarios are similar in philosophy to those described above for packet access.

Minimum integration: in this scenario the ISDN is simply used as a digital bearer circuit for connection either directly between terminals (via a terminal adapter) or directly to a Circuit Switched Public Data Network (CSPDN). Access is provided by use of either the 'hot-line' facility or a semi-permanent connection. The Terminal Adapter (TA) interfaces X.21/X.21 bis equipment to the ISDN, but neither it nor the ISDN network handle X.21 procedures. The TA may, however, perform rate adaption.

Maximum integration: in this scenario full support is given to X.21/X.21 bis DTEs by a special terminal adapter. This adapter converts X.21 signalling to the I451 D-channel signalling of the ISDN and vice versa. The I461 recommendation extensively details this conversion process including the rate adaption procedures. Interworking to existing CSPDNs is via a specialised Interworking Unit.

V-series Data Terminal Equipments (DTEs) are supported by procedures described in recommendation I463. The DTEs are connected to ISDN via special terminal adapters. Control of the call is either manually (from the terminal adapter, called by CCITT TA-A)

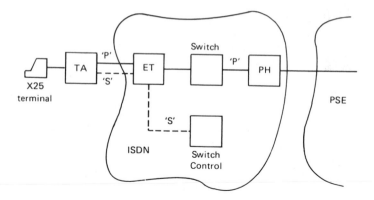

B-channel call set up

Figure 5.5a

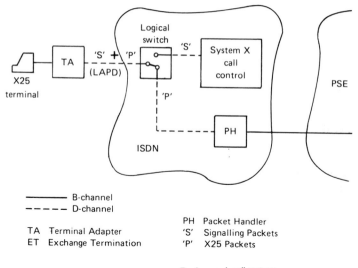

———— B-channel
- - - - - D-channel

TA   Terminal Adapter
ET   Exchange Termination

PH   Packet Handler
'S'   Signalling Packets
'P'   X25 Packets

D-channel call set up

Figure 5.5b

or via V.25 and V.25 bis protocols from the customer equipment and then mapped to I451 by the terminal adapter (called TA-B).

Connection to existing services and terminals on the PSTN is via a special Interworking Unit.

Currently no CCITT recommendations exist to cover interworking with networks (other than that described for packet data networks in I462). It is likely that the internationally agreed inter-exchange signalling system (CCITT Signalling System No 7) will form the basis of interworking arrangements between networks in the future. The UK is well placed to exploit this mechanism since the signalling system is already extensively used between System X (and System Y) exchanges.

Conclusion

As international agreements are reached on the structure of both ISDN and the interfaces and services it offers, the UK ISDN Pilot Service will be modified in accordance with I-series recommendations. Interworking between the existing networks and the latest ISDN will continue to be provided. Major changes to existing networks and exchange design(s) may need to be adopted to fully implement a completely *Integrated* Services Digital Network. It remains to be seen whether such a truly integrated network will evolve that does not require any interworking between networks, at least at the national level.

Acknowledgement is made to the Director of Technology Applications of British Telecom for permission to publish this paper.

6

ISDN in the USA: The Opportunity Begins

THOMAS J HERR &

THOMAS J PLEVYAK

Driving towards ISDN

It might be said that the three things driving ISDN are technology, technology, technology. This imposing force, in combination with end-user needs, is moving information networks inevitably towards intelligent integrated services digital networks. Technology has spawned the widespread deployment of economical digital transmission and switching systems. It has led to multiple end-to-end digital networks, tailored to meet specific customer and/or service needs. Common channel signalling, software controlled products and automated operations systems, each derived from central or distributed processing, are characterised by a common origin in technology. These current network elements combine to provide the thrust towards ISDN.

In the final analysis, technology must serve the needs of end-users. This means that ISDN must face the information productivity and corporate profitability requirements of business and the needs of residential customers. Today's networks handle a predominance of voice traffic. Business customers must cope with the more than 400 billion documents in storage in the US today. The drive toward ISDN must integrate existing voice and data services in ways which are cost effective while defining a rich menu of new services, customer flexibility and other features which ISDN can provide economically. It is these latter categories which now demand the attention of the industry. ISDN is indeed inevitable, but its service and revenue rewards will be paced by the intelligence, creativity and diligence of its stakeholders.

Study Group 18 of CCITT has established basic and primary access structures incorporating B and D channels and various line protocols.

ISDN features a separate D channel for signalling and packet data services with multiple B channels for voice and/or data. CCITT defines the 4-wire T interface as the international standard to basic and primary rate access channels. The S interface is identical to the T interface at the Physical Layer, providing higher-layer protocol services to ISDN terminals. AT&T Network Systems also supports US standardisation of the 2-wire U interface in anticipation of optional Customer Premises Equipment (CPE) or network provided NT1s.

ISDN access channels provide powerful mechanisms for defining and implementing new services. ISDN will enable integrated operations systems with improved OA&M functionality, economics and customer network control. These are widely accepted attributes of ISDN and are expected to lay the foundation for evolution into the future.

ISDN and beyond

Wideband services are expected to play an ever increasing role in integrated services digital networks. Local video services, wideband data and other applications are motivating standards bodies and the industry in general to consider wideband access channels and protocol definitions.

But integrated services digital networks must go even further to meet the full range of future customer needs. Customers will have a fundamental need for universal ports to enable true interchangeability of terminals at any port in the worldwide network. They will want network resources on demand, paying only for what they use, when they use it, with maximum economy and convenience. Architectural freedom will be a key ingredient, enabling terminal and network functions to be distributed or concentrated anywhere that is convenient to the customer or network provider.

Realisation will come about through adaptive, logically provided services with on-demand provisioning and adaptation to end-user needs. The economics of integrated access and integrated transport will combine with transport efficiency to evolve ISDN to the 1990s and beyond.

The information industry must face up to this challenge. It strikes at the core of national productivity gains. Its opportunities, once again, will be services for end-users and revenues for network providers and CPE and network systems suppliers.

AT&T Network Systems evolutionary plan

AT&T Network Systems is planning its products for an orderly and timely introduction of capabilities beginning with a broad range of digital products, available now or in the near future; then beyond to even more innovative products using emerging technologies such as wideband packet switching and integrated video access.

An evolutionary plan has been developed which maximises today's analogue and digital networks, grows gracefully to ISDN and evolves to Universal Information Services (UIS). UIS is AT&T Network Systems vision of the future. It is not a specific product offering, nor is it something scheduled to come into existence at a fixed point in time. Instead it is a vision of opportunities realised through services made possible by technology. Its attributes are those described in the preceding section and shown below.

Universal Information Services

Adaptive logically provided services

Universal ports

Architectural freedom

Integrated access and transport

Wideband access

Transport efficiency

Virtual private networks

As network evolution unfolds, a logical operations architecture will be needed which provides network operations functionality for a dynamically changing network, including network management, testing, billing and maintenance. The AT&T concept for this

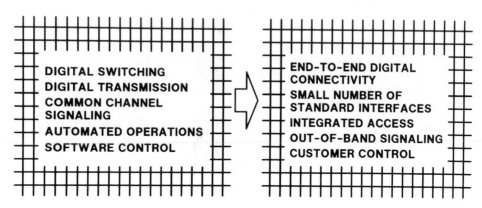

TODAY'S NETWORK

ISDN

DIGITAL SWITCHING
DIGITAL TRANSMISSION
COMMON CHANNEL
SIGNALING
AUTOMATED OPERATIONS
SOFTWARE CONTROL

END-TO-END DIGITAL
CONNECTIVITY
SMALL NUMBER OF
STANDARD INTERFACES
INTEGRATED ACCESS
OUT-OF-BAND SIGNALING
CUSTOMER CONTROL

Figure 6.1

ISDN REFERENCE CONFIGURATIONS

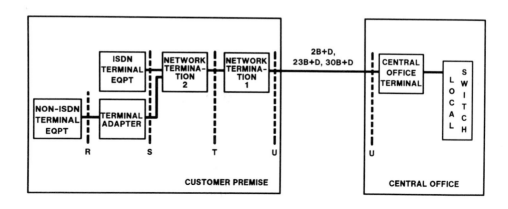

B = 64kb/s
D = 16 kb/s (BASIC ACCESS)
D = 64 kb/s (PRIMARY ACCESS)

Figure 6.2

supporting operations architecture is called Universal Operations Systems (UOS).

The operations elements shown in Figure 6.5 are driven by technology, operations demands to support new technology and services, reduce costs and increase revenues, assure flexibility and simplify processes and network imperatives to utilise existing systems and evolve to new services.

At any point in time, the network will consist of a wide range of services and technologies. Starting with the evolving network transport arrow and moving up, each layer of UOS can be defined functionally and the characteristics of products necessary to meet the needs of the layer can be identified.

Digital switching systems will be the fuel needed by network providers to take them gracefully and compatibly to ISDN and beyond. The AT&T 5ESS digital switching system offers a flexible, cost-efficient architecture with full and expanding business features, making it the ideal cornerstone for ISDN implementation and evolution to UIS.

A wide range of AT&T Network Systems products and services support its evolutionary plan:

Local Area Signalling Services (LASS)
Out-of-band signalling will be deployed at the local switch level to provide innovative customer services such as selective call forwarding and call screening. This signalling method will be important in the evolution to ISDN's D channel.

Digital Cross-Connect Systems
These are multi-purpose, microprocessor controlled electronic cross-connect and test access systems.

Digital Channel Banks
Software controlled digital channel banks are available featuring automation and mechanisation of many labour intensive tasks.

Subscriber Loop Carrier Systems
Cost-effective digital loop carrier systems will provide the basis for ISDN basic access systems.

Lightwave Systems
High capacity digital lightwave transmission systems operating at a wavelength of 1.3 microns into single mode optical fiber will greatly enhance the presence of digital transmission in the network.

Lightwave Networking Systems
Innovative lightwave networking systems will feature architectures which combine integrated transport and distributed software to provide economical centralised control and provisioning capabilities for dynamic network management.

Video Teleconferencing Systems
Digital, switched, video conferencing services are available, designed specifically for local metropolitan networks.

Focus on end-user research

In an effort to understand end-user needs, AT&T Network Systems is deeply involved in a programme of market research that reaches both business and residence customers. The focus is long range with an emphasis on customer profiles that pinpoint critical decision factors and highlight trends in information processing and handling functions. This information is fed into the development process where technology is moulded into appropriate solutions that strengthen links in the information chain.

NETWORK EVOLUTION

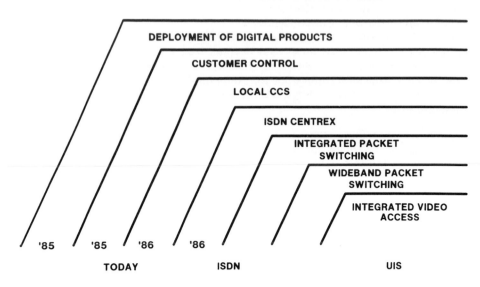

Figure 6.3

TODAY ⟶ ISDN ⟶ UIS

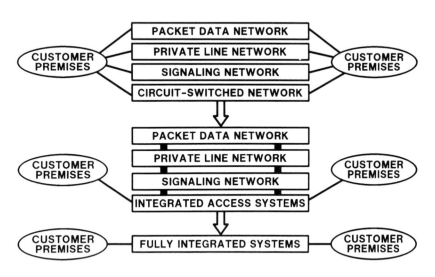

Figure 6.4

As an example of this feedback, a recent research project was undertaken to define generic information transfer needs of small, medium, and large businesses. A complete review of applicable literature contributed to the development of a set of hypothesised needs categorised by business establishment size. The set of needs was assumed to be cumulative, that is large business includes medium and small business needs; medium business includes small business needs. The set of research hypotheses tested are as shown in Figure 6.7.

In talking to business communications managers across the US, it became apparent that the most significant areas of need are independent of size. As the size of the business establishment grew, so did the sophistication of communications systems. However, the most pressing needs did not relate to sophistication of information systems. They related to cutting costs, graceful evolution as technology advances and better information from the system along with customer control capabilities.

Mapping needs into capabilities

The needs identified by communications managers have been prioritised in Figure 6.8, and an indication of the potential means of addressing those needs is shown. These needs and capabilities can be addressed by an assortment of products that may or may not be ISDN technology. The important element, however, is that ISDN products be designed with these dimensions in mind. AT&T Network Systems has incorporated these findings into its evolving family of ISDN offerings.

Numerous market research projects are being conducted by AT&T Network Systems designed to build a customer profile base. The project described above used size of an establishment as a discriminating factor. In other situations, it may be more useful to define groups of users by the types of industries they represent (health care, point-of-sales) or by the functions performed (order entry, inventory flow and control, payroll). A combination of these factors may work best to describe and group users into target segments.

Activities are ongoing that will culminate in cluster-descriptions of businesses. These descriptions will be the industrial marketing equivalent of consumer marketing's clusters of personalities that constitute innovators, early adopters, early majority, late majority and laggards. The cluster profile will include information on desired capabilities, cost/benefit perceptions and the most likely timing of new products and services. Specific applications and product introductions will be targetted to match the particular needs of each cluster.

The reality of ISDN

ISDN is no longer a concept or experiment. Today it is a functioning reality. On December 16, 1986, McDonald's Corporation became the first company in the US to transport voice, packet-switched data, circuit-switched data, and video signals simultaneously on standard twisted pair wiring using ISDN technology and production grade equipment.

McDonald's reviewed proposals from nine different telecommunications companies before choosing Illinois Bell's ISDN proposal to answer its existing and future telecommunications needs. ISDN was considered the best solution for McDonald's because it offered a very flexible and robust architecture specifying a blueprint for:

UNIVERSAL OPERATIONS SYSTEMS

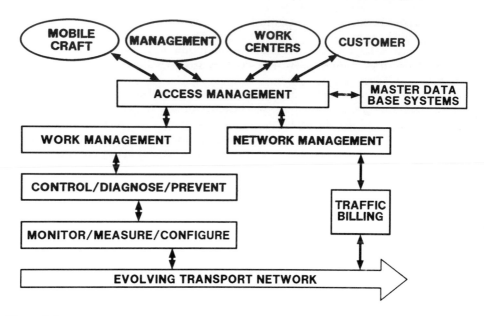

Figure 6.5

5ESS™ AND ACCESS SYSTEMS
1987 Architecture

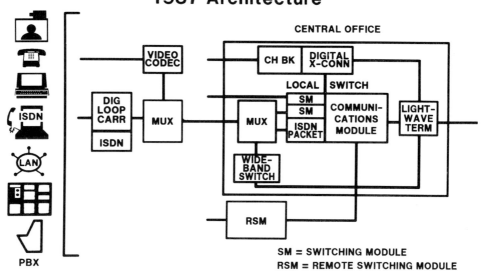

SM = SWITCHING MODULE
RSM = REMOTE SWITCHING MODULE

Figure 6.6

orderly evolution,

application diversity,

standard interfaces and protocols,

and ease of migration to voice/data environments.

McDonald's and Illinois Bell are now deep into this first large-scale customer application of ISDN services. The first phase involved cutting into service an initial configuration of approximately 100 digital subscriber lines and associated CPE devices. Initially, ISDN is being used by McDonald's for digital phones, integrated voice and data terminals, coax-elimination, facsimile, voice mail, message services systems, and modem pooling. As the application evolves, additional lines will be added and the full potential of advanced ISDN business features will be realised with the loading of new software.

By early 1988, as many as five McDonald's office locations and 400 workstations will be linked in an ISDN network. The company may eventually expand the network to include its 68 offices and 9,400 restaurants in 45 countries.

The beginning

Information is now the principal industry in American and other industrialised nations. It is the major product handled by US workers. But quantitative questions behind the statistic remain. How much of that information is useful? How much of it makes a net contribution to GNP? How much of it is just plain overhead, adding to the cost of doing business? These are questions for everyone in the information industry.

ISDN and evolution to the networks of the future will play a pivotal role in the answers to these questions. The key will lie in creative and timely planning and application of CPE and network systems products to form integrated services digital networks to meet customer needs. This is no small task; but it is inevitable, and it will be accomplished. The pace of technology will drive it and economic growth will depend on it. History may well reflect that the opportunity began now and we were the contemporaries who ushered in the 'Information Age'.

This paper concludes, therefore, not with an ending, but with a beginning.

The authors wish to express their appreciation to Nancy Kiteley and Dennis O'Neill of AT&T Network Systems for their helpful input.

INTEGRATED SERVICES END-USER RESEARCH HYPOTHESES

Business Segment	Needs
Small Business	• Reduce Auxiliaries • Reduce Hunting Arrangement • Improve Call Coverage
Medium Business	• Access Data • Reduce Rewiring Cost • Limit Extra Wiring • Eliminate Clutter
Large Business	• Protocol Conversion • Security • Eliminate Coax • Reduce Access Lines/Trunks • More Efficient Use of Lines • Worker Productivity • Cost Control • Resource Management • Distance Transparency

Figure 6.7

GENERIC COMMUNICATIONS NEEDS: BUSINESS END-USERS

Needs	Capabilities
• Transparency	• Network Functionality
• Reliable and Functioning Equipment	• System Redundancy
• Reduced Costs	• Administration Expense Management
— Equipment/Maintenance Costs	— Network Functionality
— Staffing Costs	— Network Functionality
— Wiring Costs	— Integrated Voice/Data
— Service Order Costs on Moves and Rearrangements	— Customer/Automatic Station Rearrangement
• Usage Sensitive Billing	• Dynamic Bandwidth Allocation
• Unbundled Features	• Separate Feature Pricing
• Traffic Information	• Network Station Message Detail Recording
• Customer Control	• Dynamic Bandwidth Allocation
• Modular Growth	• Standardized Interface
• Multi-Use Jacks	• Standardized Interface
• Call Coverage	• Call Management Features

Figure 6.8

7

Integrated Broadband Communications: The Programme RACE

DR ROLAND P O HUEBER

Introduction

RACE is the acronym for Research in Advanced Communications Technologies in Europe. It is an action which will accelerate the trends towards integrated broadband communication which promises more cost-effective and higher value-added communication services. The formulation of the objective chosen by operators and industry is to make a major contribution by the 'Introduction of Integrated Broadband Communication (IBC) taking into account the evolving ISDN and national introduction strategies, progresing to Community-wide services by 1995'.

RACE also embraces progress towards a single Community market for telecommunications equipment and services. What is RACE and why is it important?

Why RACE?

The importance of RACE rests on two premises: first, that the economic future of the European Community (EC) depends on making the fullest use of the new telecommunications technology over the coming decade; and second, that this objective can only be achieved on a European scale.

For the emerging global economy telecommunications represents the single most important infrastructure. The 1950s and 1960s have seen the emergence of a world market place for manufactured goods, and the 1970s and 1980s an increasingly world-wide service economy, for which telecommunications will represent the essential infrastructure and competitive factor.

This is the key element for the appreciaton of the significance of telecommunications. In addition to its importance as a major economic sector in its own right – telecommunications represented European Currency Units (ECU) 40 billion of annual sales world wide in 1985, and service revenues are approximately ECU 200 billion per year – the telecommunications infrastructure is a main determinant for the location of the high value-added activities of the future. These are communication-intensive; the international competition for these service activities will, therefore, be greatly influenced by the cost-performance of the telecommunication services which one region can offer in comparison with others.

Thus effective competition will play a decisive role for employment prospects. This extends to maintaining employment in the EC, attracting employment from other parts of the world and the chances of employment creation due to the emergence of new economic activities. Approximately half of the economically active population in Organisation for Economic Cooperation & Development (OECD) countries work in information occupations and about two-thirds of the Gross Domestic Product (GDP) of the EC depend on these activities. The international competition for this kind of high value-added employment is strongly dependent on the cost-performance and availability of advanced telecommunication services.

It has been estimated that during the next decade about ECU 500 billion (corresponding to about 5 million man-years of work or 500,000 jobs on average) will be invested in the Community in telecommunication infrastructures, services and terminal equipment, and in the next 20 years three times as much. A large part if this investment can create employment in the EC only if Europe's industry can successfully compete with international competition, otherwise it will create employment elsewhere. More importantly, however, it is estimated that for those leading in offering advanced information services the employment benefit may be 10 times as large. For Europe's employment prospects the creation of favourable conditions for new and enhanced services is the most significant employment aspect of advanced telecommunications services. Based on these estimates the overall employment at stake may be as high as five million by 1990.

Underlying these trends is a technological discontinuity associated with digitisation, which also represents a turning point in the economics of communications. The advance in digital techniques – which enable voice, data and images to be represented by a universal code – permits a much greater sharing of the resources and infrastructure of communications than has been possible previously. This effect is often referred to as 'Economies of Integration'.

These economies of integration can be realised in several ways:

multiple use of the same facilities and equipment for a range of services.

higher utility to the user by permitting services to be functionally integrated at will.

better economies in transport by combining digital streams of different origins and functions on a single path-way.

In recognition of all this, Europe's competitors are engaging in determined efforts to gain a dominating position. To meet this challenge Europe will need to draw on its collective resources. RACE is a mid- to long-term framework for collaboration and cooperation between members of the EC towards this objective.

The assessment of the situation and prospects which has emerged from the development of RACE is summarised below.

The telecommunications infrastructure is becoming all-important as the support for the world service economy of the future – but the design, manufacture and supply of telecommunications equipment and services of all kinds is also a very large and potentially profitable business in its own right. Digital technology introduces significant changes into the economics of communications; economies of integration are available from the multiple provision of services in bulk, their functional integration by the user at will, and their combined transport by optical means. The initial investment in such digital links is high. Similarly, the computer control of switching complexes, with demanding suites of software programs, implies an unprecedented investment encompassing the whole range of functions and services expected by the user of the year 2000.

Systems able to handle communications of this scope can be designed, tested, engineered and produced only within a coherent approach, that is of a telecommunications strategy conceived and executed on a European scale. This applies over a wide range of manufacturing, network operation and service provision. An uncoordinated approach and the attempt to establish interoperability after the product development stage can no longer be considered as an economically viable strategy.

The telecommunications field is not homogeneously governed by the economies of scale. Terminal equipment and services, for example, so long as they are designed as part of a consistent approach, can be supplied from a number of sources. Thus the development of the IBC offers a wide range of opportunities for medium and small companies in manufacturing and in the provision of specialised services throughout the European Community. For this to happen the efforts in establishing interworking, as addressed in RACE on technical as well as functional levels, will be decisive.

World competition is strong and growing, not only because of the changes induced by technology but also by factors such as industrial regrouping following the break-up of AT&T and deregulation in several major markets. Europe has considerable assets, but these would be dissipated if the Europeans continued, in future, to address telecommunications at the national level.

The need for the countries involved to adapt to the new conditions and to future developments is growing. In Europe, the established telecom suppliers are engaged in assessing and redefining their activities. Their position is affected either directly (for example by UK deregulation) or indirectly (removal of service monopolies like Intelsat). Operators as well as governments, realising the risks of high overheads for the economy as a whole, are increasingly looking for internationally competitive prices beyond those based on the economies of national markets.

RACE is directed towards the integration of IBC sevices and supply at the European level. The network operators and the industry have worked together on the RACE definition phase. The impetus so generated must continue if there is to be an agreed European Specification at the experimental level of the systems, equipment, subsystems and components of the new advanced networks and services.

Content of RACE

The Definition Phase of RACE, which was initiated at the beginning of 1985, prepared the ground for the work of RACE Main. The full work programme is a thick and heavy volume of documents, of which only the outline of the main headings is given below.

RACE was conceived as an evolutionary strategy distinguishing:

> *Definition Phase (1985–1986)*, to execute initial work as required to focus the research and development (R&D) work of the main programme accurately towards functional requirements of the network, terminal area and applications. It also included the assessment of the technology options of key items.

> *Phase I (1987–1992)* of the RACE Main Programme having the objectives of: developing the technology base of IBC; carrying out the precompetitive development necessary for the provision of trial equipments and services for

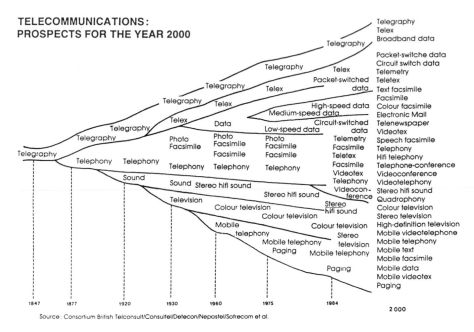

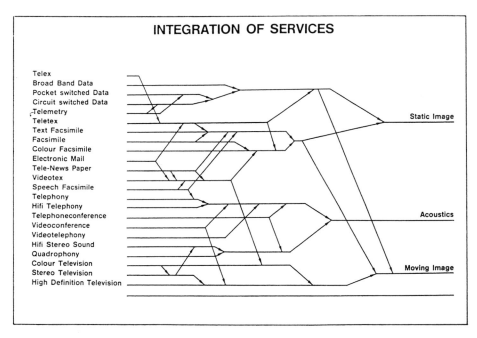

Figure 7.1 The Prospect for year 2000

Figure 7.2 Integration of Services

IBC demonstration; supporting the work of CEPT and CCITT in the formulation of common proposals for specifications and standards.

Phase II (1992–1997), depending on the outcome of Phase I, having the overall objective of developing the technology base for enhanced IBC equipment and services beyond 1995.

The main feature of RACE is its contribution to low-cost and general availability of a wide variety of advanced telecommunications services which depends on both sufficient technology progress as well as the realisation of a large market by 1995.

A useful overview emerges from a series of scenarios which have been developed: Figure 7.1 gives a view of the expansion of services which is taking place and Figure 7.2 gives a schematic representation of the concurrent progressive integration of services. The future telecommunications required to support these developments and its relationship to bandwidth is shown in Figure 7.3.

In order to achieve the underlying objectives described in the previous section, RACE Main would be structured into three main parts as explained below.

Part I: IBC development and implementation strategies

Throughout the introduction and further enhancement of integrated broadband communications, the main objectives are to achieve:

a common understanding of the evolution towards introduction of IBC and its implications including market research and promotion of the IBC concept and services in Europe and internationally.

a common definition and understanding of the IBC system and subsystems, between all main actors concerned.

guidelines for the functional specification of IBC systems and the development of integrated services.

a framework in which to identify the technology requirements and to assess the implications of technological advances and the evolution of service demands for the priorities in RD&E.

a tool for the evaluation of cost-effectiveness of various technological solutions, implementation schemes and evolutionary routes starting from the given situation.

mechanisms for analysing and assessing, at an early stage, the requirements for standardisation and functional specifications in order to facilitate and accelerate the emergence of international standards.

To meet these objectives, Part I would comprise two major areas of activity:

maintenance and further development of the European Reference Model for Integrated Broadband Communication, defined in its initial form during the RACE Definition Phase.

systems analysis and engineering work to transform the concepts derived in the Reference Model into systems and subsystems and functional specifications.

Service-integrated and Integrated Broadband Services

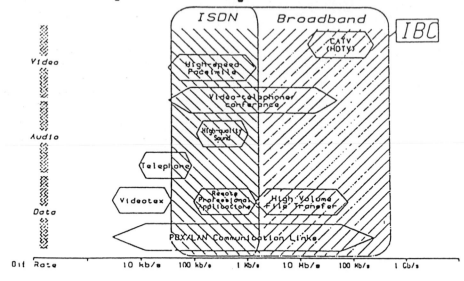

Figure 7.3

I.1 IBC Strategies: IBC is a broad field of activities which requires the purposeful work of many independent actors. They all need to be able to situate their respective work in the context of evolving objectives, conditions and rapid technological change and demand.

I.2 IBC Realisation: the Reference Model work of I.1 represents a major exercise in cooperation to produce consensus views on the evolution towards IBC and its broad functional specifications for systems, subsystems and services, and to provide a two–way link between the Reference Model and other RACE activities, Area I.2. will carry out the required systems analysis.

I.3 IBC Usage: the economic impact of IBC will depend heavily on the nature of the applications supported by IBC networks, the modes of presentation to the users, the functionalities available to users and other important parameters related to the physical and cognitive ergonomy of telecommunications usage. This work area will address these elements to the extent that they are related to work under I.1 and I.2.

I.4 Common Operational Environment: the convergence and transition to IBC represents a major problem in managing the complexity of the technical issues. This does require a specific effort which is the objective of the work under this heading.

Part II: IBC technologies

The objective of Part II is to carry out cooperative R&D on the key technologies required for low-cost realisations of IBC equipment and services. In particular, success for the IBC depends critically on the cost of the local loop optical components being within affordable limits for domestic subscribers. This presents RACE with the key objective of providing technology which, in association with standardisation, will reduce costs in mass production by a factor of 100 over today's typical costs of comparable components. Part II will be system-driven and specifically related to the functional specifications derived by Part I.

The scope of the work will include the research, test and experimentation needed to explore the techno-economic characteristics of the new technologies relevant to IBC.

II.1 Techniques for IBC System Functions: the objective is the use of advanced technology for cost-efficient implementation of IBC. The work will focus on functions which due to their generalised use form a key cost factor.

II.2 IBC Programme Infrastructure: based on advances in software technology in general, as they result from fundamental work done elsewhere, the objective here is to realise major advance in telecommunication software infrastructure so as to master the complexity of systems integration and the associated requirement of network reliability and efficiency.

II.3 Usability Engineering: the objective is to progress the technological aspects of man-machine interface and human factors so as to facilitate IBC user-acceptance linked to ergonomy and cognitive functionalities of IBC equipment.

II.4 Techniques Enabling Network Evolution: the objective of the R&D is to exploit key enabling technologies to realise advanced evolutionary subsystems, systems and networks.

Part III: Prenormative functional integration

The work is aimed at the validation of standardisation concepts and prenormative work as deriving from work done in other parts of RACE. The parts of the IBC system or subsystems will be tested by means of simulation or research-experimentation with particular reference to the needs of technological work in preparation of standardisation proposals.

Prenormative functional integration serves several important functions. It will:

permit the verification of concepts, standardisation options, reliability, security, as well as other key functional characteristics by simulation and testing at the research stage.

contribute to the reduction of risks for development and implementation by permitting the evaluation of the functional features by operators, industry and where applicable service providers and users.

provide a mechanism for demonstrating interoperability features and compliance to standards and specifications.

The scope of the work is to:

test new technology, and devices from projects in Part II RACE, ESPRIT, relevant national programmes, international projects as an integral part of an

IBC system to evaluate its functionalities and techno–economic performance characteristics.

explore relevant performance parameters and confirm the feasibility of meeting the relevant requirements of the functional entities and applications as defined within Part I activities.

The work envisaged within this part of the RACE programme is not expected to have the nature of demonstration projects or field trials. Such trials or prototype installations will be required before operational implementation of a harmonised set of IBC services can be undertaken but are beyond the scope and scale of effort under consideration for the RACE programme.

III.1. Verification Tools: work here is intended to develop verification tools related to make up operational IBC components or subsystems in order to verify design concepts, functional groups or protocols. The goal is to contribute to refinement of functional specification and/or verify standard proposals.

III.2. Development of IBC Application Pilot Schemes: early introduction of IBC services will require the diminution of the uncertainties and risks associated with new services. A key element for this is the early development of experimental situations where real IBC experimental products can be tested by service providers, network operators and users in real–life conditions. The objective of the work in this area is to contribute to the development of such experimental situations and the exploitation of the results so as to speed up EC–wide understanding of the characteristics of IBC commercial exploitation.

Conclusion

The Community has to be selective in choosing where it stakes its prestige and its resources. RACE accompanies ESPRIT as an all-important area for the future. An important criterion must be that of Community Added Value, that is 'what can the Community programme can do for the Member States better than they could do themselves?' Our answer will be clear from this review of the programme. RACE will succeed if it:

continues to get the industries of the Member States working together where it counts to establish a common base from which to compete on a global market place.

continues to enlist the cooperation of the operators in devising European and international solutions.

if both can work together with users so that the IBC can be conceived and implemented on a European scale in good time to meet growing demand of customers to improve cost-performance and sophistication of services for the benefit of economic and employment prospects.

8

Satellites: The Evolution of the VSAT

T MICHAEL KELLEY

The VSAT environment

The Very Small Aperture Terminal (VSAT) is a perfect symbol for long-distance communication in the 'Information Age'. Dramatic technological achievements in computer circuit miniaturisation and speed, first introduced by the computer industry, can now be supported by similarly small and fast VSAT equipment. VSATs give telecommunications managers a cost-effective transmission tool that permits processing and distribution of the ever-increasing volume of information they manage.

In addition to the onset of the Information Age, two other developments, one political, the other technical, created the proper environment for VSATs to flourish.

Firstly, in the United States during the 1970s, it became obvious that existing telecommunications regulations, political structures, and equipment suppliers were not equipped to offer the services that would be demanded. Sweeping changes occurred in the supply of local, regional, national, and international telecommunications equipment and services. These changes, whether for good or ill, resulted from the introduction of marketplace competition among equipment and service suppliers in a newly deregulated environment.

Not unexpectedly, a considerable amount of confusion prevailed during this period. Telecommunications managers found it difficult to plan for the future. It became increasingly difficult to find equipment suppliers, identify single points of responsibility for network quality and reliability, and to adjust scarce resources as requirements varied. In this environment, the advantages promised by one new solution, VSATs, became clear. With a VSAT network, private long-distance business networks became possible, which held out hope to provide customised connectivity, high capacity, full network control, and the flexibility to modify service connections as business expanded or contracted.

Secondly, the key to exploiting this new technology rested on its potential to be offered at attractive levels of capital investment and recurring cost. Typically, the decision to use a VSAT system (to bypass traditional long-distance transmission services) must be justified by a discounted cash flow savings of about 25%. Such levels of financial incentive finally started to become a reality in the late 1970s and early 1980s with the launch of Ku-Band satellites (14 GHz uplink, 11/12 GHz downlink). Satellite Business Systems (now owned by MCI), American Satellite Corporation, GTE Spacenet, and RCA all decided that the fundamental advantages of higher powered spot beams, smaller electronics packages, and relatively low susceptibility to terrestrial interference made Ku-Band the most attractive to serve the business community.

At the same time, the first commercial satellite networks based on the use of the Code

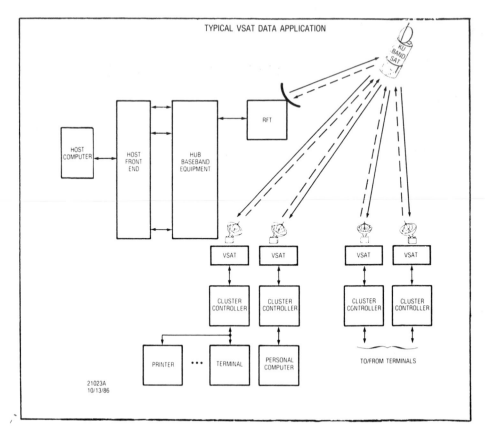

Figure 8.1 Typical VSAT Data Application

Division Multiple Access (CDMA) technique ('spread spectrum') were being built. These exploited the low cost of existing C–Band capacity, and through the use of CDMA (which defeats the problem of C–Band microwave interference), supported one-way low data rate broadcasts that could be received by very small antennae (less than 1 metre in diameter) located on a customers premises. In addition, by taking further advantage of deregulation, equipment manufacturers could become common carriers, offering end-to-end service in the United States using transponder capacity leased from other satellite system operators.

VSAT applications and networks

The major marketing targets of suppliers of both VSATs and satellite capacity were the Fortune 500 companies in the United States who were looking for opportunities made possible by deregulation. These companies included all major banks, retailers, energy companies, the document delivery industry, the lodging industry, and the insurance industry.

Though their businesses varied, they shared one common problem: how can we move data to and from our central offices from hundreds or even thousands of locations across the country in the most efficient manner? This data comes in many forms for different applications, Asynchronous data at 300 bits/s might be needed for a point-of-sale terminal to check on the status of a credit card. Synchronous data at 9.6 Kbits/s might be needed to broadcast the payroll of a major corporation; 56 Kbits/s data might be needed once each day for only one hour to provide RJE. Typically, a wide variety of communications protocols, in particular, SDLC/SNA, BSC, and X.25, must also be supported by the diverse data equipment found in a typical network. Figure 8.1 shows the key elements in a typical VSAT data network.

Of course, the problem is not only to move the data (transmission), but to move it accurately, securely, quickly, flexibly (adapting to changing conditions), and with the right protocol.

Why were VSATs such a good way to solve the above problems? Satellite transmission is a good solution because its cost is insensitive to distance, and because a satellite can broadcast one shared channel to many sites simultaneously. Many manufacturers have exploited this advantage by transmitting a single Time Division Multiplexed 'Outroute' toward all branch locations from the central site, while all branch stations share 'Inroute' channels using Time Division Multiple Access. Security is maintained by the unique addressability of individual data bursts which are under the control of the System Control Centre. Rapid response time in interactive applications is achieved by local termination of the computer protocols, while a second protocol handles transmission of individual packets over the satellite. Flexibility is maintained by downline loading of configuration and multiple access software from a System Control Centre in order to match the data ports of the central and branch site to operate in an access mode that maximises link efficiency.

Depending on the target market, each VSAT manufacturer chooses to build a standard product that solves these telecommunications problems for low per unit cost. As expected, different products solve the problems at varying levels of success. As might be expected, systems with the fastest response times, highest capacity, and most sophisticated System Control Centre will be more costly and require more commitment on the part of private operators. At times, it is difficult for even the largest companies to justify the expenditure for a dedicated satellite network, regardless of the benefits.

Faced with this environment, VSAT offerings have evolved increasingly towards a 'shared hub' concept with the target customers being common carrier and satellite system operators. In this concept, a common carrier provides the RFT baseband equipment that is needed to work with one or more VSAT products at a central site near a major city. He then sells or leases customer premise terminals to the end-user and typically bundles together all the expenses for satellite capacity, terrestrial backhaul to customer headquarters, hub investment, and the VSATs into a monthly charge per branch site. This allows amortisation of hub costs over many terminals, makes it easier for pilot networks to conduct testing, and gives the telecommunications manager the benefits of a VSAT network without becoming a carrier himself. Figure 8.2 shows a typical frequency plan for a shared hub service offering.

The deregulated environment in the United States permits variations on this theme, and in one case, the opposite scenario has occurred. Southland Corporation, after committing to VSAT technology for a private business network, saw the potential for this service from the Dallas, Texas area. They created a subsidiary, which now plans to offer common carrier service to other organisations through the same central facility.

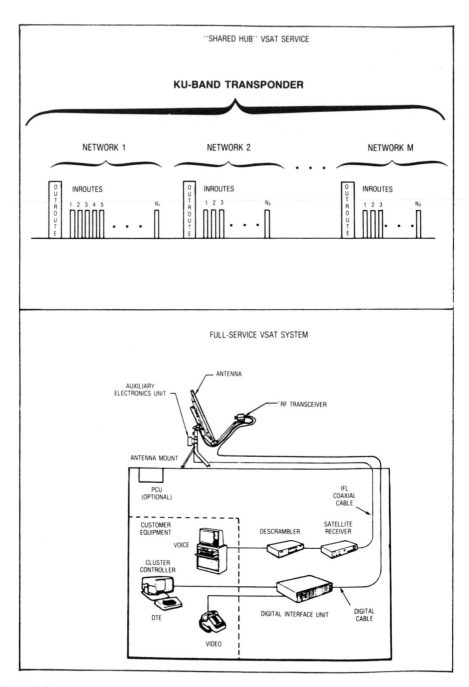

"SHARED HUB" VSAT SERVICE

KU-BAND TRANSPONDER

NETWORK 1   NETWORK 2   NETWORK M

. . .

OUTROUTE INROUTES   OUTROUTE INROUTES   OUTROUTE INROUTES

1 2 3 4 5 N_1 1 2 3 N_2 1 2 3 N_3

. . .   .

FULL-SERVICE VSAT SYSTEM

ANTENNA

AUXILIARY
ELECTRONICS UNIT

RF TRANSCEIVER

ANTENNA MOUNT

PCU
(OPTIONAL)

IFL
COAXIAL
CABLE

CUSTOMER
EQUIPMENT

VOICE

DESCRAMBLER

SATELLITE
RECEIVER

CLUSTER
CONTROLLER

DTE

DIGITAL INTERFACE UNIT

DIGITAL
CABLE

VIDEO

Figure 8.2

Figure 8.3

Finally, the winner in many VSAT procurements is often the product with the highest degree of flexibility and broadest range of applications. In particular, the ability to offer voice and video, in addition to data, gives significant added-value to the VSAT suppliers' terminal (*Figure 8.3*). In the case of Wal-Mart Industries, a major US retailer, its selected vendor offered all three services in a single package, which was an important factor in their selection.

VSAT activity outside the United States

Global data requirements, whether domestic, regional, or transcontinental, are growing at a rapid rate, as well. C-Band and Ku-Band satellite capacity is available at very attractive rates from Intelsat and from any number of domestic/regional satellite operators, such as Palapa (Indonesia), Arabsat, Insat (India) Eutelsat (Europe), Anik (Canada), Morelos (Mexico), and Aussat (Australia). The introduction of VSAT networks, whether public or private, C-Band or Ku-Band, is moving forward in areas where national policy and customer demand permit.

Among the C-Band satellite suppliers (Intelsat, Palapa, Arabsat, Insat and Morelos), VSAT activity has started to grow. In particular, Reuters has initiated low rate data broadcast services from the United States to Latin America using the spread spectrum technique and Cable & Wireless is providing similar international services in the Far East. India has also begun operating a national network for the distribution of government data. Intelsat has promoted the introduction of VSAT networks through the establishment of very attractive lease rates for its Intelnet I (spread spectrum) and Intelnet II (Rate 1/2 coded) services. However, despite the availability of very low-cost technology, start-up costs and political factors have limited development. Mexico has recently announced a new low data rate broadcast service at C-Band called Infosat I.

Among the Ku-Band suppliers, similar progress has been made. Using Eutelsat transponders, it is likely that several European countries will proceed with domestic VSAT networks in 1987. For political reasons, each country tends to guard its plans carefully, but it appears that Italy may take the lead with the first full scale VSAT network to be operational in early 1988. New telecommunications regulations in Canada, which permit private ownership of data uplinks, are likely to spawn several 'shared hub' service offerings from major Canadian cities in 1988. Mexico has announced its intention to introduce Infosat II in 1988, which will be a high-capacity two-way data service at Ku-Band. In Australia, the Australian Associated Press has already introduced a receive-only VSAT network that is designed for upgrade to two-way service over the next several years. Aussat, owner and operator of the Aussat satellite system, is progressing toward a shared hub service offering.

It is likely that the development pattern seen for VSATs in the United States could be repeated throughout the world. There is definitely a market for both C-Band and Ku-Band VSATs, since their technological/cost advantages are clear. Whether government or private industry assumes the leadership role will be decided individually within each country. In Europe, in particular, the requirement for standardisation is likely to retard progress. Hence, the pace at which this development takes place will vary.

However, the influence of the computer on the business community is so pervasive that in their own self-interest, all countries must look seriously at ways to introduce this new telecommunications tool.

9

Wavelength Division Multiplexing in Optical Fibre LANs

JOHN M SENIOR,
STEWART D CUSWORTH
& ALAN RYLEY

Introduction

An optical fibre communication system comprises a transmitter (or optical source), a receiver (or optical detector) and the communication channel (optical fibre)[1]. Optical sources represent the direct link between the electronic driving elements and the optical fibre channel. Information is delivered by appropriate modulation of the input current to the optical source such that an intensity modulated optical signal is transmitted into the fibre. The optical source is either a light emitting diode (LED), which emits diffuse radiation of broad spectral content (considered incoherent), or a laser diode, which due to the stimulated emission process emits highly directional radiation of narrow spectral bandwidth (considered coherent). The output wavelength of the emitted light is dependent on the doping and type of the photo-emissive semiconductor material (for example aluminium gallium arsenide, indium gallium arsenide phosphide) used to fabricate the optical source and extends from 780nm to 1600nm in typical devices.

The optical (or photo) detector is a device which converts the optical power into an electrical current. The two main photodetector types employed in optical fibre communication systems are the PIN photodiode and the avalanche photodiode (APD). Both device types utilise the reverse biased semiconductor junction diode. The use of different optoelectronic materials (eg silicon, germanium), produces devices whose spectral response varies with the wavelength of the incoming radiation. Clearly, to optimise a given optical system the sources and detectors should be matched in their peak spectral response. At present, the two most popular wavelength windows lie in the regions between 780–900nm and 1250–1350nm.

The optical communication transmission media is optical fibre, which comprises a central core of circular dielectric material (glass or plastic), surrounded by an concentric outer cladding region of lower refractive index material (glass or plastic). Total internal reflection at the core-cladding boundary confines the majority of the light to the core region and light is propagated down the fibre core. Fibre which has a core diameter considerably larger than the wavelength of light (50 microns or above) supports many guided modes and is termed multimode fibre. Alternatively, fibre with a core diameter in the region of 2–10 microns generally allows only the fundamental mode to propagate and is termed single mode fibre. Single mode fibre has, to date, primarily found use in long-haul telecommunications and within interferometric sensor systems and is usually excited by single mode lasers. Multimode fibre has found use in more general applications (including LANs) and fibre bandwidths of several hundred MHzkm have been achieved using a graded refractive index profile.

Optical fibres can support a wide range of different optical wavelengths, enabling the transmission of several signals in parallel on a single fibre. This technique, which is termed wavelength division multiplexing (WDM) is achieved by mixing (multiplexing) the optical signals, propagating them simultaneously within the fibre, and separating (demultiplexing) them before their subsequent detection[2]. Thus, in addition to point-to-point (simplex) operation, optical fibre communication systems allow both duplex and wavelength division multiplex operation. In duplex operation, data may be transmitted in both directions within a single optical fibre using two separate optical wavelengths. However, in multiplex operation, the data may be transmitted in the same direction, thereby increasing the overall capacity (throughput) of the system. The significance of the multiplex operation is that each WDM channel has access to the entire bandwidth of the fibre transmission medium which could be of the order of GHz for single mode fibre. Therefore, this multiplexing technique offers the potential for very high speed transmission for either point-to-point optical fibre links, or, in particular, for optical fibre LANs.

Wavelength division multiplex/demultiplexers

The purpose of the optical wavelength division multiplexer is to combine the outputs of several optical sources, operating at different wavelengths, to form a composite signal. The function of the demultiplexer is then to separate the composite wavelength division multiplexed signal into the original constituent wavelengths. In most systems the multiplexer and demultiplexer will be similar devices operating in a reciprocal manner. For successful implementation of the WDM system, crosstalk between the output levels should be 30dB or less, and devices are designed to minimise both interchannel crosstalk and insertion loss.

Wavelength selective optical multiplex/demultiplex devices may be separated into a number of categories. The most common classification is between active and passive devices. Active devices comprise either multiwavelength light sources and detectors, or arrays of light sources and detectors implemented on the same substrate utilising integrated optical techniques. Such active devices are often employed for WDM onto single mode fibre. In the passive case there are several subsets, the major two being angularly dispersive devices and dielectric thin film filter (DTF) devices.

Angularly dispersive devices

Angularly dispersive devices can multiplex or demultiplex several channels using a single dispersive element, typically either a prism or a diffraction grating[11]. This technique has a disadvantage in that it cannot be applied to both the 780–900nm and the 1250–1350nm wavelength regions simultaneously, due to the specific prism or grating characteristics.

The schematic of a typical prism demultiplexer is shown in Figure 9.1. Light from the emitting fibre is collimated by a lens and the prism angularly separates the radiation according to wavelength prior to focussing it onto the individual output fibres. Prism

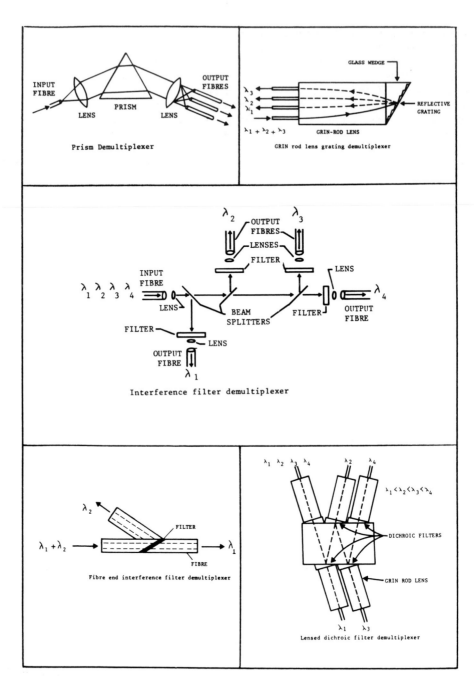

Prism Demultiplexer

GRIN rod lens grating demultiplexer

Interference filter demultiplexer

Fibre end interference filter demultiplexer

Lensed dichroic filter demultiplexer

Figure 9.1
Figure 9.3
Figure 9.4

Figure 9.2

Figure 9.5

NETWORKS FOR THE 1990s

multiplexers, however, are difficult and expensive to produce and therefore have not found widespread application. At present, the device which is widely used as an angularly dispersive element is the diffraction grating. The schematic of a reflective grating demultiplexer is shown in Figure 9.2. In this configuration the input fibre and multiple output fibres are located on the end face of a quarter pitch graded index (GRIN) rod lens[3]. Wavelength multiplexed light is first collimated by the lens and then reflected from the diffraction grating, a process which produces angular separation of the light by wavelength. The reflected light is then collimated by the lens and the different wavelengths are refocussed onto the output fibres. This configuration has been shown to produce low insertion loss (less than 3dB), and interchannel crosstalk levels less that 30dB[4].

Dielectric thin film filter devices

In general dielectric thin film filters (DTFs) can be classified into two categories, the band-pass (interference) filter, and the high- or low-pass (dichroic) filter. Both types are sensitive to the angle of the incident light beam.

An interference filter allows a narrow spectral band of light to pass through, whilst reflecting all other wavelengths. A wavelength demultiplexer using interference filters is shown schematically in Figure 9.3[5]. The incident light beam passes through a beam splitter after which a proportion intersects with the first filter, where light of wavelength λ_1 is reflected and collected by an output fibre. The remaining optical signal is transmitted and the filtering process is repeated for all the constituent wavelengths within the incoming light beam. An alternative configuration is shown in Figure 9.4 in which the fibres are cleaved at a specific angle and the interference filter is interposed between the two fibre ends[6]. The reflected light at a particular wavelength is then collected by a third output fibre.

An example of a multireflection dichroic filter demultiplexer is shown in Figure 9.5. The incoming light is collimated by a GRIN rod lens and the initial low-pass filter (generally oriented at an angle of 45 degrees to the incident light) allows the light with a wavelength less than λ_1 to pass through, but reflects all the shorter wavelengths. The low-pass cut-off point of all the subsequent filters is sufficiently diverse to allow each one to pass light of a particular wavelength.

Active devices

Both semiconductor lasers and LEDs have been investigated in order to provide multiwavelength operation for active WDM devices[7]. Furthermore, the study of multiwavelength photodetectors for demultiplexing has also been undertaken[8]. However, problems including restricted output power, coupling efficiency to the fibre and reliability for the optical sources, together with poor wavelength selectivity and high levels of crosstalk for the photodetectors, have reduced activity towards commercial devices.

An alternative approach is the use of integrated optical techniques to fabricate multiwavelength optical source arrays and multiwavelength photodiode arrays[9]. In this case the multiplexing and demultiplexing may be achieved using passive components – couplers and diffraction gratings – which are also fabricated on the same substrates. A schematic of a WDM system employing this technique is shown in Figure 9.6. The configuration uses an array of distributed feedback (DFB) lasers which couple light at different wavelengths into a single mode fibre. Demultiplexing is performed by a combination of cascaded Bragg gratings and integrated photodetectors. However, such

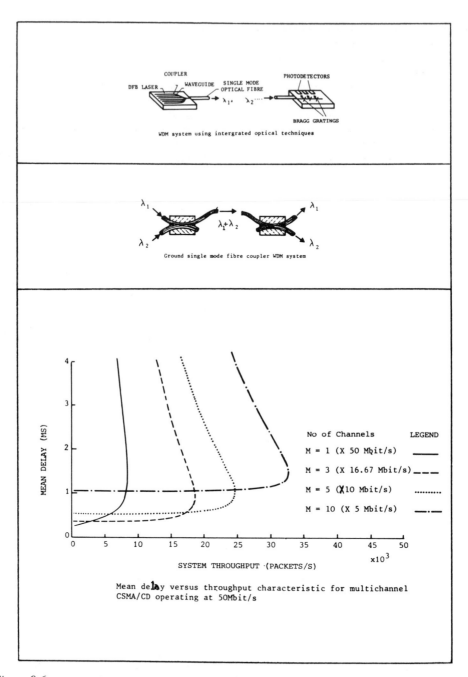

WDM system using intergrated optical techniques

Ground single mode fibre coupler WDM system

Mean delay versus throughput characteristic for multichannel CSMA/CD operating at 50Mbit/s

Figure 9.6
Figure 9.7
Figure 9.8

systems are at present experimental and have not reached the stage of commercial exploitation.

Single mode devices

Single mode WDM can be performed with passive optical filters, angularly dispersive elements, or the integrated optical techniques as discussed earlier. However, with single mode operation it is also possible to use either a WDM fibre interferometer or a wavelength selective light coupler[10,11]. The wavelength selective ground fibre coupler shown in Figure 9.7 is produced by allowing the core regions of two single mode fibres to butt together over a short length. Wavelength selective coupling occurs over this short coupling region, after which light of a particular wavelength is completely coupled from one fibre core into the adjacent fibre core.

Multichannel LANs

There is a growing interest in on-site, packet switched digital networks to provide high bandwidth communications within both modern office and industrial environments. Such local area networks (LANs) provide multiple access to a common communication channel by employing a well defined channel access scheme or protocol. Several channel access schemes have found a wide degree of acceptance. These include carrier sense multiple access with collision detection (CSMA/CD) which is utilised on the Ethernet network[12], time division multiple access (TDMA) which is employed on the Cambridge ring network[13], and token passing which behaves as a distributed polling system whereby network nodes sequentially obtain permission to use the common communication channel. In general the above schemes allocate the entire channel bandwidth of the network to a particular node for a fixed time period which is often defined by the transmission time of a single data packet.

More recently consideration has been given to a broadband network environment where a number of parallel channels may be available[14,15,16]. To date such multichannel LANs (M-LANs) have been largely implemented as broadband coaxial cable systems using frequency division multiplexing to provide multiple channels on a single cable. This involves the division of the total network bandwidth or transmission rate into a number of separate distinct channels each of which have a rate which is a fraction of the total network transmission rate. For example, a total network transmission rate of 50 Mbits/s could comprise five 10 Mbits/s channels. Delay versus throughput characteristics for such multichannel CSMA/CD arbitrated networks with overall system transmission rates of 50 Mbits/s and 100 Mbits/s, with numbers of channels where M equals one, three, five and ten are shown in Figures 9.8 and 9.9 respectively. The network is assumed to have 50 nodes, an end-to-end propagation delay between each node of 10 microseconds, a data packet length of 1000 bits and an acknowledgement packet length of 20 bits. It may be observed that an improvement in the throughput performance is obtained as the number of channels M increases. This improvement is caused by the lowering of the individual channel bit-rate, which decreases the ratio of the end-to-end propagation delay to the packet transmission time.

The characteristics shown assume the use of a broadband coaxial LAN rather than a WDM optical fibre LAN, as the total system transmission rate is divided by the number of channels. It should be noted that WDM on an optical fibre LAN would allow each channel to operate at a speed compatible with the entire fibre bandwidth. However, in the

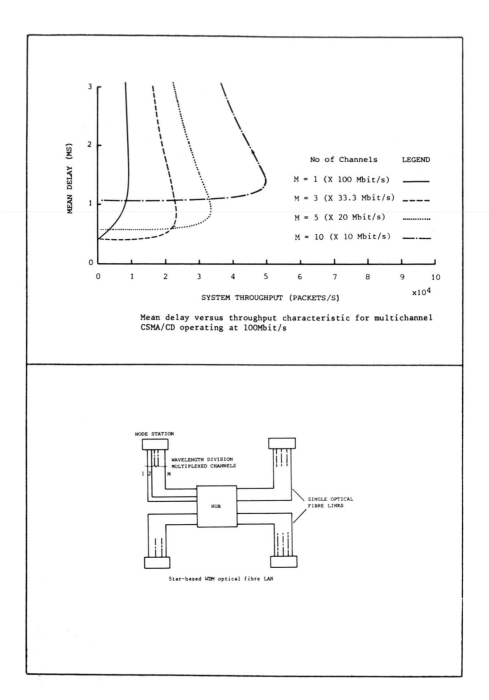

Mean delay versus throughput characteristic for multichannel CSMA/CD operating at 100Mbit/s

Star-based WDM optical fibre LAN

Figure 9.9
Figure 9.10

case of the multichannel CSMA/CD protocol this would not prove advantageous because CSMA/CD tends to become inefficient at channel speeds above 10 Mbits/s on a typical LAN.

Multichannel token passing optical fibre LAN

A single channel token passing bus (logical ring) structure is the subject of standardisation for optical fibre LANs[17]. The control packet, or token, regulates the right to access the system. The token is passed in succession between all the participating stations. Under a non-exhaustive strategy, when the token is received and a station has a message to transmit, it does so in the form of a data packet. The extension from a single channel to a multichannel LAN comprises a number of parallel channels to which all stations have access. It is clear that each individual channel within the multichannel network could be allowed to use the conventional single channel token passing protocol. However, in order to avoid the problems associated with a multiplicity of tokens, and to provide cross channel communication, a different approach is proposed to the problem of multichannel access. In this system one channel acts exclusively as the control or reservation channel, on which the token continually circulates. It is envisaged that network transient problem areas such as station initialisation and removal, token loss, token passing failure, order sequencing, token generation, etc, would be solved on this reservation channel, using similar procedures to those proposed for the conventional single channel token passing network[18]. The remaining channels (designed as data channels) are then used to transmit the data packets.

On reception of the token, the receiving station senses all the channels to determine which are idle. The sensing mechanism is assumed to be instantaneous. A channel is then selected from among those that are idle, in a predetermined cyclical manner. After transmission has commenced on a particular data channel, a busy indicator for this channel is included in the token frame. Additionally, when the data has been received, the receiving station sends an acknowledgment signal back to the transmitting station on the same data channel as the transmitted data packet. This acknowledgement is received by all the active stations and a free indicator for the appropriate data channel is then set within the token. The next station to receive the token is therefore informed of the current data channel status.

The proposed network topology for the multichannel optical fibre LAN is shown in Figure 9.10. It comprises a star configuration with M wavelength division multiplexed channels. At each node there is a requirement for M optical sources and detectors together with an appropriate wavelength multiplexer and demultiplexer unit. The star hub could be a passive transmissive device for a network with up to 100 nodes[19] or, alternatively, an active device for a network requiring more than 100 nodes[20]. With this topology every node has access to each of the M channels which includes the reservation channel and M-1 data channels.

Multichannel token passing protocol simulation

Computer simulation was used to investigate the performance of the multichannel token passing protocol on the network described above. The computer model was driven by generating random message arrivals at the constituent nodes or workstations. The message arrivals at each node were modelled as Poisson traffic having exponential interarrival

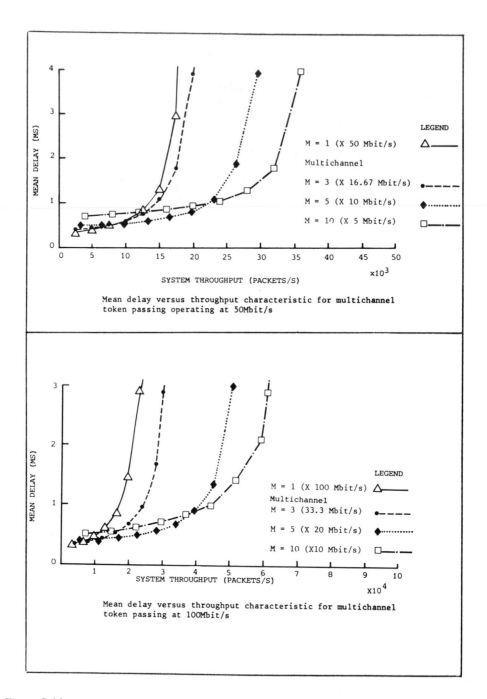

Mean delay versus throughput characteristic for multichannel
token passing operating at 50Mbit/s

Mean delay versus throughput characteristic for multichannel
token passing at 100Mbit/s

Figure 9.11
Figure 9.12

NETWORKS FOR THE 1990s

times, which was symmetrically distributed over all the nodes. Within the model both the transmitting and receiving buffers were assumed to be infinite. The number of nodes was taken as 50 and the end-to-end propagatation delay between all nodes was held constant at 10 microseconds. Constant token packet lengths of 40 bits, data packet lengths of 1000 bits and acknowledgment packet lengths of 20 bits were employed. Packet handling at the nodes was assumed to introduce no additional delay overhead.

Initially, a simulation of a conventional single channel token passing protocol including acknowledgment traffic was undertaken. The simulation was then extended to model the proposed multichannel token passing protocol. The delay versus throughput character-istics for a network with an overall system transmission rate of 50 Mbits/s with M equal to one, three, five and 10 channels (that is one, two, four and nine data channels) are shown in Figure 9.11. Similar characteristics for a network with an overall transmission rate of 100 Mbits/s are shown in Figure 9.12.

An increase in M produces a considerable improvement in throughput performance at high loads. The enhanced performance is achieved because the node receiving the token has an increased probability of obtaining a free channel on which to transmit. However, the improved performance will not continue indefinitely as M increases due to both the finite token cycle time on the reservation channel which restricts the frequency of each nodes transmission opportunity, and to the increase in transmission time incurred as the data channel transmission rate decreases.

Multichannel performance comparison

The advantages of the multichannel over the single channel approach using both CSMA/CD and token passing were demonstrated earlier. In addition the results obtained for the two multichannel protocols on networks operating at overall transmission rates of 50 Mbits/s and 100 Mbits/s which are displayed in Figure 9.8 and Figure 9.9 (for multichannel CSMA/CD) and Figure 9.11 and Figure 9.12 (for multichannel token passing) allows a performance comparison between the two techniques to be undertaken.

It may be observed by comparing Figure 9.8 with Figure 9.11 that multichannel token passing outperforms multichannel CSMA/CD at high loads when the bit-rate of an individual channel exceeds 10 Mbits/s (when M is equal to three). Furthermore comparison of Figure 9.9 with Figure 9.12 confirms this result with a throughput performance improvement at high loads when M equals three and M equals five. These observations correspond directly with the situation which occurs when comparing conventional single channel operation of the two protocols where, in general, token passing is more efficient than CSMA/CD at transmission rates above 10 Mbits/s.

Conclusions

Wavelength division multiplexing on optical fibres has been discussed and its attributes indicated in relation to high speed transmission on a single optical fibre. The possible implementation of this multiplexing technique on a star-based optical fibre LAN was described so as to allow multichannel operation together with multiple access.

A multichannel CSMA/CD protocol was compared with a novel multichannel token passing protocol which employs a separate reservation channel for passing the token. Although the multichannel passing protocol has access to one less data channel than the multichannel CSMA/CD protocol, it was shown to perform more efficiently than multichannel CSMA/CD when the bit-rate of an individual channel exceeded 10 Mbits/s. Hence the multichannel token passing protocol is far more appropriate for use with a WDM optical fibre LAN where each individual channel potentially has access to the full fibre bandwidth. It could therefore provide a method for achieving very high speed optical LANs in the future.

Currently, a major drawback with wavelength division multiplexing in optical fibre LANs is the requirement for a number of optical sources and detectors at each node together with the associated wavelength multiplexers and demultiplexers. However, developments in multiwavelength devices and integrated optical techniques will undoubtedly eventually reduce this equipment overhead.

Moreover, there is a margin for improvement in the performance of the multichannel token passing protocol on an optical fibre LAN by, for instance, operating the reservation channel at a higher speed than the data channels. This would reduce a restriction on the protocol performance caused by the fixed, finite token cycle time. The use of a higher speed reservation channel as well as higher speed data channels which are able to utilise more of the available fibre bandwidth is the subject of a continuing investigation into high speed optical fibre LANs.

The authors would like to thank the UK Science and Engineering Research Council for their support on grant number GR/D28485.

ARCHITECTURE
and
PROTOCOLS

10

Open Systems: Will the Future Ever Arrive?

RAY REARDON

'Will the future ever arrive? ... Should we continue to look upwards?'
Victor Hugo: 'Les Misérables'

Introduction

Everyone agrees with the need for standards: telecommunications carriers do; governments do; service suppliers do; manufacturers do; not least – users do.

As someone recently remarked, the nice thing about standards is that there are so many to choose from!

> There are F-series, T-series, V-series, X-series, and I-series recommendations. Within these there are scores of individual specifications and protocols, and even the individual ones can come in different flavours designated *bis* and *ter* and so on.

> There are the International Standards (IS), with the suffix number running into 4-digits, a similar set of Draft International Standards (DIS) and Draft Proposals (DP) promising even more to come; and many areas have yet to be started.

> In addition there are institutional bodies, national bodies, and manufacturers' organisations, all interested in and involved in the determination, evolution and specification of standards. Meanwhile influential user groups have started to set up their own pressure groups and to promote their own pragmatic subsets of standards.

There cannot be many other industries that hold literally dozens of seminars and conferences every year, purely on the subject of standards!

The paying customer, though, really wants 'seamless' solutions rather than construction kits as the basis for running the business. No matter how well the individual components are engineered, he just cannot digest them all and, even worse, does not see it as his job to sort out what will or will not fit together. Similarly, individual vendors or service providers cannot possibly support all permutations.

Fundamentally, standards should enable different vendor equipment to fit together – not require vendor solutions to fit different standards together. Further this prompts the question: are we making genuine progress on a broad front or spinning wheels?

In an attempt to answer this question I shall first review the architectural philosophy of OSI.

Open Systems Interconnection

In early 1977, Technical Committee 97 of the International Standards Organisation established a Subcommittee (SC16) with the stated intention of specifying an architecture to facilitate the interconnection of heterogeneous systems. This subcommittee is often referred to as ISO/TC97/SC16.

The scope of the work was envisaged as being much wider than just networking, ranging from physical transmission media to application functions such as data manipulation and word processing.

At an early stage, it conceived and defined the 7 Layer Reference Model which eventually achieved the status of International Standard 7498.

Considering the dynamic nature of the information technology industry, it is not surprising that to some extent it found itself chasing a moving target; for instance the advent of PCs and intelligent workstations, LANs, the 'connectionless' concept, ISDN, presentation graphics, the need for comprehensive network management facilities, and so on. There has been a degree of force-fitting, but the basic layered concept has proved itself versatile and resilient in reflecting change.

The OSI Reference Model

Each Layer has two major functions. Firstly to communicate with the Layers above or below it within its own hierarchical system, and secondly to communicate with its peer layers in other systems which follow the same layered concept.

Layers 1 to 3 provide *interconnection* and data transmission across various interlinked networks, which may be wide area or local area.

Layers 5 to 7 are concerned with *interworking* between information processing application systems regardless of how the network interconnection has been achieved. As such they are concerned with the meaning of the information exchanges taking place, and how the actual dialogues are conducted.

Layer 4 is the *bridge* between the network-oriented lower Layers and the applications-oriented upper Layers, allowing them to function independently of each other.

The **Physical Layer 1** is concerned with the business of transmitting a bit stream over a physical medium, between the terminal equipment and the network. It is responsible for the mechanical, electrical, and procedural interfaces involved in addition to providing for the activation, deactivation and connection of circuits to achieve a physical connection. It specifies line codes, transmission rates, signal voltage levels, and physical connectors. Standards include equipment interfaces such as V.24, the 8802.n series of standards for LANs, and I.430/431 for ISDN.

The **Data Link Layer 2** regards the transmission in terms of data instead of bits. It provides for the framing of bits into bytes for instance. It detects, and where possible recovers from, errors, or alternatively notifies the Network Layer of the existence of the error. Overall it is intended to ensure that reliable data transfer takes place between terminal equipment and the network. Standards within the layer include HDLC and LAPB, I.440/441 for ISDN, and 8802/2 Logical Link Control for LANs. For LANs it was necessary to add the concept of Medium Access Control (MAC) which is something of a hybrid in that it cuts across Layers.

The **Network Layer 3** sets up connections and is responsible for the efficient routeing of information through a network. For instance (in a packet-switched network) it works

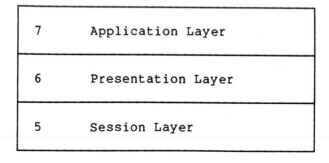

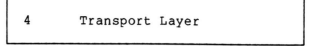

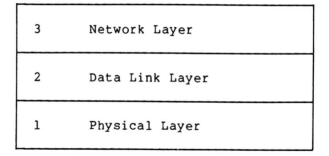

Figure 10.1 The OSI Reference Model

at the packet level rather than with bits and bytes. It is also concerned with node addressing and the routes between nodes, as well as control and acknowledgement to ensure that communication is correctly established. Standards in this layer include DP 8878 for connection-oriented X.25 networking, DP 8881 for X.25 Packet Protocol in LANs, and I.450/451 for ISDN.

The **Transport Layer 4** controls the quality of network service ensuring that reliable communication is taking place between the transmitting/receiving systems. It is concerned with end-to-end sequence control, flow control, error recovery, and multiplexing. Rather than individual bits, bytes, and packets, it is interested in the overall cohesive flow of information. The service definition and protocol specification for this layer are contained in ISO 8072 and 8073. The basic standard also defines five classes of protocol depending on the degree of error detection/recovery and multiplexing involved. The current standard is connection-mode oriented. Connectionless-mode service is under development.

The **Session Layer 5** manages the dialogue between systems. It ensures that the session is set up and terminated correctly and that, within the session, agreed protocols for turn management, synchronisation, and exception reporting are observed. It provides a tool-kit of functional units to help build the session, for example the 'kernel' which contains the service elements necessary to set up and close down the connection. The service definition and protocol specification for this layer are included in ISO 8326 and 8327.

The **Presentation Layer 6** is responsible for data formatting and code conversion to allow otherwise incompatible devices to communicate. Different manufacturers have different ways of representing data inside their machines. To enable different systems to interwork, the presentation layer sets up agreed rules at the beginning of the connection. The 'abstract syntax' relates to the sort of information being exchanged and the 'transfer syntax' relates to the rules for data representation. A special language has been specified: *Abstract Syntax Notation One* (ASN 1) in ISO 8824 and 8825. Other international standards include the T.50 international alphabet and the T.61 teletex character set. The service definition and protocol specification for this layer are included in ISO 8822 and 8823.

The **Application Layer 7** defines the nature of the task to be performed and provides the interface to user applications. It is also intended to provide a suite of service elements. The Common Application Service Elements (CASE) comprise general capabilities useful to a wide variety of applications, and the Specific Application Services Elements (SASE) provide particular facilities such as File Transfer Access & Management (FTAM). The X.400 Series for Electronic Mail also come within this group and will be incorporated within the ISO standard Message Oriented Text Interchange System (MOTIS).

Since the Reference Model was originally published it has been necessary to make some additions. The *Connectionless Addendum* was added to cover the connectionless mode of transmission needed for certain kinds of messaging services and LANs. Additional *Parts* have also been added to cover Security and Network Management, which were significant ommissions in the original Reference Model.

In summary, over more than a decade, the OSI framework has gained widespread recognition and acceptance throughout the world. Within it, an extensive range of individual standards has evolved.

However from a user's point of view OSI is not a single solution that can be taken down off the shelf and implemented directly. Someone has to select which of the many allowable components to use and how to integrate them into a real-life working system. In addition many quite fundamental functions such as network management are not yet in useable form, while some of the more ambitious areas of the Applications Layer are chasing a very dynamic market-place in which new concepts and offerings are constantly appearing.

Proprietary architectures

Most of todays corporate networks are based on proprietary architectures, that is architectures developed by specific manufacturers for their own particular product line.

Proprietary architectures control data communications within a single system of computers and peripheral devices. Specifications are often published so that other suppliers can produce compatible products and services. Sometimes conformance testing facilities may also be provided.

Proprietary architectures will persist and grow functionally richer through the 1990s for several reasons.

For many users, a fully supported end-to-end solution is more cost-effective than a self-supported 'pick and mix' approach, and gives better performance.

A specific implementation will often provide a more efficient solution with better integrity, security, and operational management facilities than more generalised approaches.

Specific implementation can and will tend to react faster to new user requirements. The user's own competitive edge may well depend on fast provision of new function.

However, proprietary architectures can be complementary and not inconsistent with standardised interconnection and interworking between different networks and systems. Most value added networks carrying out real business in the 1980s are based on proprietary architectures yet do just that. Otherwise they would not be in business. This interworking did cost a considerable amount of effort and the resulting solutions are most often very specific implementations and not portable. The OSI layered concept, with defined interface specifications and protocols, provides a very powerful architectural framework for easing that workload, widening the applicability, and improving the chances of success.

Given the commercial self-interest of vendors, and the irresistible market-place pressure for multi-vendor and inter-enterprise solutions, complementary products will undoubtedly be provided. Manufacturers will provide a useable subset of interfaces between their proprietary architectures and specific points in the OSI architecture, ideally providing the user with the best of both worlds. The interesting possibility is that a user who follows a sound proprietary architecture may well achieve practical open systems interconnection sooner than those that follow the do-it-yourself systems integration route.

User driven functional protocols

The third major force in establishing practical open systems interconnection and interworking is that driven by the user communities themselves.

The paying customer does not buy future architectures spread over a variable timeframe as such, but buys specific solutions to meet specific business needs at a specific moment in time. Certainly there are longer term incentives to adopt standards, but the practical ability to do so is often determined by existing investments as well as the desire to take advantage of newly emerging technologies and applications for which standards have yet to be specified and agreed. However, the user's voice is increasingly being heard. When large users such as General Motors and Boeing bang the table, the intelligent vendor sits up and listens. At the same time other users also tend to gather round. This is what happened figuratively, if not literally, as user companies lined up behind proposals for practical subsets of architectures and protocols.

Manufacturing Automation Protocol (MAP) user groups in the USA and Europe now have hundreds of members, and vendors demonstrate support by interconnecting and interworking their equipment at public exhibitions.

Technical and Office Protocol (TOP) has a similar objective for the general workplace.

Transmission Control Protocol/Internet Protocol (TCP/IP) was one of the earliest attempts to achieve practical interoperability, initiated by the US Defense Advanced Research Projects Agency (DARPA).

Many other governmental and inter-enterprise 'functional' profiles are being defined.

There is considerable momentum behind these initiatives, and increasing pragmatism as the paying customer is insisting that standards and protocols should correspond to actual requirements, not restrict opportunities, and be realistically and economically viable.

In conclusion

Will the future ever arrive? The answer is a very definite 'Yes'. It will arrive because it has to. The business requirements are too strong to resist.

Will it arrive exactly as the official standard-setters envisage? Probably not. What is more likely is that the eventual open systems environment will be a composite of OSI, proprietary architectures, and user specified subsets.

If we turn the clock forward ten years, it is quite possible that some of the specific recommendations currently accepted under the OSI umbrella will have turned out to be little more than wheel-spinners. On the other hand, there will also be some very powerful successes. The editor offers the following observations as purely personal opinions.

> Whether or not the Layers of the Reference Model were ideally specified and detailed sufficiently well in the first place will not matter. The basic philosophy is so powerful that unexpected new requirements will be retro-fitted (and rationalised if necessary).

> Layer 4, the Transport Layer, will prove to be the pivotal component, allowing a very high degree of contention resolution between the extremely rapidly developing realities of basic telecommunications interconnection with the extreme unpredictability of the data processing oriented interworking required by the Session, Presentation, and Application Layers.

> Proprietary architectures will persist and grow functionally richer for the reasons discussed earlier. However they will complement OSI and provide interconnection and interworking at appropriate OSI interface points, as determined by the marketplace.

> Many vendors with proprietary architectures already support the most important protocols of the first three (Interconnection) Layers. This will grow as Lans X.21, and ISDN become more pervasive and useful. In parallel new standards for very high speed packet switching will be developed.

> Similarly vendor support for X.400 and other upper layer facilities within proprietary architectures is already being announced.

> X.400 and FTAM will prove to be extremely useful useful layer standards and provide a very important base for inter-enterprise business communications. On the other hand, standards for graphics, databases, wordprocessing, spread-sheets, security, and network management will probably have difficulty keeping up with rapidly advancing concepts and technology.

The publication (and conformance testing facilities) of LU 6.2/APPC protocols will provide a very powerful and readily available approach to distributed transaction processing between OSI and SNA systems, and indeed other 'peer-to-peer' environments.

User-driven, pragmatic subsets of architectures and standards, such as MAP, TOP and TCP/IP, will continue to exercise a very strong independent commercial influence, complementing the work of the formal standards bodies.

Connecting different corporate networks together will prove to be more difficult than expected. Software release levels, network upgrades, and operational problems are a big enough problem for an intra-enterprise network of any complexity. Clearly the implications for inter-enterprise connections will be even more significant. To date the whole area of network management has tended to be underestimated in OSI.

Similarly, cross network security will place obligations on entry and boundary nodes to avoid unauthorised users from attempting to ride across the networks for fun or for free or for fraud.

Finally there is the fundamental question of whether seven layers are enough. The need for a Systems Application Architecture is increasingly being recognised.

These issues are not trivial and have yet to be analysed and defined in depth if the complex interconnection and interworking that will undoubtedly be demanded in the 1990s are to be successfully supported.

Once a standard becomes established it is part of the public domain and cannot easily be changed without public assent. Another question arises: who has the incentive and enthusiasm to keep standards up-to-date and upwards and downwards compatible as technology evolves? Immature, ossified standards can stifle industry.

There is a story about a famous landscape architect designing the layout of a college campus. Clearly the major architectural concepts had to be established early on. However he decided that the best way to establish the ideal routes for the footpaths was to wait for the students to wear them in themselves. Then after a year he laid down concrete paths where the grass had been worn away.

It is quite possible that a similar thing will happen within open systems, establishing the most effective routes with the eventual standards coming about by natural selection by users in the marketplace.

11

Message Handling as the Basis for Tele-Information Services

DR PETER H M VERVEST

Introduction

Since the early days of the telegraph, electronic mail has developed into computer-based message exchange. A new idea occurred in the early 1970s with the invention of the 'electronic mailbox': a number of researchers, brought together by the US Department of Defense via the Advanced Research Projects Agency Network (ARPANET), designed and developed the first experimental systems to exchange computer resident messages among themselves[1]. Each individual was given a computer mailbox, – a personal working area within a computer system to compose, send, receive and file messages. The electronic mailbox was an important new concept and it was totally new at that time as it meant that a computer would act as an 'agent' of the person and intervene in the communications process.

However, the early electronic mailbox systems, or Computer Based Message System (CBMS), lacked a way to exchange messages between different systems which were connected via a network. The first problem was to effect message exchange independent of the type of public or private telecommunication means being used. Secondly, agreement was necessary between the computer systems themselves with respect to the process of message communications and the types of messages to be exchanged. One of the first organisations to address these issues was the International Federation for Information Processing (IFIP), establishing its Working Group 6.5 on International Computer Message Systems in 1978[2].

International standardisation was sought to set common rules as an architecture for open systems interconnection. The International Standards Organisation (ISO) developed a general Reference Model for Open Systems Interconnection (OSI) as a framework[3]. In 1984 the International Telegraph and Telephone Consultative Committee (CCITT) set the Recommendations Series X.400 on Message Handling Systems (MHS)[4]. The Open Systems Interconnection/Message Handling Systems (OSI/MHS) model forms the basis for further agreements on computer-based message exchange. Message handling, however, can not be seen as the simple extension of electronic mail for interperson messaging. Within the ongoing standardisation work, message handling is primarily an intermediate function between system application processes on the one hand and system communication processes on the other. Message handling, therefore, is not just an extension of electronic mail for inter-person messaging, but it forms a basis for all kinds of existing and new tele-information services. It will be a way to shield the variety of networks and communication protocols from the application processes and *vice versa*.

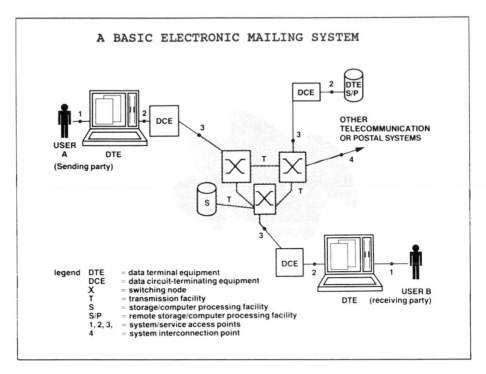

Figure 11.1

Developments in electronic mail systems

At present there are several ways to collect and distribute mail. The well-known systems include post and courier, telegram, telex, and analogue facsimile. Perhaps less well-known are facspost, store-and-forward message switching, and the telematic systems (teletex, digital facsimile, mixed-mode teletex and digital facsimile, and interactive videotex), as well as communicating word processors and personal computers, CBMS and voice mail[5]. Mail systems have in common the one-directional transfer of information in the form of a message from an identified sending party to an identified receiving party.

Figure 11.1 shows a basic electronic mailing system. It is composed of a sending and receiving party and a (tele-) communication system, enabling the transfer of mail items from one system access point to the other. There are three different modes whereby this transfer of mail items can take place:

> directly between sender and receiver, so that the intermediate (tele-) communication system is transparent for the message communication;

> store-and-forward allowing temporary storage of the message but generally only used for efficiency of the communications process;

> store-and-retrieve so that the addressee collects the messages from the intermediate system.

Because of the capturing and storage of messages inside the communication system, all kinds of message manipulations become possible. This has stimulated the interest in global message handling systems services: message handling systems interconnected on a worldwide basis can provide all kinds of message transfer and message processing services, while allowing a high degree of freedom for both sender and receiver.

The rapid development in terminal equipment, in particular communicating personal computers, and the ongoing storage of vast amounts of data in computer systems (on-line data bases), are some of the key activators of this development. Electronic mail then allows people to exchange messages among themselves as well as to access information resident in computer systems. As a result, electronic mail and message handling become vital for all kinds of tele-information services, defined as information services via telecommunications, such as data base services, electronic funds transfer, electronic publishing, electronic shopping, goods movement, and information management services. The following trends in (non-voice) telecommunications support this development:

> the implementation of global ISDN-type networks that enable the access to information by many different communication parties and for many different purposes; the concept of 'compound' document structures that can accommodate many different bit formats, such as structured data, text, voice and images;

> the design and dissemination of multi-functional, human-friendly and integrated terminals to support a variety of functions, including automated message handling;

> the construction of distributed data bases that can be accessed from the network(s) and yield information in the right format for the application processes.

CCITT message-handling functional model

CCITT has defined message handling as a function of the application layer (Layer 7 of the OSI model). It forms one of the first specifications of a user system that is part of the Application Layer in accordance with the OSI model. A Message Handling System (MHS) is defined by CCITT as the collectivity of user processing equipment, referred to as User Agent (UA), and Message Transfer Agents (MTA). A number of related MTAs constitute a Message Transfer Service (MTS), which provides the following types of services:

> interacting with originating UAs via the submission dialogue;

> relaying messages to adjacent MTAs based upon recipient designations and the networking plan;

> interacting with the recipient UAs via the delivery dialogue.

The MTS is the interconnection of distributed systems on the level of message transfer, called the Message Transfer Layer (MTL) as shown in Figure 11.2. The MTL is the conceptual boundary between the application layer and the lower-level communication layers. Its position is on the lowest part of the application layer and other application functions are positioned on top of this MTL. As of October 1984 CCITT has defined the

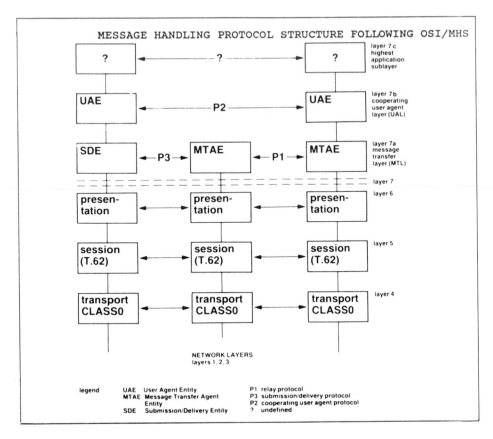

MESSAGE HANDLING PROTOCOL STRUCTURE FOLLOWING OSI/MHS

| | | | layer 7 c highest application sublayer |

Figure 11.2

Interpersonal Messaging Service (IPM) – or User Agent Layer (UAL) – for the relaying of messages for human end-users. The MTS functionality, however, extends beyond that of interpersonal messaging.

Directory services

An important extension of the MHS model are the directory services. First, the directory services enable one to identify the other party. The variety in message handling systems and the different conventions for naming and addressing, will make the compiling and maintenance of a public directory a formidable task. The updating of such a directory will be a continuous effort of processing the mutations of various directory systems. This may lead to a distributed directory system in such a way that every private MTA has an associated Directory Service Agent (DSA), to which all relevant information from the other directory systems must be copied, under the management of the overall public directory.

A second function of the directory is to include information on the type of messages (at Presentation Layer and/or Application Layer) and the method to obtain access to private or specific public systems. Moreover, the directory can be seen as a means to control access and to provide specific facilities for security. It may also provide domain management services and conformance testing services.

Protocol architecture for standardisation of tele-information services

The work of CCITT, ISO, IFIP, and other organisations (NBS, ECMA, IEEE, ANSI, etc) has resulted in an overall protocol architecture for the development of standards aimed at the interconnection of information systems. It is also the basis for the standardisation of tele-information services. The protocol structure has been laid down in Figure 11.3. It is composed of the following sets of standards (Recommendations):

IS 7498 (ISO, 1983) on Information Processing Systems – Open Systems Interconnection – Basic Reference Model and specific layer standards (including DIS 8473, 8348, DP 8602 for connectionless transmission);

CCITT Recommendations X.200, X.300 and X.400 Series;

CCITT Recommendations on telematic services as well as on bearer services;

local area network standards developed by the Institute for Electrical and Electronic Engineers (IEEE) and ISO.

A distinction is made between standardised applications and private applications. Private applications are based on proprietary architectures, developed independently of standardisation institutes by manufacturers or user organisations. System Network Architecture (SNA) and Document Interchange Architecture (DIA)/Document Content Architecture (DCA) is an important proprietary architecture developed by IBM. In general a proprietary architecture is not built for open systems interconnection and tends to exclude unlike systems from the environment. Communications across the boundaries necessitate gateway processors, which will restrict inter-system communications.

The more sophisticated inter-system applications are, the higher the level of standardisation must be. In particular three types of standards become increasingly important: office document architectures, industry-generic transaction formats, and interprocess control standards.

Office document architectures

Document interchange formats define the data structures of the information for transmission in such a way that both sender and receiver can interpret this structure. Each document will be composed of different portions of document content, with a specified relationship between these portions. This is called the document structure. ISO has been working on an Office Document Architecture (ODA) with a complementary Office Document Interchange Format (ODIF). A document is considered in two parts:

a document profile includes the parameters used to handle, process and file the document;

the content contains the information on how the document was created and which were the rules for making the document.

CCITT defines a Simple Formattable Document (SFD) in X.420 and a telematic documents interchange format in T.73 (the character set is defined in T.62).

OPEN SYSTEMS INTERCONNECTION — BASIC REFERENCE MODEL

X.200, X.210, X.250, IS 7498, DP 8509	Standardized applications			Private applications
	Telematics[2]	Office services	Data processing	

Layer 7 — application layer

Telematics[2]	Office services — DOCUMENT STRUCTURE AND INTERCHANGE T.73 DP8613	Data processing — REMOTE DATA HANDLING	Private applications [3]
TELETEX F.200, F.201, T.60, T.63, T.90, T.91, X.430, DP 9063/2, DP 9064/2	DIRECTORY, X.DS1, X.DS2, X.DS3, X.DS4, X.DS6, X.DS7	FILE TRANSFER, ACCESS AND MANAGEMENT DP 8571	
FACSIMILE T.0, T.2, T.3, T.4, T.5 DP 9063/1, DP 9063/2	MAILING F.40, F.350, X.400, X.401, X.408, X.420	JOB TRANSFER DP 8831, DP 8832	
Mixed-mode teletex / facsimile T.62, T.72, T.73	FILING DP 8571	PROGRAMMING AND INTERPROGRAM COMMUNICATIONS IS 1538, IS 1539, IS 6160, IS 6373, DP 8485, DIS 8802, DP 9007, DP 9079	
VIDEOTEX F.300, T.100, T.101	PRINTING	OTHER DP 8632, DP 8651, DP 9007, DP 9040, DP 9041	
OTHER	OTHER DIS 8879		

Layer 7a application sublayer	X.410, X.411 DP 8505 (MOTIS), DP 8649, DP 8650
Layer 6 presentation layer	T.50, T.51, T.61, T.73, T.100, X.409 IS 6937, DP 8822, DP 8823, DP 8824, DP 8825
Layer 5 session layer	X.215, X.225, T.62 DIS 8326, DIS 8327
Layer 4 transport layer	X.214, X.224, T.70 DIS 8072, DIS 8073, DIS 8602

Network oriented layers	X.213, X.244, X.300, X.310, V.100, V.110, I.120, I.210, I.211, I.212, DIS 8348, DIS 8473, DP 8648, DIS 8802/1					Private Local Area Network (LAN) and/or Wide Area Network (WAN)
	PSTN	CSPDN	PSPDN	ISDN	LAN[4]	
Layer 3 Network layer	telephone + X.25	X.21	X.25, X.3, X.28/ X.29, X.32 DIS 8208, DP 8878	I.450, I.451, X.30, X.31	DIS 8802/3, DIS 8802/4, DIS 8802/5, DIS 8802/6	
Layer 2 Data link layer	T.71 or X.25		LAPB/X.25 DIS 7776	I.440, I.441	DIS 8802/2	
Layer 1 Physical layer	e.g. V.24, V.25	X.21, X.21 bis, X.22	X.21, X.21 bis DIS 2110	I.430, I.431		

notes: 1. ISO standards are either International Standard (IS);
Draft International Standard (DIS); or Draft Proposal (DP).
CCITT Recommendations start with capital F., T., V., X., or I.
2. interworking with Telex (TWX) is foreseen, cf. F.201
3. examples are proprietary architectures such as SNA-DIA/DCA by International
Business Machines (IBM) or specific application protocols such as MAP by General Motors
4. The following LAN technologies are standardized:
DP 8802/3 Carrier Sense Multiple Access/Collision Detection
DP 8802/4 token bus
DP 8802/5 token ring
DP 8802/6 slotted ring

Figure 11.3 Protocol architecture for standardisation of tele-information services

Industry-generic transaction formats

Another important set are forms standards for business transactions. Much work for transaction standards has been performed by the Transportation Data Coordinating Committee (TDCC) in the USA. They have developed the Electronic Data Interchange (EDI) standard, with a generic software structure so that industries with similar data structures can adjust the standard to their specific requirements. EDI is composed of tables with respect to transaction set names, segments in each transaction set, segment names, data elements in each segment, and data element specifications.

Another important development by the American National Standards Institute (ANSI) addresses the issue of multi-industry transaction standards. Important ANSI transaction standards define purchase order (ANSI X12.1), invoice (X12.2), data dictionary (X12.3), remittance/pay advice (X12.4), and application control (X12.6).

Interprocess control standards

Increasingly information which is distributed over different systems must cooperate for a common task, such as for computer integrated manufacturing, data base enquiry, logistics and purchasing. Standards are needed that allow the use of distributed information as an integrated resource for certain tasks. For this reason General Motors has developed its Manufacturing Automation Protocol (MAP), based on the Seven Layer Model, but including an eighth Layer, the Manufacturing Message Format and Syntax (see also Boeing's TOP).

The introduction of electronic mail

Whereas the technology is generally available and an overall framework for interconnection is given, the question arises as to how new electronic mail and message handling systems will be introduced into society. In essence there are two important development paths: first, the new mail system can be introduced for intra-organisational applications. In this case the large organisation will take the lead. Second, new mail systems can be introduced for inter-organisational applications; in this case, service providers may take the lead.

In order to survey the introduction by large organisations, a mail questionnaire was issued to the members of the International Communication Association (ICA), which is a professional league of mainly North American telecommunication managers[6]. Figure 11.4 shows the main trends in use of mail systems resulting from this questionnaire (as unit for measurement the number of 'messages' per year – both internal and external – has been taken). The average increase over the period 1985–1995 is 5.7% per year. Some conclusions from the study are given below.

> There is a sharp increase in the use of non-standardised new electronic mail, defined as communicating word processors and personal computers, CBMS and voice mail.
>
> Telematic systems (teletex, digital facsimile, mixed-mode teletex/digital facsimile and interactive videotex) have a slower take-off, probably due to the time lag involved in the standardisation work, than non-standardised electronic mail; digital facsimile is by far the most important.

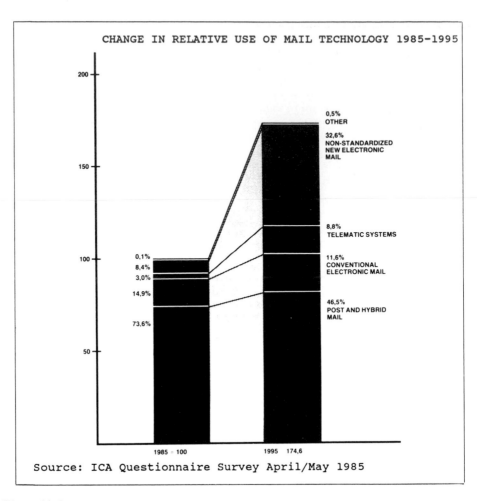

Figure 11.4

The use of conventional mail systems, that is telex/TWX, analogue facsimile and store-and-forward message switching, will decrease except for store-and-forward message switching; the growth of this latter technology (annual linear growth of 9.6%) is comparable to the newer mail systems and supports the view that telecommunication managers anticipate some major innovations here (due to MHS).

There will be a moderate increase of approximately one per cent per year in the use of post-oriented services; traditional postal services will remain about the same over the forecast period, while hybrid forms of post and electronic mail will increase at 12.2% per year.

Most of the reasons for introducing a new mail technology, as given in the ICA survey, are either need or cost driven. Need factors include orientations towards effectiveness and reliability of communication, the speed and the improvement of the information flow and information access. Cost considerations are specifically expressed in the desire to reduce costs and to improve overall operations and productivity of the telecommunications department. External factors get considerably less attention: competitive advantage, increased organisational responsiveness and the provision of new services are rarely mentioned.

The main bottlenecks foreseen with the introduction of new mail technology are in the area of organisational adaptations, user acceptance, and (lack of) standardisation. Organisational acceptance may be difficult as application requirements are different across organisations and between departments. New systems may be incompatible with already installed systems and/or current procedures; or the degree of change which is required may become too high.

Individual users may have a negative attitude towards the use of new technologies; new systems necessitate the retraining of users and result in divestiture of existing skills. User procedures are difficult and rigid, the applications are not integrated and reliability of message delivery and receipt are unproven. The introduction of new technology requires the understanding of user attitudes towards change. A phased implementation and extensive education seem to be prerequisite for successful introduction.

Another bottleneck concerns the costs associated with the introduction of new mail systems. New users may want to minimise the initial expenses and may prefer low fixed costs and high variable costs. As their usage increases, they may want to increase fixed costs in order to lower the overall costs per message. However, 'intangible' tariff structures make such a policy very difficult.

The choice and availability of equipment, software and services is also a bottleneck for many user organisations, according to the ICA. Critical for the use of new mail systems is the timely availability of a number of key technologies in the areas of workstations, network message computers, voice-mail and data communication technology in general. Workstation technologies are of specific concern as their penetration will ultimately determine the accessibility of electronic mail facilities for the individual user.

The lack of adequate standards is seen as perhaps the most severe bottleneck for the introduction of new mail technology. The findings of the ICA survey suggest that widely accepted standards are an alibi for the less knowledgeable firm to build up its own expertise. At the early stages of development, the user has in principle three alternatives:

to invest in new technology with all risks associated with that choice,

to invest in proven technology that is more or less stable and standardised,

to postpone the investment decision.

Which course of action will be taken, will depend to a great extent on the available resources in the telecommunications and automation departments of the organisation. Particularly important resources are: financial funds, in-house expertise, overall know-how in the computer and communications disciplines, including data processing and office automation, and – perhaps most important – experience in implementing systems. The

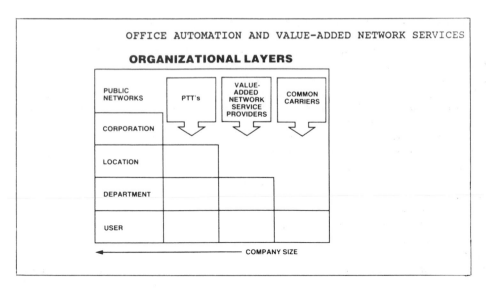

Figure 11.5

organisational attitude as well as the ability to experiment with a complicated new system seems a prerequisite for innovative behaviour. User organisations without these capabilities will prefer to postpone decisions until standardisation has been effected.

The role of value added network service providers

Large organisation will first use electronic mail as part of their office automation programmes. Office automation gradually extends its scope from the department level towards intra-site communications via local area networks. At the same time there is a development toward inter-site and corporate systems that integrate different organisational processes (purchasing, manufacturing, logistics, marketing and administration in particular) via a company wide area network (*Figure 11.5*).

The development of corporate – often international – wide area networks (WAN) by the large organisation adds a new dimension for electronic mail. The WAN becomes a company resource for access by non-members of the organisation, that is for the organisation to communicate with its environment such as suppliers and customers. The large organisation can then provide services such as information on products, organisational procedures or more general information; it can also share resources with its environment, like electronic mailbox, data bases or data processing/computer power. Even more important, transactions between the organisation and the environment can be handled electronically and procedures could be imposed upon less powerful suppliers and customers. In fact the corporate network can be used as a strategic means to increase the competitive strength of the large organisation.

Some trends are counterbalancing this possible dominance of the large organisation. Telecommunication service providers (PTT's and carriers) extend their communication-orientated services into information processing, and computer timesharing bureaux enter networking businesses. Cooperative leagues and associations of small and medium size companies seek a new opportunity to enforce the cooperative structure among their members via a concept similar to WAN.

This leads to the conceptualisation of Value Added Network Services (VANS), defined (*Butler & Cox, 1984*) as:

> 'A value added network service is a service based on a telecommunications network by which messages are processed or stored so that some value is added to the message as it is transferred from the message sender to the message receiver. In addition to the network operator, value added network services involve two other categories of participant: the service provider and the service users (or subscribers).'

Thus, the kernel of VAN services are electronic mail and message handling facilities; this usually narrows down to:

> connection of incompatible computer terminals of different manufacturers or of different models, by converting protocols, speeds, codes, formats and media;
>
> access to and from a variety of networks and the interlinking of different nets (internetting);
>
> concentration of traffic and optimal path selection;
>
> error detection/correction, improving of reliability and security;
>
> message routeing, storage and processing;
>
> access to data bases and computer application programs, including remote job entry and remote execution of jobs over distributed computer systems.[7]

It will be clear that both intra- and inter–organisational applications will play an important role in the future of electronic mail. In particular the developments in personal computers has given a new challenge to provide complementary services (the intelligent PC-Mainframe link).

Standardisation as a tool of government innovation policy

With the advent of OSI/MHS, a new technological trajectory has been advanced to manage variety in computer communications. The fundamental characteristic of this innovation can be summarised as follows:

> OSI/MHS induces the development of systems technology that shields the variety of telecommunication networks from the application processes, in such a way that distributed, formalised information systems can cooperate in order to perform a common task by 'meaningful' message exchange.

OSI/MHS constitutes the architectural design for the provision of tele-information services allowing the inter-operability of these services. As an architectural design, OSI/MHS makes a critical distinction between communication and application-oriented functions, through a common boundary, embodied in message handling. Via this architecture the pathway has been laid for the evolution of electronic mail towards worldwide computer-mediated message communications. Base technologies – network processors, computers, workstations, operating systems and programming tools – which are generally available, will have to be applied to the OSI/MHS architecture, whereas proprietary designs should be divested for their communications with the outside world ('gateway policy').

A number of rigidities exist in the process of OSI/MHS innovation. Rigidities can be observed in the development of the supporting technologies, in the existing regulatory framework for telecommunication service provision, in standardisation, and in the development of intra- and inter-organisational applications (via office automation and value added networks). Standardisation seems to have the specific role of inducing innovation as well as facilitating the transition from innovation to market diffusion. Government can therefore stimulate and lead the innovation process by way of standardisation policy. In particular the availability of expertise and the industrial interests associated with standards determine the way in which standards policy can be constructed[8].

In conclusion the most critical objectives for successful innovation in electronic mail are:

the continued development of OSI/MHS and the broad acceptance by scientists, policy makers, manufacturers, and users;

the development and implementation of network equipment and network arrangements complying with OSI/MHS;

simple-to-operate communication capabilities for workstations and private systems;

the widespread use of office automation in large organisations and the construction of company wide area networks;

the evolution of a new industry of value added network services for facility sharing, access to information and transactions;

the lowering of user barriers at the individual and organisational level, with special emphasis for the small and medium size company;

the promotion of standards, both with respect to the speed of the standards-making processes, as to the implementation and enforcement of such standards;

the creation of a new regulatory régime with respect to the provision of – new – telecommunication services, the position of traditional telecommunication service providers, and aspects of data integrity.

12

OSI File Transfer, Access and Management

S JOE HIELSCHER

Introduction

Transferring and manipulating file data between distributed systems is one of the most important underlying aspects of providing distributed information processing in open systems interconnection. Efforts to standardise a file service have been progressing now in the International Standards Organisation (ISO) for several years under the general framework of the Reference Model for Open Systems Interconnection (OSI-RM).

These efforts resulted in the progression of File Transfer, Access and Management (FTAM) to the status of Draft International Standard (DIS) in 1986. A final International Standard (IS) is expected to be available following the June 1987 meeting of ISO TC97/SC21 in Tokyo. The FTAM IS is intended to become OSI's architectural linchpin for creating, accessing, and moving structured file information reliably end-to-end between heterogeneous systems.

Purpose of FTAM

File Transfer, Access and Management is part of the OSI family of standards, produced to allow the interconnection of computer systems through communications methods. The aim of OSI is to minimise the amount of detailed technical information that must be determined about a system before a meaningful communication can be established. FTAM defines services for file information interchange through communications, and does not apply to the interchange of files on physical media, such as diskettes and tapes.

Requirements for FTAM, frequently cited by users:

> to provide distributed access for record-oriented (hierarchical) files, thus allowing programs resident and executing on one system to access data files on another system.

> to retrieve, store, distribute and manage files and file data in a distributed multi-vendor network.

Systems that differ from one another in terms of their structure or the conventions used to represent information are termed heterogeneous. The heterogeneous nature of most real file systems, file services, and even the semantics used to describe these systems, presented the greatest obstacle to achieving a distributed file service standard. Assured transportability of the file information between heterogeneous operating systems, without the user being concerned with the different aspects of data representation, was a subject for many years of study before the FTAM standardisation effort even began.

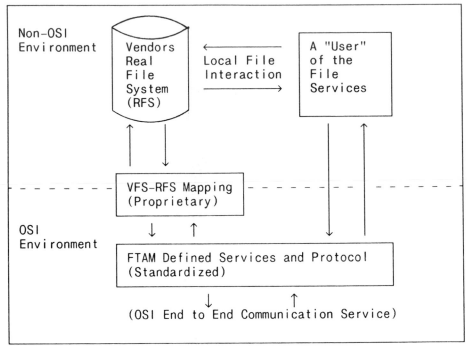

FTAM Architectural Model

Figure 12.1

The FTAM approach to file interchange involves the standardisation of the interactions between a file service user and a file system (the file service provider). In the case of FTAM, this operation is a distributed one – thus allowing for a very powerful approach to file access, as well as file transfer and management within an OSI network.

The FTAM-provided file services could be implemented in a vendors' product to provide a core component for user applications (for example accounting and payroll) or system applications (for example distributed data base management). A great benefit, only realised with such an architecture is that the apparent complexity of the FTAM file service providers to the file users may be reduced.

An architectural model

The FTAM service and protocol is an Application Layer standard (OSI-RM Layer 7). The OSI-RM and associated protocols and services for Layers 1–6 define an architecture for communication of the information needed in order to provide the services of Layer 7, the Application Layer. Because Layer 7 provides services which have meaning to end-users, and not just to the protocols of a layer above, FTAM must deal with the behavior of the local operating systems (its processing and storage capabilities) which are by definition outside the scope of OSI.

The non-OSI aspect of the file services required the developers of the FTAM standard

NETWORKS FOR THE 1990s

to study the scope of existing proprietary file systems in great depth before standardisation efforts could progress. The study resulted in the definition of an abstract model for a file system, called the Virtual Filestore (VFS). The VFS defines a whole vocabulary for FTAM, which allows for a definition of the required file services and protocols in well understood terminology. Indeed, the concept of the VFS has connected the conceptual services of OSI with a real user need.

In a real implementation, that is any product which uses FTAM protocol, the VFS is an invisible abstraction that implies the appearance of file information to the users of the file service. The VFS exists only in terms of a mapping function which the local system implements between its real file system (RFS) and the FTAM user. Therefore, the architectural model for FTAM allows the differences in real file systems to be absorbed into the VFS-RFS mapping function.

Figure 12.1 shows the relationship of the OSI aspects of FTAM to the non-OSI aspects of the local (ie proprietary) file system.

FTAM itself does not define how the human user interfaces to the services that it provides. For example, an implementation of FTAM may be invoked directly by a human user, by a subsystem processing a queue of requests, by transparent mapping to an operating system, or by a user-written application program. In each case, the same file protocols will be used, and the same file model applies.

An analogy to record-oriented files

The Virtual Filestore concept, when compared with a record-oriented proprietary file system, is easily mapped to represent the hierarchical structural nature of real files in its own abstract OSI terminology (*Figure 12.2*). The common concept of a file-record becomes the VFS Data Unit (DU) and the concept of fields within a record corresponds to a VFS Data Element (DE).

Organisational aspects of the VFS describe how DUs are related in terms of a hierarchy, or tree-structure. Sub-trees within this structure are referred to as File Access Data Units (FADUs) which are the smallest unit of data within the VFS which may be transferred. In fact, all operations on a file's content are performed on an FADU basis – the FADU being either all of the contents of the file or a single record/DU.

Each DU, like a record, has a structure of its own and, as is usually the case with real files, the DU structure is consistent across all of the DUs in a particular VFS file. DU structures are defined on a file-by-file basis when a file is created. The FTAM implementation uses the services of the Presentation Layer to identify the data types of each DE within the DU. When a VFS file is selected by an initiator, the responder communicates this structural information along with the document type definition, file name, and attributes.

In order to ensure that the file contents exchanged by FTAM can be interpreted with the same meaning by all implementations, FTAM represents its data according to ISO's standardised ASN.1 Primitive Data Types. Each DE is a specific instance of one of the abstract data types shown in Figure 12.2. Because of this common representation, FTAM exchanges are independent of the local file systems code set and storage architecture.

Required supporting services

In order to establish, control, and terminate application dialogues (FTAM Associations) with remote applications, FTAM uses ISO Layer 7 Association Control Service Element

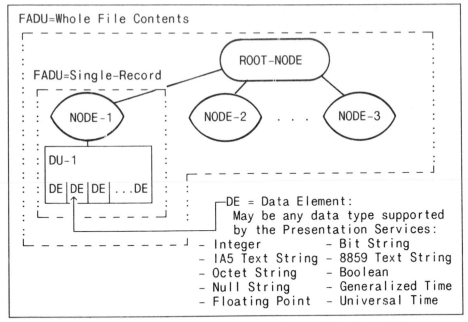

VFS File Representation of Typical File

Figure 12.2

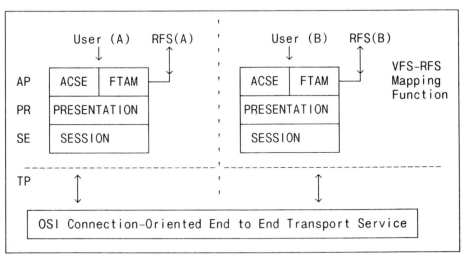

FTAMs Position in the OSI Reference Model

Figure 12.3

(ACSE) protocol. Additionally, an ISO Presentation Layer protocol (Layer 6) manages the transfer syntaxes required, and the data representations involved, and in turn, relies upon the Session Layer which performs connection and synchronisation services for the FTAM user. Because the functioning of the upper three layers of an FTAM implementation are interdependant, an FTAM product will usually encompass the services of Layers 5 through 7 together.

Further, an FTAM product requires a reliable end-to-end OSI Transport service. This service will be specified by Functional Standards according to ISO Transport Class 4 protocol. Physical interconnection of the distributed system is invisible to FTAM. For example, the actual connection may run over any X.25 wide area network or any 802.3, 802.4 or 802.5 local area network (*Figure 12.3*).

The file service

Exchange of file information in FTAM is performed by use of the file service. FTAM defines the file service in terms of file service users and file service providers. The file service providers assume a master-and-slave relationship, and are referred to as an Initiator and a Responder. FTAM specifies the services performed by the Initiator which issues file service requests, and the Responder which acts on the VFS files in response to those requests (*Figure 12.4*). File service users always obtain file service through an FTAM initiator.

The act of transferring file data can be considered as being performed by a copying application. The Initiator, which may have local access to a file in its own VFS, or its non-OSI filestore, and remote access to the Responder VFS selects and opens the file of interest, and then locates and copies the desired information. This operation may be performed on the entire contents of a file, resulting in a file transfer, or on a portion of the file contents (for example a record), resulting in file access.

The file protocol carries only information about the virtual filestore at the Responder side of the connection, and thus any exchange of file data is asymmetrical – controlled by the user at the side of the Initiator (*Figure 12.4*).

An implementation of FTAM may support either the Initiator or Responder role, or may optionally support both. As an example, a file server application would probably support only a Responder role, and may service a number of secondary systems which will read and write file information to it as Initiators. A general purpose system which wishes to support open file transfer with peer OSI systems is likely to support both roles.

Exchanges between the Initiator and the Responder lead to the selection of at most one file in the Responders VFS at any one time. Each Responder supports one VFS and its associated files.

Quality of service

The file service defined by FTAM allows the user to specify its quality of service requirement. Based on the users' requirement, and the services available at the Responder and Initiator side of an exchange, the requested level of service may be rejected or accepted. FTAM defines an architecture for the file service in which the quality of service may imply that error-recovery procedures are needed (*Figure 12.4*).

The FTAM IS will contain error-recovery procedures, however it should be noted that no current implementation work on FTAM, nor Functional Standard, specifies use of the

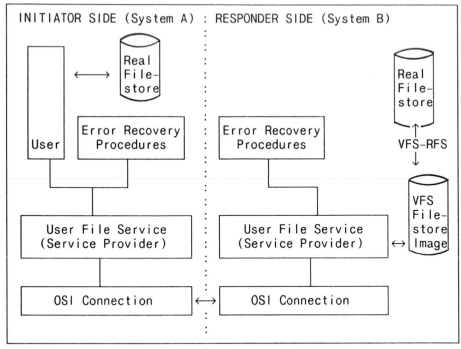

File Service Architecture

Figure 12.4

error-recovery mechanism. The recovery process will eventually allow restarting and synchronisation of failed transfers at predefined checkpoints. Because it is assumed that any FTAM application profile rests on a reliable end-to-end communication service, the user visible service is never impacted by non-interrupting communications errors between the involved machines.

In order to allow the definition of inter-operating subsets of the FTAM standard, provisions are made for an implementation to limit itself to one or more Service Classes.

Five file Service Classes are defined in FTAM in terms of the Functional Units they provide. Functional Units are the abstract definitions for the functions provided within the protocol and are considered either mandatory, optional or not supported in the definition of the FTAM service classes.

In the following table (*Figure 12.5*) the five Service Classes and the nine Functional Units are associated. The FTAM standard allows a great deal of flexibility in how an implementation may select the optional Service Classes, and which Functional Units may then be implemented within those Service Classes. Furthermore, the FTAM File Protocol itself provides a negotiation mechanism by which the Initiator and the Responder agree on the least common denominator of support for the Service Classes so that they may inter-operate.

Optional functional units are negotiated immediately following association of the FTAM application dialogue. The cooperating applications establish a least common

NETWORKS FOR THE 1990s

denominator of the requested, mandatory and commonly agreed functional units available.

FTAM specifies an extensive set of attributes for VFS files. Attributes that are associated with the files' existence and thus are always present are called File Attributes. Some attributes exist for a file only while that file is being manipulated or read by one of the file service users; these are called Activity Attributes.

FTAM defines a general hierarchical model for describing the structure of files. In the model, a file structure is an ordered hierarchical tree, and the file data is assigned to the nodes, or limbs, of the tree. This is a powerful file model, because its use can be extended to represent the majority of file structures that exist in real systems. There are four aspects of the File Structure in FTAM.

> *File Access Structure*, which describes how the file is composed from individual Data Units (DU).

> *Presentation Structure*, which describes the abstract syntax of DUs.

> *Transfer Structure*, which describes how DUs are to be serialised for communications purposes.

> *Identification Structure*, which describes how the naming of nodes in the File Access Structure can be transferred.

Not all real filestore implementations will map successfully to all imagined file structures. In order to allow the users of the FTAM file service to limit the scope of structures which must be supported, and to allow implementation on systems with simple and complex file systems, FTAM allows for the identification of Constraint Sets. Constraint Sets are used to accomplish two ends: to limit the range of file structures allowed and to identify how basic actions can modify the structure without changing its essential nature.

The FTAM DIS identifies the seven specific constraint sets outlined in Figure 12.6 which serve to represent some common file structures known to be implemented in real systems today. The ISO Constraint Sets are always identified by name.

Document types

In order to simplify the identification of implementation options – in the structure of file information, the Constraint Set, syntax and semantics for the transfer of information in files – FTAM allows for the identification of a broad range of options for each file into a limited number of Document Types which are in turn each identified by a single unique Document Type Name.

The use of the Document Type Name further enhances the likelihood of two FTAM implementations being able to inter-operate by selecting the series of options available to the implementor.

An important feature of Document Types is a feature that identifies how a complex file structure may be accessed by a simplification method, where the more complex types may optionally be read as a simpler subset of the File Access Structure, for example reading a sequential text file as a simple text stream.

Document Types may be defined by ISO, in the FTAM International Standard, or by one of the organisations defining functional standards. Ideally, the final FTAM IS will define a limited number of document types which will satisfy all user requirements, and

S C E L R A V S I S C E E S				

Unconstrained Class (U) ↓

File Transfer and Management Class (TM) ↓

File Management Class (M) ↓

File Access Class (A) ↓

File Transfer Class (T) ↓

FUNCTIONAL UNITS

	T	A	M	TM	U
• Kernel	M	M	M	M	M
• Read	*	M	–	*	O
• Write	*	M	–	*	O
• File Access	–	M	–	–	O
• Limited File Management	O	O	M	O	O
• Enhanced File Management	O	O	M	O	O
• Grouping	M	O	M	M	M
• Recovery	O	O	–	O	O
• Restart Data Transfer	O	O	–	O	O

"M"=Mandatory / "O"=Optional / "–"=Not Supported
"*"=One or more starred functional unit must be supported.

Service Classes and Functional Units

Figure 12.5

which may then be mapped to many real file systems by the implementors.

At this time ISO has defined five Document Types, and in a parallel effort, the National Bureau of Standards OSI workshop (NBS) has defined nine. While the NBS and ISO document types are very similar, NBS has structured a more limited set which are simpler to implement than ISO's, and has added one document type which serves to define an interim FTAM function – that of remote access to the VFS file directory or catalogue (NBS-9). Eventually, remote access to an FTAM file directory may be provided by another Application Layer function, Directory Services.

As with file structures, the actions that FTAM defines derive from the study of real file systems. An action in FTAM effects either the file attributes or contents, or both. By their nature, actions on attributes are said to affect complete files such as naming or file usage parameters, while actions on file content allow the user to read or modify the data contained in the file. FTAM defines eight actions on complete files and six actions for file access which are listed in Figure 12.8.

Implementation

The speed of development for many of the OSI Standards and their related Functional Standards has been unprecedented. Implementors and users have contributed, at significant expense, to the development of this effort hoping to profit from the resulting solutions. Because FTAM was recognised very early as an important OSI application service, it was widely implemented while still in its early draft stages. This was due largely to the influences of the MAP and TOP organisations and has resulted in a phased implementation of the FTAM protocol.

The combination of complexity in the standards, the widespread demand, the speed of development and the range of capabilities and applications to be supported has lead to a set of difficult problems for the implementors related to implementation choices, conformance and compatibility.

Because ISO standards have been developed through a consensus process responsive to a wide range of requirements, each contains multiple classes of service and many options. Because the standards must work in a variety of communication situations and satisfy diverse application requirements, each contains parameters or values that must be assigned or negotiated for a particular situation.

The result is an extremely large number of implementation alternatives for each standard and an even larger number of alternatives associated with the OSI seven-layer stack of protocols. Implementors have to agree on what options to implement, and how to ensure that their products will work with each other.

Functional standards emerge

Inter-operating requires selection of a common set of options and services in the base standards, and also upon common usage of several layers of the OSI protocols. Thus the need for a standard for standards, or a Functional Standard becomes apparent which;

satisfies a given functional requirement, and the needs of a particular market, for a given set of standards;

ties together the usage of several Layers of the OSI Reference Model.

A number of organisations have convened experts to draw up Functional Standards (also known as Functional Profiles, Specifications, or Implementation Agreements). Frequently these are practical reference implementations around which manufacturers can design viable products. The intent is that products built to conform to a certain Functional Standard will inter-operate with other implementations built to the same Functional Standard. In this sense, Functional Standards bring greater value to the notion of conformance, and enhance the meaning of any conformance test result or certification statement made by a vendor.

The natural inverse of the above situation is that, if there are multiple Functional Standards, there may be multiple, incompatible, products. The later would be undesirable to the implementors, and so the organisations involved in Functional Standards have significantly coordinated their work – hopefully to ensure that the resultant Functional Standards allow an area of overlap, where the two are identical, and products conforming fully to either Functional Standard will be able to inter-operate.

The MAP, TOP, NBS and SPAG specifications for the implementation of OSI protocols provide examples of Functional Standards which specify the implementation aspects of the Seven Layer OSI Reference Model. Specifically, these Functional Standards define the requirements FTAM application services impose on the supporting protocols for OSI Layers 5, 6 and 7.

ISO CONSTRAINT SET NAME	COMMON FILE TYPE REPRESENTED
• Unconstrained	For use with any file type where the user wishes to transfer the whole file without having any access, or conversion of the internal structure of the file.
• Sequential Flat	Simple sequential, or consecutive file types.
• Ordered Flat	Indexed sequential file type, index field serves as name of individual FADUs and in the case might not be unique.
• Ordered Flat-Unique Names	Same as above, but index names are unique.
• Ordered Hierarchical	Hierarchically organized files, where the children of each node of the file are ordered according to their node name.
• General Hierarchical	Full Hierarchical with no constraints.
• None	The root node in Hierarchical structure only with no data.

ISO Constraint Sets

Figure 12.6

The important effect of the General Motors Manufacturing Automation Protocol (MAP) and the Boeing Technical and Office Protocols (TOP) groups, which have done much to pressure OSI into the implementation stage, is well publicised. In 1985 both MAP and TOP published specifications, in effect the first North American OSI Functional Standards (MAP version 2.1 and TOP version 1.0). Some FTAM products were built to conform to these specifications, and many more prototypes were demonstrated. Late in 1986, based on significant technical advancements in OSI, both MAP and TOP announced their plans to release new versions of these specifications in 1988, which would supersede the earlier versions (MAP version 3.0 and TOP version 3.0).

In parallel efforts, a number of European companies have cooperated in efforts to create a European Functional Standard for many aspects of OSI. The result of much of this effort is the Standards Promotion and Application Group – Guide to the Use of Standards (SPAG – GUS) which is currently in its third revision.

Much of the technical background work for the SPAG, MAP and TOP FTAM specifications had been done at the National Bureau of Standards (NBS). The NBS sponsored a workshop for developers of OSI products, which has been doing work since 1984 on Functional Standards based on the forthcoming ISO standards. These Functional Standards are documented in an evolving 'Implementors Agreements' document, which specifies three implementation phases for FTAM. These agreements are the basis for the work in MAP, TOP and SPAG.

Versions of FTAM products

There have been several Functional Standards for the implementation of the FTAM protocols defined by the organisations mentioned earlier. These were completed to various degrees prior to the resolution of the ISO Draft Proposals and working papers for FTAM, and well before the impending International Standard had stabilised.

It must be stated that while experimental work can be carried out on unstable International Standard drafts, provided they are sufficiently advanced technically, it is extremely difficult for a manufacturer to invest in a product for which the commercial lifetime may be short; it will be unsaleable when 'stable standard' products are on the market. This has proven to be the case with some early products implementing the FTAM first and second draft proposals. The prospect of an FTAM DIS, which is now complete, and a forthcoming IS, makes long-term commercial investment by the vendors and users feasible.

There have been five Functional Standards for FTAM that are known to be implemented, but few systems vendors have made these products generally available. As will be shown, there is significant overlap between each version identified below:

Autofact '85

MAP 2.1/TOP 1.0/NBS Phase One

NBS Phase Two FTAM

MAP 3.0/TOP 3.0/GOSIP (See Phase Two)

SPAG GUS 3.0 (See NBS Phase Two)

Autofact '85 FTAM

Autofact '85, a trade show held each year in Detroit, Michigan, was a demonstration of practical inter-operating in an automated factory environment based on the MAP 2.1 and TOP 1.0 specifications. General Motors and the Boeing Company put significant resources behind the planning of this demonstration. Some 21 vendors demonstrated inter-operating of FTAM and Manufacturing Messaging protocols (MMFS) at this show. The event was meant to be a demonstration of feasibility of inter-operating open systems.

ISO	=	NBS	Document Type Common Characteristics
FTAM-1		None	Unstructured Text File Single FADU Character String Unstructured Constraint Set
FTAM-2		NBS-2*/3* 4/5	Sequential Text File Multiple FADU Character String (Records) Sequential Flat Constraint Set *Required only for backward compatib.
FTAM-3		NBS-1	Unstructured Binary File Single FADU Octet String Unstructured Constraint Set
FTAM-4		None	Sequential Binary File Multiple FADU Octet String Sequential Flat Constraint Set
FTAM-5		NBS-6	Sequential File (Flat File) FADU DU Syntax Follows ASN.1 Ordered Flat Constraint Set
FTAM-5		NBS-7	Random Access File (Relative) FADU DU Syntax Follows ASN.1
FTAM-5		NBS-8	Simple Hierarchical File (Indexed) FADU DU Syntax Follows ASN.1 Unique Node-Name Identifier Strings Multiple FADUs
No Equiv.		NBS-9 (Interim)	File-Directory File Non-stored Only SELECT/OPEN/READ/CLOSE/DESELECT Only access allowed is Sequential

ISO and NBS Document Types

Figure 12.7

The Autofact demonstrations were based on an early Draft Proposal FTAM and a document produced by the MAP Task Force (General Motors) to further define the incomplete portions of the standard. This was the Demo Agreements Document – Autofact '85 which defined the following FTAM capabilities:

simple file transfer

binary and flat (ASCII) files only

limited File Management (create, delete and read attributes)

The Autofact '85 FTAM variation allowed the exchange of demonstration files between the participants, along with filenames and very limited structuring information on the files.

Autofact FTAM was implemented in the absence of supporting protocols for the Presentation Layer, because the technical work at that Layer was too unstable and incomplete to be implemented.

MAP 2.1 and TOP 1.0 FTAM

The MAP 2.1 and TOP 1.0 version numbers identify the specifications, or Functional Standards, whose release followed the Autofact '85 demonstrations. Functionally, these documents are identical with the Autofact agreements; however, minor changes were made in the FTAM specification in order to align more closely with the second FTAM Draft Proposal which was released by ISO for balloting during MAP and TOP preparation for Autofact '85.

There are, therefore, slight differences between the specification used for FTAM at Autofact and the final MAP 2.1, TOP 1.0 and NBS Phase One implementations of FTAM. These differences are sufficient to not allow inter-operating between the Autofact implementations, and MAP, TOP or NBS versions. These versions, although practically identical in terms of the file service, are effectively incompatible and will not inter-operate.

NBS Phase One FTAM

The NBS FTAM Phase One specification is the result of work done in coordination with the NBS Workshop for Implementors of OSI, General Motors and the Boeing Company in preparation for Autofact '85 and to some extent, thereafter. The completion of Phase One in NBS signified an attempt to formalise early work into an NBS document. This specification is also based on the FTAM 2nd Draft Proposal. NBS Phase One implementations are identical with MAP 2.1 and TOP 1.0 FTAM when certain errata are considered to align the latter with the NBS specification.

The NBS Phase One specification was also developed in the absence of a sufficiently stable Presentation Layer specification, and therefore, maps the protocol for FTAM directly onto the Session Layer services. This mapping, and the total lack of a presentation protocol is the reason that NBS Phase One FTAM is incompatible with DIS or IS versions of the FTAM standard, and is a cause for great concern where it has been built into MAP or TOP networks based on the current MAP/TOP specifications.

NBS Phase Two – the first full product
(SPAG, MAP and TOP versions 3.0)

Following the feasibility demonstrations of 1984 and 1985, the NBS workshop began to define a second specification for FTAM – Phase Two. The workshop based the Phase

Actions on Complete Files	Actions for File Access
• Create a File • Select a File • Change Attributes • Read Attributes • Open File • Close File • Delete File • Deselect File	• Locate an FADU (First, Next, Previous, Key) • Read FADU • Insert FADU • Replace FADU • Extend FADU • Erase FADU

Virtual Filestore Actions

Figure 12.8

Two Functional Standard on the FTAM Draft International Standard of February 1986. In March 1987 the Phase Two Functional Standard was frozen in draft status, and the decision was made for Phase Two to be finished in late 1987 when the final ISO FTAM International Standard becomes available. Some implementors are proceeding to develop products to the current draft Phase Two specification.

The most significant aspect of Phase Two FTAM is that it is the first FTAM specification designed to produce meaningful products. Phase Two FTAM has become the preferred remote file access method for MAP and TOP in their next general revision. In fact, MAP version 3.0, TOP version 3.0 and the SPAG GUS version 3.0 specifications will essentially be the same, and will each reference the NBS Phase Two FTAM Functional Standard. A new specification, also based on the FTAM work done at NBS, is the US Government OSI Profile (GOSIP) – which defines only Phase Two FTAM implementations will be accepted for US Government procurements.

The members of the NBS workshop again realised the original file service problem when a final definition of systems conforming to the NBS specification was drafted. Not all FTAM systems would need the same level of functionality, but those used for the same purpose would need to be built with compatible services!

To satisfy this need, NBS and SPAG jointly defined the five implementation classes, within the FTAM Phase Two Functional Standard, that are documented in Figure 12.9. MAP, TOP and GOSIP went one step further and recommended which implementation classes, and which file types, would be needed by the users.

The NBS implementation classes are:

> T1 (SPAG Profile A111), Simple File Transfer, provides a minimal level of file transfer, and allows only unstructured binary, and flat text file exchanges.

> T2 (SPAG Profile A112), Positional File Transfer, which adds the capability to transfer record-oriented text and data files, and includes Document Types NBS-6 and NBS-7 which allow complex records (DU-Syntax) to be exchanged, and individual records to be transferred or 'read'.

NETWORKS FOR THE 1990s

T3 (SPAG Profile A113), Full File Transfer, adds to T1 and T2 the ability to transfer indexed files (Document Type NBS-8).

A1 (SPAG Profile A122), File Access, provides the ability to read a complete file or a record, to locate within a file based upon position, record number or key, and to write or erase information in a file. This implementation class supports only the document types also supported in T2.

A2 (SPAG Profile A123), Full File Access, adds support for Indexed files (NBS-8) to implementation class A1.

M1 (SPAG Profile A13), Management, provides the services required for an Initiator to perform VFS filestore management, including the functions of create a file, delete a file, read attributes, and change attributes.

The NBS/SPAG implementation classes (in SPAG they are called Profiles) differ from each other mainly in the functions required (File Transfer, File Access, or File Management), and in the complexity of file types supported (Unstructured Binary Files, Sequential Files, or Indexed Files). Indeed, it will be important for users to understand fully which of these capabilities are required, and which the products they buy may support – as all Phase Two FTAM products may not provide the full suite of FTAM functionality.

MAP, TOP and GOSIP will require that all implementations used for general purpose remote file access and transfer should support at least implementation class T1/A111, and Document Types FTAM-3 through NBS-5. These user specifications also recommend that users should only buy products that also support Document Types NBS-6, NBS-7 and NBS-8. Implementors are 'highly encouraged' to build-in NBS-9 remote filestore file-directory access.

What is more, all general purpose MAP, TOP, and GOSIP implementations should be able to both send and receive files, and should be able to act as either Initiator or Responder. Special purpose systems, like file servers, should identify clearly what subset of this functionality will be supported.

Figure 12.10 shows some of the significant added functionality of the Phase Two implementation in terms of the features provided in comparison with Phase One. It should be apparent from this summary why many users are awaiting the Phase Two products.

Conformance and compatibility

Both vendors and users have agreed that conformance tests represent the best vehicle for achieving compatible implementations and, as a result, multi-vendor inter-operability. Conformance testing is also the principal technique by which ISO experts expect implementors to achieve reliable compatible implementations of OSI protocols. Inter-operability testing may further assure compatibility between specific OSI products, but is not a substitute for conformance testing, which is required to ensure that each vendor's implementation fully adheres to the OSI standards.

In May 1987, under the auspices of an NBS project called OSINET, several vendors completed initial FTAM inter-operability tests using their implementations of FTAM Phase One, but no testing has been done yet for Phase Two product implementations.

OSI conformance testing is expected to be provided by the Corporation for Open

NBS Phase Two/SPAG Version 3.0 Classes/Profiles	T1/ A111	T2/ A112	T3/ A113	A1/ A122	A2/ A123	M1 A13
Service Class:						
Transfer	S	S	S			
Management						S
Access				S	S	
Unconstrained	O	O	O	O	O	O
Functional Units:						
Kernel	S	S	S	S	S	
Read	*	*	*	*	*	
Write	*	*	*	*	*	
Ltd. File Mgmt.	O	O	O	O	O	S
Enhance File Mgmt.						S
Grouping	S	S	S			S
File Access				S	S	
Document Types:						
FTAM-3 Unstructured Bin.	S	S	S	S	S	
NBS-2 ASCII Text (CRLF)	S	S	S	S	S	
NBS-3 8859 Text (CRLF)	S	S	S	S	S	
NBS-4 IA5 Text		S	S	S	S	
NBS-5 8859 Text		S	S	S	S	
NBS-6 Sequential DU-Syn		S	S	S	S	
NBS-7 Random DU-Syn		S	S	S	S	
NBS-8 Indexed DU-Syn			S		S	
NBS-9 File_Directory	O	O	O	O	O	

S = Support Required
O = Support Optional/Recommended
* = Either Read or Write, or both, Func. Units Required

NBS Phase Two & SPAG Implementation Classes

Figure 12.9

Systems (COS) to its members in late 1987. The COS conformance tests will be useable by many different types of organisation: by vendors for self testing of the systems they sell, by customers for the acceptance testing of systems they buy, and by third-party organisations that may be offering various types of certification services.

FTAM conformance test efforts

Prior to Autofact '85, no sufficiently complete implementation work of the FTAM standard had taken place to have required a conformance testing methodology. Therefore, there were no conformance test facilities against which to test, and no verified correct implementations.

To achieve the objectives of the Autofact demonstration, participants worked together to build conformance testing programs which ran on a single reference system. All participants in Autofact '85 were required to pass testing with this system, and then to succeed in further testing against each of the other participants. This tedious process took up to sixteen weeks of testing to achieve 21 partially inter-operable demonstrations at the Autofact show.

In April 1986, COS initiated a contract with the Industrial Technology Institute (ITI) for the development of testing software for a MAP Version 2.1 test-bed based on the Autofact test systems. This initial test-bed was intended to provide more complete testing of the six Layers of OSI protocols which were demonstrated at Autofact and later formalised in the NBS, MAP and TOP specifications. The ITI test-bed for MAP Version 2.1 is available to today to test MAP version 2.1 products only.

However, there are significant differences between the MAP 2.1 protocols and the COS-endorsed protocol combinations. Therefore, parallel work has been done in COS to define conformance testing requirements for NBS Phase Two FTAM and the supporting protocols.

The parallel efforts will provide COS members with test systems for Phase Two FTAM in early 1988. COS has defined a protocol stack for product implementations which will be consistent for MAP 3.0, TOP 3.0, NBS Phase Two and SPAG levels of FTAM.

FTAM's future

The NBS Implementors Workshop has progressed to define objectives for FTAM Phase Three, which will build upon, rather than replace, Phase Two implementation specifications. Vendors are recognising the opportunity that will exist when Open Systems Interconnection is extended to the distributed information arena with the full realisation of the FTAM capabilities, and are expected to implement inter-operating, and meaningful, FTAM based products in the near future.

However, users will need to be aware of what FTAM products will provide for them, and what they will not. In their fullest implementation, an FTAM product may provide greater distributed file service than is available from proprietary methods today. It is more likely, though, that early FTAM products will be somewhat more limited, and achieving matching services from each vendor in a multivendor network may not be an easy task – at least for the next two years.

FEATURES PROVIDED BY FTAM PHASE	Phase One	Phase Two
File Level Access (Transfer Only)	■	■
Record Level Access:		
- Locate (1st, Last, Prev, Next, Current, Begin, End, Node-Name)		■ ■
- Insert, Replace, Extend, Erase		■
Security:		
- User Identification and Passwords		■
- Permitted Actions List		■
File Types Supported:		
- Unstructured (Binary Stream)	■	■
- Flat File (Var Length, Simple)	■	■
- Text File (IA5 Text, Simple)		■
- Sequential File (Flat, DU-Syntax)		■
- Random File (Record Number, ")		■
- Indexed Files (Single Key, ")		■
- File Directory (VFS File List)		■
Access to Files:		
- Stream	■	■
- Sequential		■
- Indexed Sequential (Key)		■
- Record Number (Relative)		■
Compatible With what Phases?	None	Forward
Performance (Larger PDU, Grouping)	No	Enhanced
Negotiation of Services	None	Yes
Error Handling and Diagnostics	Some	Expanded
Checkpointing	No	Future
Concurrency Control	No	Limited
Error Recovery Procedures	No	Future

A Functional View of the FTAM Phases

Figure 12.10

13
SNA Trends

ANTON MEIJER

Introduction

The SNA that was announced in 1974 was not at all the same as the SNA known today. It was very limited in scope and function, but did provide the basic mechanisms and framework that were needed for the overall design of a communication system. In later years additional functions were added and the architecture was expanded as experience grew and customer requirements for more functions increased. It is, however, interesting to note that no fundamental change was made to the architecture in the 10 years of its existence. The basic communication protocols that were initially defined are still the basis of the architecture. This illustrates IBM's view, that 'SNA' means three different things:

> *a strategy*: it is IBM's approach for coherent systems design, which provides continuity across releases;

> *an architecture*: it defines the rules for connection and interaction between nodes in a network, to increase the connectivity choices;

> *a set of products*: it represents a spectrum of hardware and software implementations.

In the following a brief overview of the SNA history is presented. A detailed description of SNA is not given, it is available elsewhere[1,2,3,4].

History

The first releases of SNA, generically known as SNA-0 and 1, provided fairly limited function. The major purpose was to set the direction and the concept of an all-encompassing, well-structured architecture. In these releases, a network could consist of a host computer (with the VTAM access method), one or more channel-attached Communications Controllers (IBM 3705) and, attached to these, some of the Cluster Controllers (*Figure 13.1a*). In short, an early SNA network was a very limited tree network, but it exhibited all the important communications concepts of SNA.

SNA-0/1 defined three types of nodes (Physical Units – PUs):

> the Host node (PU-5),

> the Communications Controller node (PU-4),

> the Cluster Controller (PU-2).

Communication takes place between Logical Units (LUs) that serve either application programs in the host, or terminal programs in the cluster controllers. Before Logical Units can communicate, a session must be established between them.

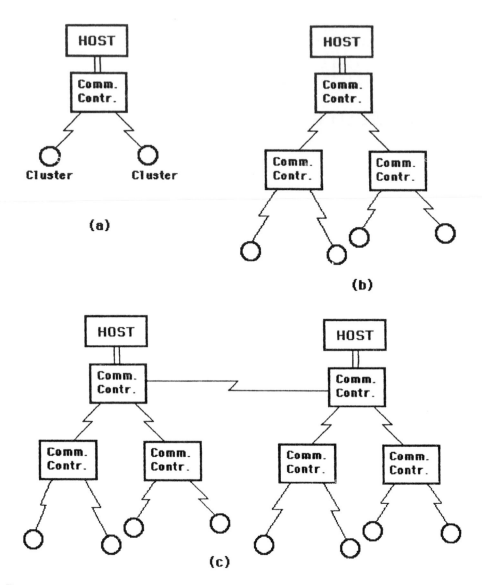

Figure 13.1

In the next major release, SNA-2 (also announced in 1974, but for later availability), the most significant enhancements were:

local attachment of cluster controllers,

remote communications controllers (but never more than one local and one remote in tandem),

Terminal Nodes (PU-1, simpler than Cluster Controller nodes),

support of switched communication lines.

These enhancements, however, did not really extend the scope of the architecture (*Figure 13.1b*). That happened with the next release, SNA-3 (1976), also known as Advanced Communications Functions (SNA/ACF). Until that time, SNA was often said to be a centralised architecture: a tree network with a general purpose computer as the root. The network manager (SSCP – System Services Control Point) was located in this host computer. The network was more a terminal access network than a computer network. Now, with SNA-3, several host computers could be interconnected via their local communications controllers (*Figure 13.1c*). Each of the host computers contains a System Services Control Point (SSCP), which is responsible for the control of the set of resources allocated to it. These sets of resources constitute 'control domains' or, briefly, domains. Internally in each domain, the SSCP exercises centralised management, as in earlier SNA networks. Between domains the SSCPs cooperate on a non-hierarchical basis.

Logical Units anywhere in this network can have a session with LUs in one of the hosts. Once an LU is in session with an application in another domain (host) than its own, the data traffic to that application bypasses the own–domain host. Domain host involvement is required only to establish the session.

In the following release of SNA, SNA-4 (1979), first of all, some restrictions were removed that existed in earlier versions. An important enhancement from an architectural point of view was the introduction of parallel sessions between host-resident LUs. The most important enhancement however was undoubtedly the addition of full networking capabilities to SNA[5,6].

Central in this release (*Figure 13.2a*) is the possibility to use more than one physical path (called an Explicit Route) between any two network nodes and to have, on top of these, several end-to-end transport connections (called Virtual Routes), independent of the network in between. Between adjacent nodes there can be multiple transmission links. These can either behave as separate links or they can be grouped into Transmission Groups in such a way that a Transmission Group behaves as if it were one link, but with a greater capacity.

In 1983 SNA Interconnection (SNI) was announced as a way to interconnect independent SNA networks via a gateway node (*Figure 13.2b*)[7]. As somebody remarked at that time, 'Only IBM would come up with a network architecture that needed a gateway to talk to itself'. There were several reasons for the gateway. An important one is that in an SNA network all resource names must be unique. For large networks, it is not simple to ensure this uniqueness. With interconnected networks, each network has its own name and address space. For cross-network traffic, the names are prefixed with a network ID. This is also attractive when one wants networks that are controlled by different organisations to communicate with each other. The addresses are translated between the two address spaces by the gateway node, in order to isolate both address spaces.

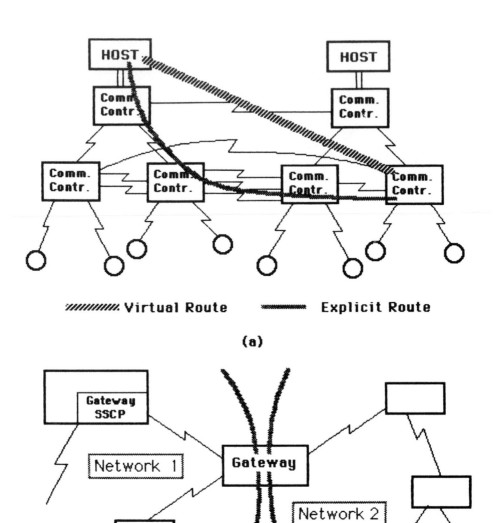

Virtual Route ////////////   Explicit Route ══════

(a)

(b)

Figure 13.2

SNI also provided a temporary solution to a problem that IBM had committed to resolve but had not yet done: the limitation of the SNA address structure which is a severe problem for large networks. Although in SNA-4 the required space for larger addresses was defined in the headers, Extended Network Addressing was not announced until September 1984. With SNA Interconnection, large networks can be partitioned into a number of smaller ones that are interconnected via gateways.

In 1982 an announcement was made under the name Advanced Program to Program Communication, (APPC)[8]. This announcement had to do with more extensive function for the communication between Logical Units. SNA Logical Units are classified in Logical Unit Types, depending on their characteristics and the protocols they use. Logical Unit type 6 (LU-6) was used for communication between LUs in host subsystems, such as CICS and IMS. APPC defined a new Logical Unit type, LU-6.2. Together with the new Physical Unit PU-2.1, it made program-to-program communication available to non-host based products, like Cluster Controllers. Current LU-6.2 implementations in clusters can however only take advantage of this capability on point-point connections. Nevertheless, LU-6.2 and PU-2.1 set the basis for new capabilities, as will be shown later in this paper.

An important aspect of the announcement of LU-6.2 was also the publication of a formal Service Description[9]. This meant that programmers could now make one and the same design for different systems, based on the service description and translate that into the characteristics of a specific machine. Until that time IBM had always been reluctant to specify the service interfaces. (The accompanying description of the protocols used by LU-6.2 were revealed much later[10]. Their publication was one of the requirements made by the European Commission in the anti-trust agreement with IBM in 1984).

When the LU-6.2 architecture was released, IBM announced two other architectures, Document Content Architecture (DCA) and the Document Interchange Architecture (DIA)[11]. These architectures give a general framework for the description of documents as they may be created in textprocessing systems or in electronic mail systems and the like and for the exchange of such documents between these systems. The systems need not even be SNA systems but one can assume that in an IBM product-line they are likely to be. However, if other manufacturers also implement DCA/DIA, and several have indicated that they will do so, their products could communicate at the document level.

The announcements of DIA and DCA were followed in 1983 by the announcement of SNADS, SNA Distribution Services[12], based on DIA and DCA. With SNADS, IBM defined an architecture for the asynchronous exchange of documents. These documents can conceptually be any type, text, data, voice or image or any other form of non-coded information. Where SNA is aimed at communication between partners that are simultaneously present (synchronous exchange), SNADS provides the framework for communication between partners that do not participate at the same time (asynchronous exchange). This architecture is the basis for IBM's office products for the years to come. SNADS is highly equivalent to the X.400 series of Recommendations from the CCITT. One can expect that gateways between the two will appear in the market once there are sufficient numbers of implementations of both.

So far, the various releases of SNA were described in terms of architectural additions. There are, however a number of additions to the IBM product-line, that are indicative for the direction that IBM is now taking. Until only a few years ago, many inside IBM did not recognise that anything of interest could be happening outside the company. To them there was no need for IBM equipment to interface with other, non-IBM equipment.

Several factors, among them the widespread use of microcomputers and intelligent workstations, have created an environment in which even IBM believes that it is important to be able to interconnect to the outside world. In recent years IBM products have been showing more than a marginal interest in the interconnection of non-SNA equipment.

Traditionally, SNA products have always been able to accept IBM's own non-SNA equipment, to various degrees of architectural cleanliness. The old NCP/EP (Emulator Package) was the farthest away from integration; it created a separate network for BSC equipment, that only physically shared the 3705 controller. With the Network Terminal Option (NTO), Start/Stop, BSC and even the Teletype were accepted. Next, the announcement of Non-SNA Interconnection (NSI) gives users more flexibility to attach BSC and S/S workstations using the transport functions of SNA. Whereas with the Emulator Programs, the BSC and SNA worlds only shared a common communications controller, in NSI the BSC devices can be attached to any Controller. The data and control is wrapped in an SNA message and routed through the SNA network to the controller attached to the destination host. There it is unwrapped and passed on to the host as BSC again. The main advantage of this approach is that existing BSC workstations and workstation control programs can still be used, with the advantage of the SNA network management tools even for the BSC environment.

In the late 1970s IBM supported X.25 as a valid way to connect terminals through public data networks based on X.25. In 1977 limited support for the then existing networks (Canada and France) was made available[13]. SNA 'founding father' Edward Sussenguth[13] made a statement at the Kyoto ICCC in 1978, saying 'It is our objective to provide attachment to such networks where the attachment is consistent with IBM's overall business plans.' IBM also made a formal statement of direction to this effect in May 1980, the same year the CCITT ironed out the differences in X.25 interpretations. A formal IBM X.25 product was released in 1981.

The various ways in which X.25 can be used, either as a transport means in an SNA network, or to connect non-SNA equipment into SNA, are described very well in the literature[14]. In the case of SNA equipment, the X.25 circuit is used similar to a switched or leased telephone line. In the case of non-SNA attachment, the X.25 virtual circuit is concatenated to the SNA session, with or without protocol conversion for the higher layers. In the latter case, it is the responsibility of the SNA application programme to understand whatever protocol the attached equipment uses. The GATE and DATE options of the NCP Packet Switching Interface (NPSI) product, assist users in designing applications for X.25 connectivity. This is also used in the Open Systems Network Service product, that enhances the X.25 interface to the level of the OSI Network Service, and the implementations for the German interim standards EHKP4 and EHKP6. GATE and DATE will probably also be used for further OSI products. In September 1984 IBM issued an 'OSI Statement', from which the following two quotations are taken.

> 'IBM has software under development in Europe which will provide support for selected functions in the OSI 4 and 5 layers. ... This effort is directed towards offering an IBM product to customers.'

> 'This represents a further step in IBM's commitment to providing products capable of system interconnection in conformance with OSI standards.'

Another major announcement in the interconnection arena was made in 1984, when the IBM 3710 Network Controller was announced. It provides for the attachment of a number of terminals, SNA, BSC, Start-Stop (like the IBM Personal Computer), and X.25. It is also based on the PU-2.1, but has some additional features. Normally, a PU-2.1 attaches to only one sub-area node; the 3710, however, can attach to more than one sub-area node (multi-tailing) while still remaining one PU. Furthermore, 3710s can be cascaded, that is they can act as path-through nodes to the sub-area. This seems to be in line with a possible new network philosophy, which will be explained later in this paper. This new philosophy also accommodates another 1984 IBM announcement, the various Local Area Networks, which do not yet have a place under the SNA umbrella.

Past trends

From the overview of the history that has been presented here, a number of conclusions can be drawn that will help to understand SNA's future directions. First of all, it is clearly IBM's policy to be evolutionary rather than revolutionary. This is understandable if one only looks at the number of SNA installations around. Recent figures indicate some 20,000 host machines being tied into an SNA network. Anything but a non-disruptive policy would not be acceptable.

SNA started off with a simple tree-shaped network. Then it expanded into a multi-host environment. After that, more networking was added with multiple routes. Then, interconnection made it possible to build networks of networks.

From the communications point of view, SNA started with the asymmetric, synchronous session with a Primary LU in the host and a Secondary LU somewhere in the network. Next, more generality was built in through LU-6.2, making the session partners equivalent. This paved the way for another major addition, SNA Distribution Services, which fulfills the requirements for asynchronous (non-simultaneous) communication.

What will be next? There are still many requirements that users have and there is a wide variety of complaints about certain aspects of SNA (or at least it's implementations). Often, a clue about what to expect next can be found in contributions that IBM people make to conferences, magazines and so on. Two interesting papers were published by IBM authors that do give an indication as to what IBM may be up to. The first paper[15] was presented to SHARE in February 1985, the other[16] was an invited paper for the Personal Computer Communications Special issue of the IEEE Journal on Selected Areas in Communications. Both reflect what IBM sees as requirements for the future of SNA; although they describe only possible solutions, it is an indication of the way key people in IBM are thinking.

Future Trends

Some of the key SNA issues addressed in the papers, are:

> full session symmetry (PLU in the Peripheral Node)
>
> parallel sessions between any two LUs
>
> routing functions not only in subarea nodes
>
> connectivity flexibility, including LANs, X.25 and ISDN arbitrary topologies
>
> better directory services

dynamic route establishment

less cumbersome network generation

The solution proposed in the papers is called SNA Low Entry Networking (SNA/LEN). It is based on LU 6.2 and on an enhanced version of PU-2.1. It is not possible to give a full description of the ideas behind SNA/LEN in the context of this paper, but some of the major points are described below.

In today's SNA, there is a hierarchy of two networks: the sub-area network, with host nodes and communication controller nodes, in which all routing takes place. Attached to sub-area nodes are the peripheral networks that have a star-topology and thus no real routing. In SNA/LEN it is proposed to have only two types of nodes: Network Nodes and Peripheral Nodes (*Figure 13.3a*). Both are built on top of PU-2.1 in such a way that even a small system (like a personal computer) can act as a full Network Node. An important point is, however, that SNA/LEN nodes are fully capable to participate in an 'Ordinary' SNA network (a sub-area network), thus making it possible to interconnect both types of network in a transparent fashion.

The configuration of the SNA/LEN network is not pre-generated, as it is in today's SNA. The configuration is built up dynamically, while nodes are added by establishing contact with a network node that is already part of the network. This can be through SDLC, but also via a LAN, X.25 or even Asynchronous ASCII. Once the contact is established a session (LU-6.2) is set up between the control points in both nodes. If the new node is a network node itself, the nodes exchange their topology information. This implies that all network nodes maintain full knowledge of the topology of the network. This is required, since each network node is expected to be able to perform best-route calculations.

The topology database contains information about each node in the current network and the links it has to other network nodes. In addition, a network node has two directories, one including its own resources and those in the peripheral nodes attached to it, the other (the 'cache' directory) including resources in remote nodes, that were most recently located.

Peripheral Nodes also contain directories, but these only describe the local resources. When a Peripheral Node wants to connect to the network, it must establish a connection with the network node at the link level. Here, security enters the picture. Only certain Peripheral Nodes (pre-defined to the network node as 'authorised') may send in a description of their resources dynamically. For other Peripheral Nodes, all local resources must be pre-defined in the directory of the network node.

When an LU in a Peripheral Node wants to establish a session with another LU, somewhere in the network (which it only knows by name), it sends a request to its own network node(s) to locate the resource. If the resource is found in the local directory, the network node can immediately forward the request to it. If it is not found, the cache directory is inspected, to check whether the resource was located before. If it is, a message is sent to its network node, to verify the entry. (The resource may have become disconnected after the last reference). If the resource is not in the cache either – or if the cache entry turns out to be invalid – a search through the network is performed, trying to locate the requested resource. The technique proposed in SNA/LEN is the 'breadth-first' search, which means that a 'flooding' routing technique is used for the search: each network node sends the locate request it receives from a neighbour to all other neighbours. Only after a reply, either positive or negative, is received from all neighbours, is a reply sent to the neighbour from which the request was received. This technique ensures a response time for the request that is proportional to the diameter of the network instead of being proportional to the number of network nodes. Another advantage of this search technique is, that it allows the use of generic resource names, such as 'printer' or 'quality printer'.

All positive responses are returned to the node that made the original request. This node will then select which resource to use – if there is more than one available – and calculate the preferred path to it. This is not the place to elaborate on the actual route calculation. The proposal uses a variant of Dijkstra's shortest path algorithm, using various weights for the characteristics of the route.

Once the route is established, the SNA BIND message is sent to the destination, along this route. This BIND also contains the route description, to make all nodes along the route aware of it. A permanent route description is left behind in each intermediate node, by using a 'session connector swap' in each node. This is a well known technique, similar to what was used in networks like TYMNET and ARPANET. Since SNA/LEN uses PU-2.1 nodes, the message format between the nodes is the SNA FID-2 format. This format is normally used between a sub-area node and the attached peripheral node. It allows for two one-byte addresses, called the 'local addresses'. In SNA these local addresses are mapped to full network addresses in the Boundary Function. In SNA/LEN a pair of local addresses is called a 'session connector'. It is proposed, to assign an independent free session connector for each node-pair along the session path, and swap these session connectors as the message progresses through the network (*Figure 13.3b*). The advantage is, that no overall addressing is required, and that there is no basic restriction on the size of the network.

The LEN proposal also includes session priority and a flow control scheme. The session priority is selected when the session is established and it is added to the session connectors (the 'swap pairs') in each node when the route is established. It does not have to be carried on each message. Flow Control is defined as a mix between session level pacing, as it was used in SNA before, and per-hop pacing with a variable window, similar to techniques used in other networks. The mechanism implies commitment by the receiver of buffers it needs for the traffic allowed, thus avoiding deadlock situations.

Since SNA/LEN uses the FID-2 message format, an SNA/LEN network can be attached through a Boundary function to a sub-area SNA network and therefore become part of the SNA community. All session level protocols are the same as they have always been in SNA, so the real advantage is in giving more flexibility to the peripheral nodes in doing peer-to-peer communications. Since each node – both network and peripheral – will contain a control point, network management can still be exercised as before. The papers make a distinction between network control (which has to do with the actual operation of the network, which must preferably be decentralised) and network management, (which involves problem determination, change management and accounting). These can still be centralised using the standard SNA tools, if a network owner chooses to do so.

Conclusion

Not all aspects of SNA could be covered in this paper, nor could all issues related to today's SNA be discussed. The intent has been to show how SNA, over the years, has evolved as a powerful architecture which has gained wide customer acceptance. Starting as

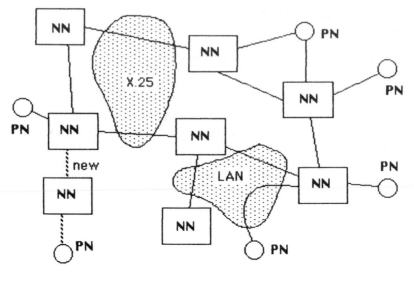

PN = Peripheral Node   NN= Network Node

(a)

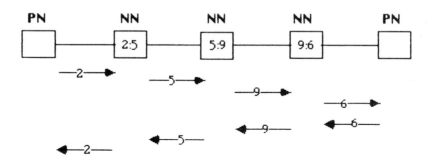

Session Connector Swapping

(b)

Figure 13.3

a simple architecture, more powerful functions were added gradually, based on IBM's deliberate philosophy to solve not too many problems at once. Based on the recent additions to the SNA product-line, one may expect a further growth towards a network-architecture, that is more open and more flexible than it has been until now. The potential extension to SNA discussed in this paper, based on IBM publications, suggests that SNA will evolve in the direction of networks of autonomous nodes, tied together in a variable topology *where users want it to be variable*, while still retaining the strongly controlled environment that is required in other situations. It is clear, that IBM will continue to be committed to SNA or compatible extensions of it. SNA will for years to come remain the 'glue' holding IBM products together. As one of the author's former colleagues at James Martin Associates expressed it:

'SNA may have its faults, but as a glue it sure is sticky'.

14

Interworking with LU Type 6.2

CHRIS MAIRS

Introduction

As the SNA and OSI architectures have evolved, Data Connection has had continuing substantial involvement in SNA and OSI interworking, including:

> feasibility/design studies for PTTs and computer manufacturers;

> specification and implementation of a general purpose SNA to OSI gateway;

> development of a portable SNADS/X.400 gateway product.

This has provided a unique insight into interworking requirements, problems and possible strategies.

The need for SNA/OSI interworking

OSI is now a reality and, over the next five years, the recent growth in its market acceptance will be reinforced by the increasing availability of OSI products from a wide spectrum of computer manufacturers. Nonetheless some of these manufacturers, particularly the largest ones, will retain their own network architectures. In particular IBM's Systems Network Architecture (SNA) is extremely unlikely to be superseded by OSI since:

> SNA is a mature architecture, benefitting from over a decade of intense architectural and product development.

> IBM and its users have invested vast resources in the development of SNA-based application software.

> features of network control and management, embedded deep within the architecture, and fundamental to the operation of large SNA networks, are not yet fully addressed within OSI, and may never be addressed in a manner conducive to the convergence of SNA with OSI.

> SNA development is partly driven by market pressure from IBM's largest users, which can often conflict with OSI convergence.

IBM's established market and its commitment to the strategic positioning of SNA has created an installed base of over 20,000 SNA mainframes throughout the world. Most other large computer manufacturers have recognised the marketing benefit of connectivity to IBM systems and thus provide varying degrees of SNA support. These two facets have jointly established SNA as a *de facto* industry standard, which is unlikely to be dominated by OSI.

This will lead to a world population of networks, a very large number of which will be OSI and a very large number of which will be SNA. The advent of public information networks and the increase in transfer of electronic information between organisations, is creating the need for user access to more than one network, or access to a network of one architecture via a network of the other architecture. Therefore there is a real, increasing, need for products that facilitate this dual access.

Common interworking problems

Interworking can be considered in two categories: specific application layer interworking (Figure 14.1) or general purpose gateways (*Figure 14.2*). The problems that arise when considering application layer gateways include:

each separate application layer function requires additional software in the gateway.

it is not always possible to identify the appropriate SNA application to which a gateway should be built. For example there are many IBM file transfer products (eg DSX, RJE, ADCS, SSS, CICS/BDI); it is not clear whether FTAM can be mapped on to any of them.

there is not always a compatible pair of existing applications (one in each network). This tends to lead to severe subsetting of function when going through a gateway.

this strategy does not address the provision of an interworking capability for 'user written' applications, since for each application, new software is required in the gateway.

General purpose gateways suffer from the following problems:

it is not possible to build a truly general purpose gateway at the Application Layer since any such gateway would be the sum of all possible specific application gateways, and would hence be unacceptably large, or possibly infinitely large.

a general purpose gateway at a lower layer implies awareness of the 'foreign' architecture in at least one of the networks as shown in Figure 14.3

a perfect mapping is not possible because the layers of the two architectures are not semantically equivalent. For example although data flow control and the Session Layer perform a similar role in the architectures there is no equivalent in the Session Layer to the SNA concept of brackets.

While LU-6.2 is certainly not a panacea for all these problems, it does have characteristics that may facilitate many aspects of interworking, as will be shown in the remainder of this paper.

Overview of SNA LU Type 6.2

In SNA, a Logical Unit (LU) is a port into the network through which an end-user can communicate with other end-users. For example the terminal on someone's desk is the

Specific Application Layer Gateway

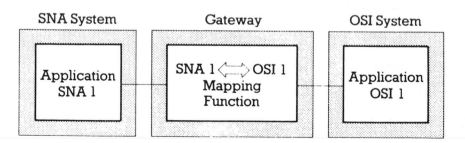

Figure 14.1

General Purpose Gateway

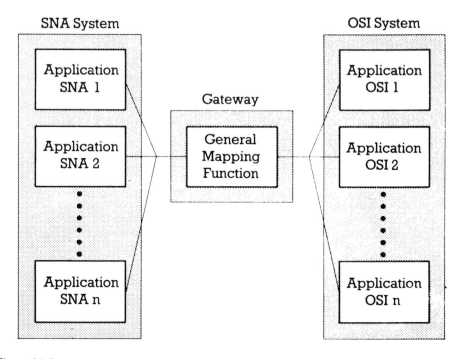

Figure 14.2

port or LU giving access to the network. Similarly CICS is a port or LU giving transaction programs access to other transaction programs across the network. The type of an LU characterises the sessions which the LU supports, by identifying subsets of the protocol at various layers within the architecture.

LU-6.2 is a relatively recent addition to the architecture, which goes further than previous LU types. In addition to defining a rationalised subset of the protocols, it also:

> provides a distributed operating platform for transaction programs (*Figure 14.4*),

> presents a rigorously defined service boundary to transactions programs,

> interfaces with other facilities of the local environment such as database managers, to coordinate synchronisation and security,

> provides many performance features and options.

High performance throughout has been a fundamental objective in the design of the LU-6.2 service and protocol.

The importance of LU-6.2 within SNA

While there will remain for many years a large installed base of systems and software implementing previous LU types, LU-6.2 is of key importance because it is the basis for all IBM's office automation products, it will be used in future for all end-user (and IBM-provided) distributed transactions, and most other LU types will be superseded by LU-6.2.

Above all LU-6.2 is important because IBM is promoting it as 'strategic' and have already gained the support of many of their largest users.

The state of OSI transaction processing

In 1986 the European Computer Manufacturers Association abandoned a proposal to adopt LU-6.2 lock, stock and barrel as the OSI TP service, utilising the existing ISO Layers 1 to 4, but making little use of the ISO defined Session, Presentation and Application services.

This decision, after considerable technical work, involving cooperation from IBM, was made for primarily commercial reasons, in that many of the manufacturers thought that the use of LU-6.2 would strengthen IBM's marketing position and give them a two year implementation lead, as they already had developed the LU-6.2 software.

In September 1986, transaction processing formally became a work item for the ISO committees under the title of OSI-TP and the first meeting was held in January 1987. Several proposals were put forward, including one that again defined the OSI transaction processing service boundary as equivalent to the LU-6.2 verb set (*Figure 14.5*). This proposal, however, differed crucially from the ECMA work in that it made use of existing OSI session, presentation, association and commitment concurrency and recovery (CCR) facilities.

Although this 'LU-6.2 compatible' proposal received considerable support, some countries felt it was inappropriate since:

Awareness of "Foreign" Higher Layers Caused by Lower Level Gateway

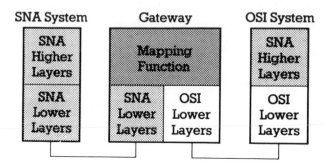

Figure 14.3

The Distributed Operating Platform of LU 6.2

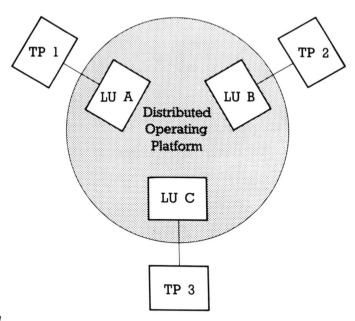

Figure 14.4

LU-6.2 has its roots in CICS transaction processing which has been around for many years and therefore does not represent the latest thinking on how best to meet the TP requirement;

an LU-6.2 verb set will necessarily restrict access to some OSI facilities that TP's may legitimately wish to use;

specifically, LU-6.2 is currently a strictly half-duplex protocol, and there is an argument that full-duplex transaction processing can be more efficient.

There are, thus, still major questions as to the fundamental nature of OSI-TP and its compatibility or otherwise with LU-6.2. The work will not reach Draft International Standard (DIS) status until mid-1988 and consequently 1989 is the first realistic date for implementations to become available.

LU-6.2 interworking strategies and issues

The mechanism depicted in Figure 14.6 provides a possible platform for the implementation of distributed transactions, in which portions of the distributed transaction may be arbitrarily located in SNA or OSI networks.

This strategy clearly requires a transaction processing interface in the OSI model. If the OSI interface adopted is functionally equivalent to the LU-6.2 verb set the interworking software would be comparatively straightforward. If, on the other hand, a different transaction processing strategy is adopted, the complexity – and indeed feasibility – of this interworking strategy becomes uncertain.

The interworking software is to some extent a user of the SNA and OSI TP services, but may also require hooks into the service providers, primarily for performance and to aid in the resolution of resource allocation and synchronisation issues that affect both service providers.

In the special case where no local TP interface is provided, this interworking software will act as a gateway as shown in Figure 14.7. However, if the local common application interface is not implemented, then a system with the physical capability to access both network architectures will suffer from one of the following deficiencies:

there will be two different interfaces which a transaction will have to access, requiring knowledge of where the conversation partner is located;

a single interface will be provided but the pathlength overhead indicated in Figure 14.8 will be incurred for all accesses to the foreign network.

Interworking solutions with a common application interface have the following benefits:

distributed transactions can be designed without regard to the network architecture of the system supporting each component;

components of a transaction may be migrated from OSI to SNA systems or *vice versa* without affecting the rest of the transaction;

one TP program can communicate with partners in SNA or OSI systems without awareness of the architecture of the partner's system.

CO-TP in the OSI Model

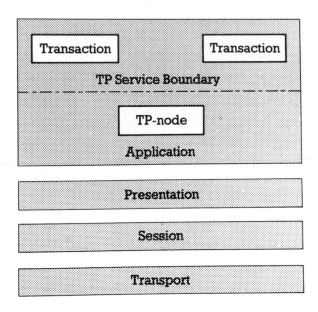

Figure 14.5

Interworking Software to Enable Mixed Network Distributed Transaction

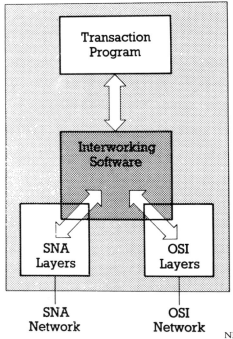

Figure 14.6

NETWORKS FOR THE 1990s

In short, this is a genuinely open architecture for distributed systems embracing both SNA and OSI networks. However, this strategy raises two important issues.

It is unclear whether the TP service eventually adopted by ISO will lend itself to this strategy.

No account is taken of the many OSI applications such as X.400 that do not utilise a transaction processing service.

It is important to realise that LU-6.2, in the same way as the OSI Presentation Layer, is only a platform upon which applications that perform useful functions can be built. It is not in itself a complete facility, but only the plumbing. Some of the applications that reside above LU-6.2 will be provided by IBM and others will be user written transactions.

A good example of an IBM product that resides above LU-6.2 is DISOSS – the mainframe resident component of IBM's office automation strategy. One of the major functions of DISOSS is its mail distribution capabilities, based upon DIA and SNADS, similar in many respects to the electronic mail functions of X.400.

A specific application gateway between DIA and X.400 is depicted in Figure 14.9. Conceptually this gateway is no different from the specific application gateways discussed earlier. However the implementation of an LU 6.2 application gateway is made simpler by:

the rationalised protocols used by LU-6.2,

a greater similarity between the LU-6.2 protocols and the OSI protocols than is the case for previous LU types,

the well defined protocol boundary for LU-6.2.

Nevertheless, these LU-6.2 gateways suffer from:

dissimilarity of function at the application level (for example distribution features available in DIS/OSS that have no equivalent in X.400);

applicability restricted to stable, well defined products – providing no relief for the interworking of user written transactions.

LU-6.2 is not a panacea for interworking problems, since the older LU types will be widely used for many years. However, the advent of LU-6.2 is encouraging, as it may facilitate development of:

a platform upon which mixed OSI and SNA distributed transactions can be built,

useful specific application level gateways such as DIA/SNADS to X.400.

The first of these benefits, however, is totally reliant on the adoption of a transaction processing service for the OSI model which is functionally compatible with LU.

Timescales and sources for solutions

Timescales for provision of interworking capabilities between LU-6.2 and OSI will be dictated by two factors: the user requirement for this capability, and the manufacturers' ability to deliver.

Pure Gateway Created by Deleting Local Application Interface

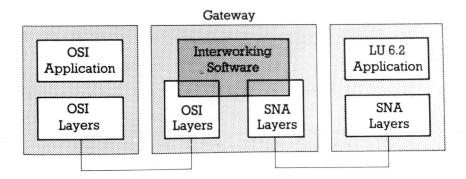

Figure 14.7

Extra Path Length Incurred Without a Common Interface

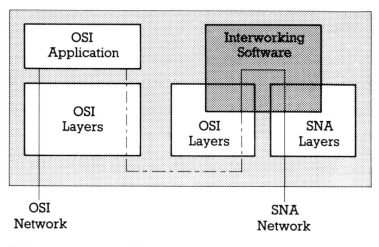

Key: — – — – — Extra Path Length

Figure 14.8

A Specific DIA-X.400 Application Gateway

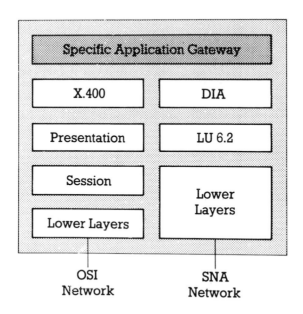

Figure 14.9

As the number of products implementing OSI grows, and the number of products implementing LU-6.2 grows, so the user requirement for interworking between the two will increase. This requirement is already becoming evident in the area of document interchange – specifically interworking between DISOSS and X.400. The requirement for these document interchange gateways will be met by products available from 1988 onwards.

A more general requirement for LU-6.2 to OSI gateways providing the capability for 'mixed' distributed transactions will emerge when an OSI transaction processing interface is agreed and implemented. While these gateways will be of immense benefit to end–user organisations such as banking and retail, it is unlikely that the OSI standards will be stable before 1989. Consequently we should anticipate the first such gateways reaching the marketplace in the early 1990s.

From the manufacturer's point of view, the timescales for product availability are constrained by the complexity of the problem. In particular development of an interworking capability requires: SNA LU-6.2 skills, OSI skills, and a clear understanding of interworking issues and problems.

Users will tend to look towards the large manufacturers, including IBM, to provide coherent solutions. Many of them will do this by acquiring generic portable software from specialist organisations who can pull together the necessary skills, thereby shortening their timescales and decreasing their development risk.

15

The MAP/TOP Initiative

NICHOLAS C L BEALE

In 1979 Mike Kaminski started an activity at the GM Technical Centre in Warren, Michigan to provide standard communications protocols for plant-floor communications within GM. From this, a communications architecture movement called Manufacturing Automation Protocol (MAP) has evolved. A related activity at Boeing, has become Technical and Office Protocol (TOP). What began as a 1.5 person effort has now become arguably the most significant user initiative in the history of computing.

Stimulated by GM and Boeing, 21 vendors including IBM, AT&T and Siemens, spent an estimated $70 million on developing the OSI-based software and hardware to demonstrate MAP and TOP at Autofact '85. Representatives of over 250 companies attend the US MAP Users Group. In Europe about 100 companies, including BP, Daimler-Benz, FIAT, Philips, Renault, Shell, and Unilever are members of the European MAP Users Group (EMUG). GM has already stated that all the factory automation equipment that they buy will have to be MAP compatible: Dupont has announced that purchasing preference will be given to MAP compatible equipment. Most other major manufacturing companies are expected to follow suit in the next few years. Why?

For the user of automation equipment, MAP and TOP offer the prospect of being able to build integrated, evolving automation systems with equipment from many different suppliers. These are essential to compete in large scale production in the late 1980s and 1990s.

Information as the key economic resource

The key economic resource today is information. Many organisations have no product except information, and the value of their information assets are substantially greater than the value of their tangible assets. Consider a pharmaceuticals company (Glaxo), an advertising agency (Saatchi & Saatchi) and an information distribution company (Reuters). Figure 15.1 shows their sales, profits, fixed assets, net tangible assets and market valuation. The 'Information Valuation' has been calculated as the difference between the market valuation of the company and their net tangible assets.

They could sell their tangible assets to a financing company, and lease them back, with minimal effect on profitability. The value of the company comes from the market information, the product information, the legal information and the other information that makes the difference between a heap of hardware and a very profitable company.

In each case this information valuation represents about 80% of the valuation of the company. Hence the gathering, distribution and use of that information is the key economic issue for such companies. But information can only be distributed with common protocols: you need to 'speak the same language'. This helps to explain why MAP has become an issue for top management in the US.

Given that information is the key resource, the acquisition and effective use of that information is key to the success of any enterprise. Effective communication is thus essential. With effective communication it is possible to build integrated automation systems, for Computer Integrated Manufacturing (CIM). Early US experience in CIM[1] showed benefits listed in Figure 15.2 as well as substantial gains in product quality, capital equipment operating time, and engineering productivity.

The reduction in lead time is perhaps particularly significant. In increasingly volatile markets the need to plan a new product several years in advance makes it extremely difficult to be sure that it is the product that the market requires: design times of the same order as product life times lead to unstable control.

In theory a user can achieve integrated communications by buying as much equipment as possible from one vendor, as much as possible of the rest from vendors which communicate with that vendor, and then building protocol converters for the rest. This clearly constrains purchasing, and the user has to settle for less than ideal equipment in order to maintain compatibility. In the highly competitive conditions of large manufacturers, this in itself may be bad enough.

No single Western vendor makes the complete range of equipment required in a factory, and the very large vendors typically have communications incompatibilities even amongst their own products. In practice the high cost of developing and maintaining protocol converters tends to restrict the communications to the perceived 'essential requirements' of the application. There are also significant project costs and project risks associated with such a strategy: testing the communications can be on the critical path.

By using an agreed set of common standards the costs of communication in a control system can be substantially reduced. In practice this means using MAP/TOP. Studies at Dupont and Eastman Kodak[2] have indicated projected savings on automation projects in the range of ten to 20%. The level of communications integration is also greatly increased.

Evolving systems

However the most important aspect of the MAP initiative may well be its prospect of being able to build evolving integrated systems. It has been clear for many years that large computer-based systems are not static, but evolve from initial design through to implementation, installation and use. Unless a system is designed to evolve it will be hopelessly unwieldy. The spate of new automation applications over the last 10 years shows no sign of abating. Factories whose automation systems cannot evolve and develop to take advantage of the latest cost-effective technology will rapidly become obsolescent.

There is really no prospect of having a rapidly evolving automation system unless MAP/TOP is used. Every major vendor will support them, most do already. It is probable that the vast bulk of new automation products over the next 10 to 15 years will be using MAP/TOP communications. The vendors cannot all support another 'standard'.

This paper has indicated why the use of MAP/TOP is essential for integrated, evolving automation systems, and why this is considered so important by major users. Not only are the general arguments compelling, a major manufacturer who does not adopt MAP/TOP risks being at a significant disadvantage compared with competitors.

A vendor who does not adopt MAP/TOP faces an additional problem. If a user decides to switch to purchasing MAP/TOP products, the policy can (in principle) go into effect the next day. But it will take a vendor six to 24 months and a great deal of effort to implement MAP/TOP products. The US companies are well ahead but the majority of

US Experience of CIM

5 - 20%	reduction in	Pesonnel Costs
15 - 30%	reduction in	Engineering Design Costs
30 - 60%	reduction in	Lead Time
30 - 60%	reduction in	Work in Process
40 - 70%	gain in	Overall Productivity

Figure 15.1

Information Companies

	Glaxo (30/6/84)	Saatchi (30/9/84)	Reuters (31/12/84)
SALES	1200	855	313
PROFITS	256	20	74
FIXED ASSETS	347	22	116
NET TANGIBLE ASSETS	676	27	146
MARKET VALUATION	3184	200	829

(source: Robert Wigram & Co)

hence
'INFORMATION VALUATION'	2508	173	683
(% of Market Valuation)	79%	86%	82%

Figure 15.2

European manufacturers were barely aware of MAP until 1986. The creation of EMUG and the ESPRIT CNMA project help somewhat to remedy this gap, but the challenge is still serious.

MAP content

MAP and TOP are firmly based on the existing and emerging OSI protocols. They are both evolving architectures, which will incorporate new standards as they develop and are seen to be appropriate to the user needs. There is a MAP Specification, currently version 2.1, which defines precisely which standards are referenced at any moment.

The MAP and TOP standards selected at each of the seven Communications Layers of the ISO OSI model are currently shown in Figure 15.3. It will be seen that MAP and TOP are essentially common at the middle layers, but diverge at the top and the bottom. Below each of the layers is discussed in turn and an indication of the rationale for the choices made.

The main Local Area Network standards are being generated by a project of the Institute of Electrical and Electronic Engineers (IEEE) called Project 802. This is developing standards for three types of LAN:

802.3 CSMA/CD (*very similar to Ethernet*),

802.4 Token Bus (*as used in MAP*),

802.5 Token Ring (*as used by IBM*).

It is also developing a common standard for Logical Link Control (LLC) so that all the 802 LANs present the same interface to Layer 3. The IEEE Standards quickly became ISO Draft International Standards. Thus IEEE 802.4 has become ISO DIS 8802/4.

Summary of the three types of LAN

In 802.3 CSMA/CD (Carrier Sense Multiple Access with Collision Detect) all the stations are attached to a common bus (usually a piece of coaxial cable). If a station wants to transmit, it waits until the bus is clear and then transmits. If two stations do this at about the same time a 'collision' occurs: this is detected and the two stations wait for a random time and then try again.

This protocol works very well if the probability of collisions is low, but if the network is loaded heavily so that the probability of collisions becomes high, then the performance deteriorates sharply. It is also impossible to give a maximum time within which one can guarantee that a message will be transmitted. This is not a serious problem in the drawing office, but is serious in real time applications such as the factory. To overcome these limitations, Token Passing LANs were devised.

In the 802.4 Token Bus, all the stations are attached to a common bus, but control of the bus is passed by messages in a cyclical order between the various stations. At any one moment, a given station 'has the token' which gives the right to control the bus. In this way collisions are avoided in normal operation, and an upper bound can be given to the time it takes for a message to be transmitted.

The 802.5 Token Ring connects all the stations into a ring, so that a Token can pass in a definite physical order between stations. It therefore is inherently simpler and has much faster response times than a Token Bus. It is supported by IBM, but not currently specified in either MAP or TOP.

TOP chose 802.3 because the Ethernet is so widely available, and the limitations are not considered sufficiently serious for Technical Office work. 802.3 is slightly incompatible with the Ethernet, but all Ethernet vendors are (believed to be) migrating to 802.3.

General Motors chose 802.4 for MAP for two main reasons. They were not prepared to accept the limitations of Ethernet: specifically the lack of a guaranteed response time. Also 802.4 supported Broadband, and GM had substantial experience with broadband networks in their plants, which offer superior noise immunity and the ability to span greater distances than Ethernet.

The 802.2 Logical Link Control (LLC) offers 3 types of service: connectionless (1), connection oriented (2), confirmed (3).

Type 3 is not in the current published standard but is being added. MAP and TOP

MAP/TOP Protocols

OSI Layer	MAP (Version 2.1)	TOP (Version 1.0)
7:Application	ISO Case* ISO File Transfer* MMFS Messaging MAP Directory MAP Network Management	(X.400 Messaging)
6:Presentation	null/MAP Transfer	
5:Session	ISO Session Kernel	
4:Transport	ISO Transport Class 4	
3:Network	ISO CLNS*	
2:Data Link	IEEE 802.2 LLC I IEEE 802.4 Token Bus	8 0 2 . 3
CSMA/CD 1:Physical		
Baseband	IEEE 802.4 Broadband	8 0 2 . 3

* indicates that a subset of this protocol is used.

Figure 15.3

currently require only type 1 service, so are said to support LLC I. Type 3 service is likely to be included in the MAP 3.0 specification for the Real Time Segment.

MAP and TOP specify the ISO Connectionless Internet protocol, but on the same subnetwork MAP uses an inactive subset. This reduces the overhead if two stations on the same LAN are communicating. Inclusion of a connection-oriented Network Layer is under study.

MAP and TOP can get away with using reasonably lightweight protocols at Layers 1 to 3 because they specify the heaviest ISO protocol at the Transport Layer, Transport Class 4. The Transport Layer is responsible for reliable end-to-end delivery of data, and deals with setting up connections, missing, duplicated and mis-sequenced packets, multiplexing and de-multiplexing.

The ISO Session Kernel gives two way simultaneous transmission between session users. It is the smallest subset of an ISO session protocol.

The Presentation Layer is concerned with format conversion of data. MAP currently has a null Presentation Layer, which effectively means that they use the same transfer syntax.

The Application Layer allows user programs to exchange information (as opposed to data). The protocols selected here allow the specific types of information transfer required by the application. These are: File Transfer (MAP/TOP), Manufacturing Messaging (MAP), Electronic Mail (TOP), CAD File interchange (TOP).

To support these Special Application Service Elements (SASEs), there is an ISO Common Applications Service Element (CASE) which allows one to form 'Application Associations' to control and coordinate the flow of information, and to establish the universe of discourse within which the exchange of information operates. There was thus essentially no alternative to selecting ISO CASE.

The Manufacturing Messaging protocol, however, was generated by the MAP effort to fill the specific need of being able to send such messages as:

STOP (Manual Restart Required)

What is the value of NUMBER OF GREEN WIDGETS MADE?

Initially an interim messaging protocol (GM Message Format) was defined, and this quickly became Manufacturing Message Format System (MMFS) which is specified in MAP 2.1. However in the course of submitting it through the EIA project RS511 towards ISO standardisation at TC1/84, it has become modified substantially into a different and improved system called Manufacturing Message Service (MMS which equates to EIA 1393A). This used the X.409 notation, and is a considerable improvement on MMFS but is incompatibile with it. MAP 3.0 will specify MMS, and thus MMFS must be used with caution.

MMS has its own file access mechanisms, so there is some overlap with ISO FTAM. However ISO FTAM is conceived as working in a mainframe type environment, whereas MMS is in the culture of Industrial Minicomputers and Programmable Controllers.

Developments in MAP

MAP has moved impressively through various stages:

> Tech Centre project; GM Project with NBS support; GM Project with strong US industry support via 'MAP User Group'; International project with strong industry support via US, European, Canadian and (soon) Japanese 'MAP User Groups'.

As the MAP constituency has broadened and experience is gained with demonstration and pilot implementations, the MAP architecture is expanding and is being refined as Version 2.2 of the MAP specification is superseded by Version 3.0.

An Enhanced Performance Architecture is being developed for real time use. This is likely to consist of the PROWAY style 802.4 Carrier Band LAN with LLC III and MMS directly running over the LLC, eliminating the middle layers of protocol. Inclusion of Connection Oriented network services is under study, to make it easier to connect MAP networks through wide area networks. Virtual terminal protocols, and full X.400 messaging will no doubt be incorporated into the MAP/TOP architecture. Token rings are also likely to be included initially in TOP, but fibre optic token rings can be expected in MAP in due course. Fibre optics are beginning to be studied actively within MAP.

As the higher layer protocols become better understood through implementation and use, developments are expected in these areas. The performance implications of current implementations will also generate new ideas to be included in the overall architecture.

European MAP Users Group

An ad-hoc steering committee was formed in 1985 under the chairmanship of Vic Gregory of Unilever, and this has presided over the creation of The European MAP Users Group (EMUG). EMUG now has over 150 corporate members, a secretariat and elected steering committee. The inaugural Annual General Meeting to approve the constitution took place in Paris in April 1986.

EMUG has a Steering Committee, a Technical Committee, and three technical working groups. These working groups liaise closely with the US MAP Task Force working groups, and participate in the international definition and evolution of the MAP specifications.

WG1 (Full Architecture) concentrates on Layers 5, 6 and 7 of the OSI Seven Layer Model (Session, Presentation and Application) as well as management issues.

WG2 (Networking) deals with Layers 1 to 4 (Physical, Media, Network and Transport) as well as having specific responsibility for Installation, Redundancy, and Fibre Optics. Work programmes have begun on Relays and on Fibre Optics, and it has been agreed that EMUG WG2 should have the primary role within the international MAP effort on Fibre Optics.

WG3 (Real Time) has responsibility for the Real Time (Proway) segment, the RS511 Messaging protocol, and MAP for process control.

There are encouraging signs that close liaison will be established with other relevant European projects connected with the ESPRIT work. A strong willingness was expressed by all parties to work together to avoid unnecessary duplication of effort or divergence from the overall international MAP specification. European companies interested in this area are strongly urged to join the group, and more information can be obtained from the EMUG Secretariat at Cranfield Institute of Technology.

A number of companies in the US and Europe are currently implementing MAP. General Motors devised a five step implementation plan, which has allowed them to phase in MAP gradually without delaying essential automation projects. They are now implementing in earnest, with 17 plants having committed MAP implementation schedules and an estimated 10,000 MAP nodes being installed at GM during 1986.

Other companies are putting in pilot implementations, including IBM and Deere & Co. The ESPRIT CMNA project is understood to include a MAP demonstrator at British Aerospace, and a number of other European companies are planning MAP implementations. Nevertheless it is most unlikely that there will be as many as 10,000 MAP nodes installed in Europe before mid-1988, so in this respect Europe is one or two years behind the US. This is likely to be serious but not catastrophic. It will give some opportunity for Europe to learn from the teething troubles of earlier MAP systems. But unless determined efforts are made to catch up, the consequences for what is left of Europe's manufacturing industry will be very unpleasant.

Conclusions

The economic importance of MAP and TOP have been described, the protocols selected for MAP and the main reasons for their selection have been discussed, some probable developments have been indicated.

MAP, more than any other single factor, has taken OSI out of the realm of theory into the heart of the economic world. It would be tragic if, having talked about OSI for so long, Europeans failed to grasp the opportunity.

16
The Emergence of TCP/IP

STEVE SPANIER

Introduction

Like the unknown actor who lands a prime-time TV series after labouring in obscurity for years, Transmission Control Protocol/Internet Protocol (TCP/IP) is riding the wave of networking interest into the public eye. Contrary to the idea that it is a recent phenomenon, TCP/IP has actually been in existence for over ten years. During the period preceding its 'discovery', few had heard of TCP/IP because networks of any kind were scarce.

Over the last five years, substantially reduced computer prices have resulted in an influx of computers into virtually every conceivable arena. Personal, single-user machines have become extremely popular and have stolen a large market share from mainframe manufacturers. Less expensive computers can be used effectively to divide a problem into smaller, more manageable pieces. The single assumption, however, is that these machines must be able to communicate with each other. Communication between small computers is not a serious problem if all the machines are purchased from the same manufacturer. Unfortunately, the networking of computers from many different manufacturers is a non-trivial problem, because of different bus structures, file systems, input/output systems, character sets, and many other factors.

With the realisation that heterogeneous networking is a critically important issue, companies are looking for network technologies that satisfy their needs. Typically, these needs include ease of implementation, performance, reliable data exchange, useful utility programmes and, perhaps most importantly, the ability to connect computers from different vendors. An in-depth look at today's network marketplace reveals that TCP/IP is part of the only fully specified, heterogeneous protocol family currently available. The XNS protocols are not specified above the OSI Transport Layer. DECNET and SNA, although large and powerful networking implementations, are not heterogeneous. Finally, the much heralded International Standards Organisation's Open System Interconnection (OSI) protocols are not yet ready. This situation left little alternative for prospective network users in the early 1980s – they chose TCP/IP, thus creating a *de facto* industry standard.

Luckily, TCP/IP has more going for it than merely being in the right place at the right time. These protocols were derived from a real need and have been thoroughly tested over the last 12 years. In fact, the OSI protocols have largely been fashioned after TCP/IP and some of its sibling protocols (FTP, TELNET, UDP). The Internet protocol family (of which TCP/IP is a member) is a solidly defined, market-tested suite. The history of this protocol family is a lesson in the effectiveness of usefulness and availability.

The history of TCP/IP

In 1973, the Defense Advanced Research Projects Agency (DARPA) decided it needed new host-to-host protocols on the ARPANET to support different underlying communication techniques. DARPA therefore funded experimental implementations of TCP/IP by both Stanford University and Bolt Beranek & Newman Inc. (BBN). These implementations were completed in 1974 on a PDP-11 running TENEX, respectively. In 1978, after four years of testing and refining, the Department of Defense (DoD) promulgated versions of TCP/IP and mandated their use as DoD standards.

By 1982, 75% of the ARPANET community was using TCP/IP in its hosts. At about the same time, the 4.2BSD operating system incorporated TCP/IP into its kernel. Since then, 4.2BSD has become one of the most popular derivatives of the very successful UNIX operating system, and TCP/IP support has grown with it. 4.2BSD's popularity in the engineering community has forced vendors dealing with this market segment to offer TCP/IP support as a matter of course. 4.2BSD developers also incorporated Address Resolution Protocol (ARP), a protocol mapping Ethernet to Internet addresses, into their operating system. This served to bond TCP/IP firmly to Ethernet; Ethernet has subsequently become a *de facto* industry standard at the media-access Layers of the OSI reference model.

Today, TCP/IP implementations can be found on everything from IBM mainframes to the Apple Macintosh. TCP/IP is supported by well over 60 vendors, and exists on over 2,000 major Defense Data Network (DDN) nodes and many hundreds (possibly thousands) of subnetworks. The TCP/IP-Ethernet combination has found its way into office as well as engineering environments and continues to gain in popularity.

TCP/IP's important features

TCP/IP's popularity may be attributed to five essential characteristics the DARPA identified as design goals: reliability, inter-operability, security, flexibility, and the ability to allow easy transition to new protocols. All but security have proven to be critical needs in the commercial marketplace as well.

Reliability is certainly one of the most important of TCP/IP's features. As designed by the Internet development team, IP has no responsibility for reliable data delivery; it simply ensures proper delivery between networks. TCP provides reliable, full-duplex, connection-oriented communication between cooperating processes. IP permits this even if the processes exist on machines on remote networks.

The TCP portion of TCP/IP maintains data transmission reliability by using a positive acknowledgement with retransmission (PAR) mechanism. TCP is designed to allow upper layer protocols (ULPs) to channel continuous streams of data through TCP for delivery to peer ULPs. TCP breaks these streams into 'segments' (a segment is the basic unit of transmission for TCP) containing appropriate addressing and control information. TCP then passes these segments to IP for transmission through the network (and possibly to other networks).

The strategy of TCP's PAR mechanism is for a sending TCP to retransmit a segment at timed intervals until a positive acknowledgement is returned. TCP uses a checksum to detect segments that may have been damaged in network transit. Damaged segments are treated as if they were lost segments: they are discarded without acknowledgement. TCP assigns sequence numbers to each data byte, thereby enabling a receiving TCP to detect duplicate and out-of-order segments. Sequence numbers also allow a single acknowledgement to cover many segments of data.

TCP's reliability is further aided by a flow control mechanism called a 'window'. The receiving TCP uses windows to regulate the amount of data dispatched by the sending TCP. The window specifies a contiguous interval of acceptable sequence-numbered data. As data are accepted, TCP slides the window upward in the sequence number space. The window may grow and shrink based on the acceptance pattern.

A final feature contributing to TCP's reliability is an acknowledgement scheme that coordinates ULP synchronisation. When ULPs wish to communicate, they use the corresponding TCPs, which use the acknowledgement scheme to open a connection. In the simplest connection establishment process, the two TCPs synchronise sequence numbers by exchanging three segments (hence the use of the term 'three-way handshake' to describe this process).

Inter-operability was one of the Internet development team's most important goals. In this context, inter-operability refers to the ability of different computer systems to communicate with one another. Inter-operability is achieved with three standardised utility programs: FTP, TELNET, and SMTP. These utilities define the interface between the user software and the transport and network layer software, and allow different vendor implementations to be compatible. Without them, users on computer systems from different vendors could not communicate effectively.

FTP provides file transfer capabilities. Using this protocol, users on one computer system can move binary or ASCII files from one computer to another on the network. TELNET provides a virtual terminal emulation package. In a broad sense, the TELNET protocol supports a standard method of interfacing terminal devices and terminal-oriented processes. With the TELNET protocol, a user on one computer can cause a terminal or monitor device connected to that computer to appear as a dumb terminal that is directly attached to a remote computer on the network. The SMTP protocol provides a mechanism for transferring mail between network hosts reliably and efficiently.

Because so much of the information passed through the DoD is compartmentalised, security was another important TCP/IP design goal. IP includes several fields within its header that allow for selective protection of information. In order for a TCP connection to be established, the modules at each end of the connection must agree on the security information to be associated with the connection.

Also important to the DoD is the ability to send 'urgent' data. Any ULP can indicate that certain data is urgent, and a bit will be set in the TCP header. Also, 'push' commands force TCP to package and send any data it has been given up to that point without waiting for additional data. This mechanism is intended to prevent possible deadlocks where a ULP waits forever for TCP data and also to provide ULPs with time-critical information (such as interrupts or breaks).

Precedence refers to the ability of the system to allocate adaptively network resources so that network performance is related to the importance of the function being performed. The TCP/IP specification refers to security and precedence together. Connections are not established when one side of the impending connection has a higher precedence than the other. If an attempted connection is aborted because of mismatched security or precedence information, that result is logged. So far, very few vendors have implemented the security and precedence features of TCP/IP, because most commercial TCP/IP implementations don't require them.

Another important feature of TCP/IP is its flexibility. TCP/IP makes very few

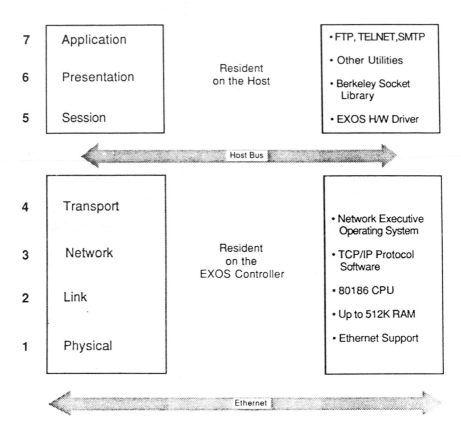

ISO/OSI Reference Model   **EXOS Implementation**

7	Application		• FTP, TELNET,SMTP
		Resident	• Other Utilities
6	Presentation	on the Host	• Berkeley Socket Library
5	Session		• EXOS H/W Driver

Host Bus

4	Transport		• Network Executive Operating System
3	Network	Resident on the EXOS Controller	• TCP/IP Protocol Software
2	Link		• 80186 CPU
			• Up to 512K RAM
1	Physical		• Ethernet Support

Ethernet

Figure 16.1

assumptions about either the lower or higher layer protocols. Therefore, the use of TCP/IP does not dictate either the media or the applications one may use. When TCP/IP does require things of other protocol layers, it uses primitives that allow many different combinations. Also, because TCP/IP was designed from the outset to be heterogeneous in nature, it is reasonably general in orientation, permitting easy migration to new protocols. This is extremely important to the DoD, as they do not want to exclude commercially implemented protocols from their future plans.

TCP/IP implementations on intelligent controllers

Because TCP/IP deals primarily with network rather than application parameters, and because it is specified in such a way as to allow substantial implementation modularity, TCP/IP does not necessarily need to run on the host computer. Recently, several companies have experienced success in marketing implementations of these protocols that run on intelligent network controllers. A typical 'front-end' implementation dedicates a board to the running of TCP/IP software and media access protocols (such as Ethernet). This board has its own resources (including a central processor, memory, and a link-layer controller chip) so that is doesn't constantly interrupt the host during network transactions.

Figure 16.1 illustrates a typical intelligent controller architecture. The model for this figure is the Excelan Open System (EXOS) Intelligent Ethernet Controller. The EXOS architecture includes a real-time, multi-tasking network operating system designed to give the transport layer code a common interface to the board, the host, and the network. Because the on-board protocol code has no interaction with the host operating system, it does not 'break' when new versions of the host operating system are introduced. New transport protocols such as OSI can easily be added, and will not conflict with the protocols already being run on the board.

The intelligent controller approach has many advantages over traditional host-based implementations. Because network transactions can occur simultaneously with host-based processing, network throughput does not degrade as quickly with an intelligent controller-based implementation. As the host CPU becomes more heavily loaded, it is less able to devote attention to network activities. If those network activities are being handled by a dedicated processor, however, network throughput does not suffer drastically. To the users, this means less response-time variance when the computer is busy.

Figure 16.2 depicts the results of an experiment run at Excelan to determine the effects of host CPU load on network performance for both host-based and intelligent controller-based implementations. The graph shows a 20% reduction in throughput for the host-based approach under a moderate host load (one CPU-intensive task) and drastically lower throughput under a heavy host load (two CPU-intensive tasks). In contrast, the intelligent controller-based approach degrades a maximum of 20% under heavy host load. Because most hosts are at least moderately loaded during most of the working day, these results imply that running TCP/IP on an intelligent controller will generally yield faster network throughput than traditional implementations that run TCP/IP on the host.

Other advantages inherent to intelligent controllers include more efficient use of host memory, a 'cleaner', more modular implementation, and the ability to migrate quickly to new protocols. This last advantage has major implications for the impending gradual inclusion of the OSI protocols into the worldwide networking picture.

TCP/IP and the OSI protocols

TCP/IP has served the needs of network users for over 10 years. In the last three years, however, the National Bureau of Standards (NBS)-backed OSI protocols have gained a large following, particularly in the European communications community. The impending clash between the OSI and Internet protocols was forseen by both the NBS and the DoD. These government organisations therefore commissioned a study to provide recommendations on 'Transport Protocols for Department of Defense Data Networks'. The study was performed by the Committee on Computer-Computer Communication Protocols (CCCCP), and their final report was presented to the DoD and the NBS in February of 1985.

One conclusion of the CCCCP study is that 'the DoD has a large and growing commitment in operational TCP networks, and this will increase by 50 to 100% in the next 18 months. This rate of investment will probably continue for the next five years for new systems and the upgrading of current ones'. Elsewhere in the report, the committee

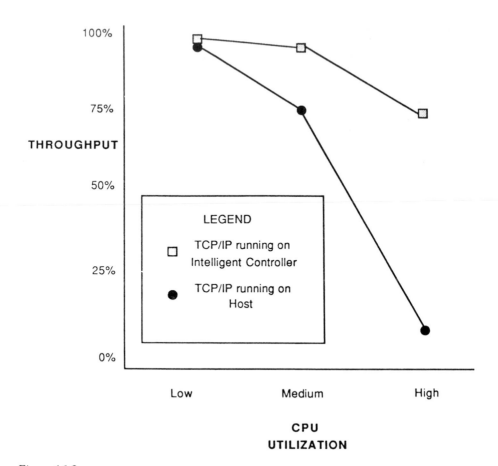

Figure 16.2

states the 'if DoD does not make a firm commitment to TP-4 (the OSI transport protocol) by mid-1985, the number of systems that will move ahead with TCP will probably constitute almost half of the growth of the DDN in the next five years. In other words, delay of a decision to move to TP-4 until 1986 would mean that most of the DDN subnets that will exist in the late 1980s will be based on TCP.'

In fact, the DoD did not commit to a decision to use the OSI protocols until late 1986 ('*Feds Weighing OSI Compatibility In All Net Buys,*' *Computer Systems News, September 8, 1986*). Commercial vendors, recognising the implications of this delayed decision on OSI, have flooded the TCP/IP market. In the last year or so, intelligent controllers, gateways, terminal servers, and other products based at least in part on the TCP/IP protocols have been introduced. Very successful TCP/IP conferences have been held. All of this implies a long and bright future for TCP/IP. Network experts now predict a minimum of five to ten more years until OSI approaches TCP/IP's popularity.

When OSI products finally become available in the mass market, TCP/IP will not become obsolete immediately. Because of its substantial (and growing) installed base, vendors will begin to offer products that allow a smooth transition from one protocol to the other. These products will include intelligent controllers that allow simultaneous running of both the TCP/IP and TP-4 protocols. Intelligent controllers make migration less difficult because they isolate the intricacies of the networking code from the complexity of the operating system kernel.

TCP/IP's strong foothold in the engineering and government communities, coupled with its rapidly increasing penetration into the office marketplace, will ensure that some time will pass before TCP/IP's growth slows. Even more time will pass before other standardised protocols replace it. For users, the important point is that they can confidently purchase TCP/IP products now while still ensuring easy migration to other protocols as they become popular.

17

Standards & Compatibility in LAN Integration

DR GEE SWEE POO

A local area network (LAN) aims to interconnect a variety of data communication devices together. These devices may be made by many different manufacturers using different hardware and firmware architectures and possibly supporting very different ranges of software. However, as long as they possess proper interfacing mechanisms that meet the requirements of the LAN's access method, then they may exchange data across the LAN. The ability to interconnect heterogeneous devices via a LAN offers users a great deal of flexibility in designing networks. In practice, it represents a potential source of problems. Current LAN systems provide only low level connectivity but not higher level functions. Consequently, devices connected to a LAN may not be able to communicate cooperatively. This situation creates serious problems in planning for an integrated network. Careful planning is essential to ensure that the equipment and software purchased are capable of supporting compatible standards, whether international, national or *de facto* standards. This paper aims to address the problems of network integration in relation to standards in addition to outlining the compatibility issues currently facing the CSMA/CD baseband LAN.

The Standards

The key to the successful development of the LAN market is the availability of a low cost interface. The cost of connecting a device to a LAN must be much less than the cost of the device alone. This requirement, coupled with the complexity of the LAN protocols, dictate a VLSI solution. However, chip manufacturers will be reluctant to jump on the LAN bandwagon unless there is a high volume market. A LAN standard will assure that volume and also enable devices of a variety of manufacturers to intercommunicate.

This is the rationale behind the work of the IEEE Project 802 Committee. A draft set of standards for LANs has been produced and endorsed by both the IEEE and ISO[1]. The standard specifies a three-layer tree-like communication structure as shown in Figure 17.1, which corresponds to Layer 1 and 2 of the ISO-OSI Reference Model. The distinct feature is that two Layers, Logical Link Control (LLC) and Medium Access Control (MAC), are defined for a single OSI Data Link Layer. The LLC Layer is described in document 802.2. It provides for the exchange of data between service access points (SAPs), which are multiplexed over a single physical connection to the LAN. Both the connectionless datagram and connection-oriented virtual circuit services are provided. For the same LLC layer, there are three MAC standards: CSMA/CD Bus, Token Bus and Token Ring. These are described in documents 802.3, 802.4 and 802.5 respectively. CSMA/CD has converged with the Ethernet specification and is well suited to office applications. A 10 Mbits/s baseband coaxial cable physical layer has been approved. The broadband options are still under consideration. On the other hand, the definitions of token bus and token ring are useful for time-critical as well as office applications. For token bus, three physical options are provided: the single-channel broadband system of one, five, or 10 Mbits/s as well as the multi-channel broadband with similar speed options. For token ring, both twisted pair and baseband coaxial cable options have been defined. The former gives data rates of one to 4 Mbits/s. The 4 Mbits/s option has been implemented in IBM Token Ring System. The latter is capable of supporting up to 40 Mbits/s. The relationship of the standard to the OSI model is described in document 802.1.

The range of options offered may seem alarmingly excessive, given the original alleged rationale for standards. Nevertheless, the standard has at least narrowed the alternatives. It is anticipated that future LAN products will conform to the scope laid down by IEEE 802.

The IEEE 802.3 standard has embodied the Ethernet specification. These are not, however, identical. There are subtle differences between them. Ethernet has been around the marketplace for some time. Its history can be traced well back to the experimental work in Xerox's Palo Alto Research Center in early 1970. In 1980, the first Ethernet technical specification release 1.0 was announced jointly by Digital Equipment, Intel and Xerox Corporations.[2] Consequently, quite a number of products were built according to this specification. In fact, it was the closest thing to a *de facto* industry standard at the time. With the announcement of IEEE 802.3 standard, many manufacturers have joined the bandwagon and IEEE 802.3 products have begun to mushroom. To align with the international standard, the Ethernet 1.0 specification has been revised with subtle changes, yielding Ethernet 2.0. The new specification handles all functions required by IEEE 802.3. The remaining differences are inconsequential.

Low level compatibility

Today, in the LAN marketplace, there are three types of baseband products: Ethernet 1.0, Ethernet 2.0 and IEEE 802.3. As mentioned above, Ethernet 2.0 is functionally identical to IEEE 802.3. Quite often, the two are made synonymous and the name IEEE 802.3 is quoted instead. In fact, most companies with CSMA/CD LAN products are shipping Ethernet 1.0 or Ethernet 2.0 products but not IEEE 802.3. Genuine IEEE 802.3 implementation is still not commonplace.

In order to identify the major differences among Ethernet 1.0, Ethernet 2.0 and IEEE 802.3 the physical, MAC and LLC layers, which concern with the low level compatibility issues, are examined.

Electrically, IEEE 802.3, Ethernet 1.0 and Ethernet 2.0 are all compatible at the cable level. IEEE 802.3 and Ethernet 2.0 are essentially identical at this level and include a number of features not included in Ethernet 1.0 such as 'jabber control' in the transceiver, a 'heartbeat' function in the transceiver and controller and tighter tolerances. Ethernet 1.0 system may transmit bit stream to Ethernet 2.0 or IEEE 802.3 but may not be understood by either.

Two types of coaxial cables are currently used. The thick cable is specified in the standard. It has a propagation speed of 0.78c and can cover a distance of 500 metres. The thin cable is not in the standard but offers the same electrical characteristics as the thick cable. It has a slightly lower speed of 0.66c and covers a shorter distance of 300 metres. The bit rate remains 10 Mbits/s. The thin cable, however, is more attractive than the thick one as it is cheaper, more flexible and easier in installation. Consequently, a new proposal

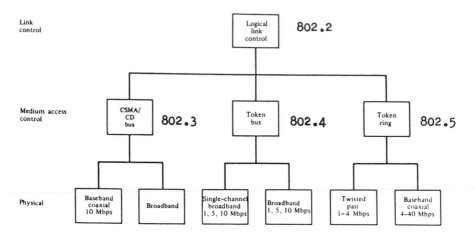

Figure 17.1

IEEE 802 local network standards.

Ethernet	DA	SA	TYPE	DATA	CRC
IEEE 802.3	DA	SA	LENGTH	DATA	CRC

Figure 17.2

DA	SA	LENGTH	DSAP	SSAP	CONTL	DATA

Figure 17.3

Controller/transceiver compatibility matrix

Transceiver / Controller	Ethernet 1.0	Ethernet 2.0	IEEE 802.3
Ethernet 1.0	yes	no	no
Ethernet 2.0	no	yes	yes
IEEE 802.3	no	yes	yes

Figure 17.4

148   NETWORKS FOR THE 1990s

called Cheapernet has been made, calling for the inclusion of thin cable in the standard. Nevertheless, these two types of cables can be intermixed at will with no compatibility problem except in this case, the distance constraint of thin cable applies.

The MAC frame format is the main incompatibility between Ethernet and IEEE 802.3. This is illustrated in Figure 17.2.

Ethernet uses the TYPE field to determine which client protocol the frame is for. IEEE 802 uses the LENGTH field to do additional error checking. However, if the LENGTH field is greater than 1500, it may be viewed as a TYPE field. Thus, IEEE 802.3 and Ethernet can coexist but not necessarily communicate.

A LLC frame format has been defined by IEEE 802 on top of the MAC frame format, providing a similar function to the TYPE field in an Ethernet packet. Thus, a complete 802.2–802.3 packet is shown in Figure 17.3. Ethernet does not define a LLC-like protocol.

The interface between the controller and the transceiver unit is basically the same for Ethernet 2.0 and IEEE 802.3 whereas Ethernet 1.0 is different. The compatibility matrix is shown in Figure 17.4. Thus, Ethernet 1.0 controller must operate with Ethernet 1.0 transceiver. Ethernet 2.0 or IEEE 802.3 controller can usually run with either Ethernet 2.0 or IEEE 802.3 transceiver. The key differences involve the heartbeat function and voltage levels.

Tests have been made on a number of controller and transceiver products from DEC, 3Com, Interlan, TCL and Bridge. Some combinations of the products are not compatible. For instance, the DEC DEUNA controller and 3Com transceiver combination fails. This is because the 3Com transceiver eats a few bits of the 'preamble' which is apparently legal, but the DEUNA self-test microcode cannot deal with that.

It is obvious that compatibility is a cause of concern. As many different versions of IEEE 802.3-Ethernet-compatible products are available in the market, innocent users may well commit themselves to the wrong boxes if not careful!

Higher level compatibility

The IEEE 802.3 standard which embodies Ethernet specifications provides a low level connectivity for multivendor devices. However, the standard does not specify higher level protocols. Without a common higher level software, devices from different manufacturers are still not able to communicate. This is because the true differences between computers are not addressed by the standard, but only their ability to exchange bits on a physical level. It is at these higher levels that many who venture into LAN products are sorely disappointed. Figure 17.5 shows a comparison of various higher level implementations based on the common IEEE 802.3 standard. Among them, Xerox XNS and DARPA TCP/IP are open architectures whereas the others are proprietary protocols. Consequently, the XNS and TCP/IP protocols have been adopted by many leading IEEE 802.3-Ethernet-compatible product manufacturers. These include Bridge, Communication Machinery, Excelan, Ungermann-Bass, 3Com and Interlan.

The Xerox Network System (XNS) is the most prevalent of the higher level protocols employed in IEEE 802.3-Ethernet products today[3]. It is a derivative of the software developed by Xerox for handling network messaging and logical session management between network devices. The Transmission Control Procedure/Internet Protocol (TCP/IP) is a set of network software utilities performing network and transport functions[4]. It is borrowed from the software developed by US Defense for ARPANET applications. In an effort to market the LAN products, manufacturers have chosen one or

ISO-OSI Model \ Systems (Host)	XEROX XNS UNIX VMS DOS	DARPA TCP/IP UNIX VMS DOS	DEC DNA VMS	ATT UNIX	ICL IPA VME DRS	HP MPE
Application	Mail FTP	Mail FTP	↑	↑	↑	↑
Presentation						
Session			DECNET	3BNET	IPALAN	HPLAN
Transport	SPP	TCP				
Network	IDP	IP	↓	↓	↓	↓
Link	IEEE 802.3-Ethernet					
Physical						

Comparison of higher level implementations
based on IEEE 802.3 standard

Figure 17.5

other of these higher level protocol sets. The drawback is that systems implementing XNS cannot communicate with those adopting TCP/IP even though they may share the same cable. One possible remedy is the provision of protocol conversion for the different protocols. This may be satisfactory in the short term but is certainly not a long term solution.

As for the proprietary implementations like DECNET, 3BNET, IPALAN, and HPLAN the situation is rather discouraging. Not only are the protocols inaccessible but the connectivity is limited to specific vendor's products. It is obvious that the strategy adopted is purely a marketing decision. Ironically, such strategy tends to negate the effort of universal interconnectivity which is the whole spirit of local area networking.

Application level compatibility

For the application level, the hope for a common standard is rather remote. There exist different types of protocols for different applications: file transfer, virtual terminal, distributed TP, electronic mail, and so on. None of these follow any common standards.

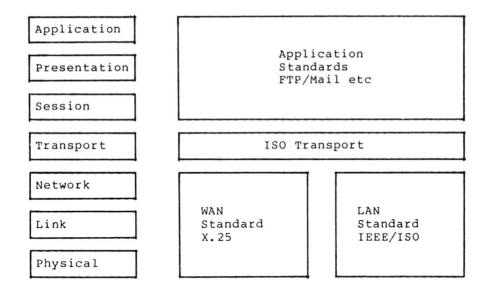

Application		Application Standards FTP/Mail etc	
Presentation			
Session			
Transport		ISO Transport	
Network			
Link		WAN Standard X.25	LAN Standard IEEE/ISO
Physical			

A possible trend of Networking Standards

Figure 17.6

Above all, the most confusing is the operating system of computers, on which most application programmes reside. Where on earth can we find a standard operating system acceptable to all machines? Adoption of a universal operating system has the following advantage: programmes developed on one system in the network can be readily transported and executed in other systems, thus achieving a high degree of inter-operability. Such is the Utopia of distributed computing. In reality, most organisations possess a mix of machines from different manufacturers operating with diverse operating systems. It is unlikely that an ideal solution can be found.

Typically, an end-user has two choices for implementing a baseband LAN: either a single-vendor solution or a multivendor plug-compatible solution. The first choice is less hazardous: the vendor will generally come with complete hardware and software for specific processors and network applications. However, this approach dictates an environment with identical or uniform hosts, for instance DECNET for VAX machines and 3BNET for 3B5 machines. It is not applicable to a mixed-host environment.

The second choice is more flexible and, in general, cheaper. One can get plug-in boards from a number of vendors to fit different host processors. This gives a high speed host-to-host communication. However, some modification of host software may be required. On the other hand, there exist general purpose controller boxes, offering low speed RS232 links. Quite often, a combination of both types of controller is needed. This approach is attractive but requires networking knowledge to combat compatibility problems. Careful planning is needed at the early stage to acquire compatible hardware and software. This is to ensure a proper network integration in order to attain a high degree of interoperability.

Future trends

The IEEE 802 standard has managed to narrow the alternatives but has failed to remove confusion. The many options within the standard are highly undesirable, they tend to aggravate the compatibility issues rather than eliminate them. Standards relating to higher level protocols are not yet defined. With the mushrooming of LAN products, there is an urgent need for the higher level protocols to be standardised.

Nevertheless, some progress has been made in the ISO-CCITT front. An international standard for the Transport Layer has been defined by ISO[5]. This standard has gained the endorsement of CCITT and is to be adopted by PTTs worldwide for international telecommunication[6]. A natural scenario would be to adopt the ISO transport standard for local area networking. Figure 17.6 depicts a likely trend for networking standards. A common ISO transport layer may be acceptable to all. The attraction is that, with the common interface, it would be possible to achieve transparent communication not only among multi-vendor LANs but also across LANs and WANs worldwide. The spirit has been pioneered by General Motors and Boeing in defining the Manufacturing Automation Protocol (MAP) and Technical and Office Protocol (TOP) respectively using the ISO transport protocol[7,8]. It is a move in the right direction.

APPLICATION &
IMPLEMENTATION

18

Corporate Networks

RAY REARDON

Towards the corporate network utility

In the past, corporate networking needs arose from two different areas:

  data processing applications

  traditional telecommunications

In most corporations, data networks started with terminals being owned by the individual data processing applications. The traditional telecommunications network, however, was separately implemented and separately managed. Both of these characteristics are changing as companies view all aspects of their communications as a whole: be it voice, data, text or image.

Fundamentally it is the business applications themselves, and their communities of users, that drive the need for any kind of network. So it is useful firstly to examine the major drivers determining the nature of corporate networks in the late 1980s and into the new decade (*Figure 18.1*) before discussing the characteristics that corporate networks will require for the 1990s.

Voice and conferencing

Voice is the classic area of direct person-to-person communication. In any medium-to-large work location there will be a need for a switchboard or private branch exchange (PBX) to handle telephone calls. This does not necessarily imply the need for a private voice network, which will generally be justified on two main grounds: the ability to manage and reduce overall transmission charges and, equally important, the ability to provide direct desktop-to-desktop dialling between locations which, in turn, can lead to significant reductions in switchboard operators. Similarly, some companies establish telegraph switching systems to reduce internal and external message handling costs.

Three major trends are taking place in this general area: the evolution of new generations of powerful digital PBXs with the ability to integrate data as well as voice; the growth of electronic messaging systems which are starting to supersede traditional telegraph transmission for text oriented communications; and the advent of the videophone and slow-scan videoconferencing.

Studio-quality videoconferencing requires many megabits per second of bandwidth and significant set-up and operational costs. However quite adequate conferencing facilities are being installed within companies using compression techniques at speeds as low as 4.8 Kbits/s over a normal public network dial-up connection. Even at these speeds, a colour image can be refreshed in about 40 seconds which is quite adequate for successful business presentations. The widespread availability of the higher speed 64 Kbits/s ISDN switched facilities planned for the 1990s will make videoconferencing a significant, and comparatively cheap, service within the corporate network manager's portfolio.

Business process systems

In many companies, there is already a considerable penetration of on-line systems to support every area of the company's business process from product design, manufacturing, marketing, and technical support, to billing and administration. This type of application was the largest driver of processing (and networking) capacity through the 1970s and into the 1980s. Previously each system tended to own its own terminals, but increasingly such systems are coming to assume the existence of generalised facilities which requires only that the new business process application has to join the network.

It is a paradox that whereas most employees work in small geographically dispersed units, most of today's data processing users tend to work in large centralised organisational units. This is not so surprising, since the earliest waves of information technology were aimed at the information workers in headquarters or central administration groups. However this is changing as business process systems reach out to the 'sharp end' of the business into the front office or the retail outlet in the High Street. Technology is not the limiting factor here: it is primarily a question of cost justification and the technical support required at the location.

The evolution of field networks took place relatively early, where the transaction itself had very obvious intrinsic value or was a service or commodity in its own right and processed within a formal branch office organisation (as in banking or insurance). Network connected point-of-sale retail systems came rather later, a major justification being the extra management information and control made possible. These will become more pervasive into the 1990s as the High Street (or Main Street or the Shopping Mall) goes on-line.

In both these examples the volumes and justification were high enough to develop specific systems solutions. For lower volume applications, videotex has been an important enabler (although significantly less so in the USA compared with Europe). Essentially videotex is a graphics-based, menu-driven system that uses simple paging and indexing methods usually via dial-up over the public telephone network. Its major advantages are its low cost and its simplicity. Today it is relatively low-speed and inelegant compared with purpose-built systems ... but it does do the job! Whole industries, of which the travel industry is probably the best example, have been affected by videotex. It will be interesting to see what impact the availability of higher speed 64 Kbits/s ISDN dialled transmission and higher resolution graphics will have on the future expansion of this unassuming technology.

Decision support systems

A big driver of processing capacity since the early 1980s has been the emergence of decision support systems. These provide the ability for planners, managers and professionals to create their own applications for goal-setting, planning, tracking, reporting and presentation, etc, without the necessity for traditional application development and central code writing.

They may be based on large mainframes or use personal computers. However, once the corporate user has got beyond the initial excitement of using spreadsheets on a stand-alone personal computer, access to corporate data, and the ability to update that data is needed as

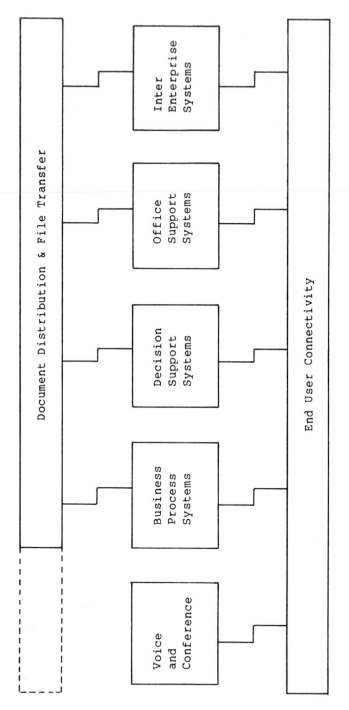

Figure 18.1

well. As the enthusiasm first felt for setting up programs and re-keying data diminishes centrally distributed software and down-load/up-load of data files are required as well as on-line help. In short, despite their original independence, the users will look to the corporate network to sort it all out.

From a purely networking point of view, 'expert systems' will probably follow a similar course. They will gain acceptance in a stand-alone mode but will then move on to the second stage of requiring access to corporate data, central software and technical support, as have many PC users.

Office systems

The most recent driver of capacity has been the area of office support systems. They can be stand-alone local systems but the leading edge users integrate office systems with their other network-based business systems as they move towards the era of the 'computer integrated office'. Office systems comprise electronic mail, diary scheduling, filing and retrieval as their basic functions. They require not only workstation access but also document distribution and file transfer between other users, who may or may not be served by the same host processor, and who may be in other geographical locations, or indeed in other organisations.

Most of the technology and architecture needed for network based, integrated office systems already exists. The most important thing is for a company to have a clearly articulated strategy for office systems and to achieve pervasiveness across the whole company as quickly as possible.

However there is one rapidly evolving technology that has not yet even started to achieve its full potential or its eventual integration with the overall office systems infra-structure. It is a technology that tends to be ignored by the mainstream data and text oriented networking fraternity. That technology is facsimile, otherwise known as fax or image transmission. It is one of the fastest growing areas of inter-location and inter-enterprise communication. In the 1990s the number of terminals installed will exceed the size of the world-wide Telex network. Any office system or electronic messaging system without fax capability will be a very restrictive system indeed.

The travelling user

As business process, decision support, and office support systems become a fundamental prerequisite to the way that a company carries out its business, many of its personnel will need access to those systems whether or not they are actually at their normal place of work − just as they assume the use of the telephone today.

This access may be required from home, from a hotel, from the client's or supplier's office or, in some cases, from a car or other vehicle. Once again, the technology certainly exists today (albeit at lower transmission speeds and less convenience than that enjoyed at the user's normal workplace) and the pressure on the network manager to provide such facilities is building up. Apart from the technology there are several other considerations.

Firstly, technical support. The corporate network will have to provide access gateways into the network at one or more geographical points. There is a trade-off between external call costs and the cost of providing wide geographic coverage of access points.

Secondly, security. External access − whether from the normal switched public network, packet switched networks, ISDN, or cellular radio − raises additional security implications for protection against 'hackers', serious or otherwise. Protection methods include call-back to verify calling location identity, sophisticated access profile and password management, and evolving techniques for session authorisation and encryption.

Thirdly, but not least, cost. A quick calculation of the cost of a user doing an hour a day of interactive electronic mail from home at 09:30, or via cellular radio from the car, multiplied by the number of users and the number of working days a year can be a salutary exercise! Clearly attention will need to be given to the design of application systems to allow upload/download to an intelligent workstation rather than automatically extending the existing interactive, conversational methods. The difference in call charges will be enormous.

There are undoubtedly extra implications to address, but some things are clear: the transmission technology to support travelling users exists. They will demand it and justify it. But the network and application implications are not trivial. It is an extra dimension for the corporate network that is coming, and coming fast.

Inter-enterprise systems

Probably the most significant additional area of demand for corporate networks in the late 1980s and into the 1990s is the rapidly accelerating trend towards extending information systems beyond the traditional boundaries of the enterprise, and the interconnection between enterprises.

Working away from the workplace, as discussed above, is one example. Externalising corporate information or 'electronic brochures' for sales support is another.

Extending the business process directly to the agent or even the customer is proving to be a great source of competitive advantage. Of course this is nothing new. Airline reservation systems have used electronic marketing channels for years and classic case studies such as American Hospital Supplies and Swedish Tobacco testify to the commercial benefit that can be achieved from giving the customer direct access into the product selection and ordering process.

Extending the business process in the other direction to service suppliers or to manufacturing vendors can also contribute significantly to a company's competitive edge and 'just–in–time' component and stock management systems.

Requests for the interlinking of corporate office systems for electronic messaging between organisations are also starting to accelerate. In addition new opportunities for electronic data interchange (EDI) between business partners and business communities of interest are being developed, often via an industry sponsor.

The era of the extended enterprise and inter-enterprise information systems is already upon us. The essential prerequisite is the ability of the corporate network to support this additional dimension, possibly via a Value Added Network service supplier.

Characteristics needed

Network function

In order to support the above application drivers, the corporate network needs to have four basic capabilities:

    end–user connectivity

    document distribution & file transfer

    easy application attachment

    interworking with other networks

End-user connectivity must provide transparent support of workstations and their associated devices such as printers and plotters and allow *any* user in *any* location to use *any* terminal to sign on to *any* application that might be in *any* centre supported by the network.

Document distribution and file transfer are necessary to provide basic communication between users, centres, host systems, and office systems, both within and outside the corporate enterprise as well as for the distribution of software.

A network is only as useful as the applications it serves. Therefore some means of efficient and easy application attachment without additional development is required. The applications themselves need to be attachable at several levels: workstation, department, location, national and international. Proprietary architectures are probably the most cost effective approach for most user companies as the need to move towards comprehensive and cohesive systems *application* architectures is becoming increasingly recognised.

Gateways will be required to allow interconnection and interworking with other networks. In addition to the integration of networks, it is most important that these gateways also provide isolation in order to protect the security and technical integrity of the individual networks.

Network performance

There are many areas that need to be addressed in the area of network performance. Here we will consider three of the major ones:

capacity

service levels

flexibility

Network capacity objectives must be designed in from the outset. Clearly the number and distribution of applications and workstations as well as their projected growth is a fundamental design parameter, but one that is often underestimated. It is likely that during the 1990s many companies will reach the stage where they will have as many workstations on the network as they have telephone handsets. Some have reached that point already.

Similarly, the service levels to be achieved need to be clearly defined. In practice there will be little option here. As users become totally dependent on network-based applications to do their jobs they will require and expect the same level of service as they get from their desk lamps. That is: '24/7/100/SSRT', which means 24 hours a day, 7 days a week, 100 per cent availability, and sub-second reponse time.

As well as achieving high performance levels, the network will need to provide the flexibility to manage change without disruption. Workstations and applications need to be added quite regularly. In addition people move, workstations move, applications move, and offices and centres get relocated.

Network design

The 'network' will seldom be a single network, but rather a hierarchy of networks and subnetworks. The following elements will be common in many companies:

digitally integrated backbone

managed data network

digital PBXs

local area networks

The availability (and tariff economics) of high-speed digital circuits is enabling network managers to rethink their basic network topography and to integrate both voice and data traffic over the same digital highways between major locations. In parallel the rapid evolution of megaspeed multiplexers and transmission resource management hardware is providing the capability to allocate and manage the bandwidth across different types of usage.

Within this digital backbone network, physical integration can be achieved while keeping a considerable degree of logical separation between the voice traffic and the traffic on the managed data network.

The managed data network (or sub-network) has several functions. It owns the data oriented devices on the network, performs packet multiplexing, and establishes the session between workstation and host application, or between host application and host application. It also manages the actual operational service. As network management facilities become more powerful and provide end-to-end visibility across the whole network, the managed data network may also carry out network management for non-data oriented devices, including the basic telecommunications hardware and PBXs.

The modern digital PBX has the ability to switch both voice and data, although for data it is not as efficient or as powerful as a specifically designed managed data network approach. Nevertheless, the PBX can share the integrated digital backbone network with the managed data network within the overall design. 'Smart' PBXs with the ability to make dynamic decisions on routing calls and data over leased circuits or over the public network or ISDN at direct primary rate (1.54–2.048 Mbits/s) will fundamentally alter the range of options in the telecommunications manager's toolbox.

At the location level, the need is not only to provide connectivity between devices, but also a flexible and easily managed approach to the general problem of cabling and wiring. In this respect, probably the most significant recent event has been evolution of the token-passing ring architecture for local area networking and the cabling systems that support it. Bridges are also becoming available so that individual rings can be interconnected into a hierarchy of networks, allowing complex buildings to be wired for optimum manageability and resilience. This hierarchy of local networks in turn fits within the overall hierarchy of the corporate network.

In conclusion

For many companies, the corporate network is already critical to the business. As we enter the 1990s, this will become even more so as the network is seen as a fundamental corporate utility. Whether it predominantly uses private, leased transmission facilities or whether it predominantly uses public facilities such as ISDN, a corporate networking strategy is essential.

19

ISDN Basic Access Terminal Adaptors

PAUL FREUCK & JOHN KUTNEY

Introduction

To achieve the goal of universal ISDN service, it is important that ISDN be able to interface to a great number of existing terminal types and protocols and be able to handle a multitude of call types. As ISDN becomes more universally applied, many ISDN terminals of various capabilities will become available. However, during the introduction of ISDN and for a number of years afterward, it will be necessary to adapt existing terminal devices to ISDN. ISDN terminal adaptors (TAs) will have to be conceived, designed and implemented to permit existing terminals and data network devices to interface ISDN through the basic access S/T reference point.

To maximise the market penetration of ISDN, ISDN Terminal Adaptors should be designed to meet a majority of existing data applications. Some of the more prevalent applications must be considered.

Replacement of:

asynchronous and synchronous modems and data sets for use over public dial and private leased lines.

private dedicated facility, such as is used in cluster controller to host applications.

Support of:

X.25 data communications.

protocol conversions, such as asynchronous to packet.

transport of personal computer generated data.

integrated voice/data terminal (IVDT), and workstation functionality.

communication with data subscribers on the analogue network.

analogue tip/ring interfacing.

synchronous computer networking via SNA.

central office based local area network (LAN) implementations.

To meet such a mixture of applications in a market optimised manner, it would be necessary to develop a large family of ISDN terminal adaptors. However, due to a present lack of specific data concerning the requirements of ISDN customer premise equipment

(CPE), universal, flexible hardware designs for both stand–alone and PC in–slot based adaptor requirements, with software focussed on specific applications, is the most prudent initial approach. These initial designs would later be market optimised via reconfiguration, redesign and repackaging once the requirements of the CPE marketplace start to crystalise.

The rest of this paper will address in detail the envisioned applications for ISDN terminal adaptors and the technical factors to be considered for terminal adaptor development.

ISDN terminal adaptor application environments

Our market research has identified four prime areas for ISDN terminal adaptor application; modem replacement, packet services, computer host/terminal networking, and integrated voice and data requirements.

Modem replacement

Use of the ISDN basic access interface and the ISDN central office transport to replace the existing analogue modem access and connection arrangements can provide for substantial improvements in data transmission quality, efficiency and connectivity. For widespread application the Terminal Adaptor must be able to serve all standard low-to-intermediate data rates up to 19.2 Kbits/s for both asynchronous and low speed synchronous modem replacement. The Terminal Adaptor will adapt the incoming data bit rate on to one of the ISDN basic access 64 Kbits/s B channels.

For asynchronous applications, variable character lengths (which include the start, stop and, optionally, parity bits) must be supported. Full duplex or half duplex operation, with a selectable ready–to–send/clear–to–send delay, also should be supported. Call set-up will be accomplished via conversion from the *de facto* standard. Hayes autodial modem commands into the ISDN Q.931 Layer 3 protocol. This will provide for the transparent replacement of modems and allow existing dialling procedures and programmes to work with ISDN. For synchronous modem applications the Terminal Adaptor must be able to provide a dial-up type capability.

Isochronous transmission should also be provided for speeds of 300 to 19200 bit/s in lieu of asynchronous stop/start operation.

Due to the widespread use of the asynchronous data communication mode with existing personal computers (PCs), it is imperative that this key market segment also be addressed by addition of an ISDN terminal adaptor as a PC in-slot board. This subject is discussed further in the *ISDN terminal adaptor technical considerations* portion of this paper.

The modem environment applications just discussed are summarised in Figure 19.1.

Packet services

The use of HDLC-based X.25 packet techniques is integral to the successful introduction and development of ISDN services. Packet handling, through its statistical multiplexing techniques, makes the most efficient use of existing central office and transmission facilities. To maximise these efficiencies it is important that packet services be integrated with voice and other data services as far out towards the end-user as possible. The packet handling provisions of the ISDN signalling protocols allow its integration at the S/T reference point. To take advantage of this the ISDN terminal adaptor must include X.25 packet handling capabilities.

To maximise X.25 packet applications, the ISDN terminal adaptor must support X.25 data communications on both the B and D channels of the ISDN Basic Access Interface. The terminal adaptor should support X.25 LAPB data terminal Equipment (DTE) functions along with the X.3 Packet Assembler/Disassembler (PAD) function for asynchronous interfaces.

To provide for maximum packet connectivity from asynchronous terminals, external multiline PADs can also be attached, as shown in Figure 19.2. This implementation, in conjunction with the ISDN packet handling capabilities, clearly illustrates the routing flexibility and facility efficiencies provided by packet services.

The asynchronous to X.25 packet protocol conversion capability provided by the X.3 PAD can also find wide application in the PC environment. The PC in-slot version of the ISDN terminal adaptor equipped with X.3 PAD capability will be able to make use of existing PC asynchronous communication software to send data via packet mode.

Computer host/terminal networking

The 64 Kbits/s capacity of ISDN B channels is sufficient to support many existing computer/terminal network scenarios. In conjunction with a high speed ISDN terminal adaptor, the ISDN transport can be used to support synchronous communication at 48K, 56K and 64 Kbits/s. This application replaces dedicated special service facilities such as cluster controller to host leased lines, and can be used for other synchronous data communication applications, such as replacement of synchronous data sets.

An example of this application would be a terminal adaptor that emulates IBM 3270 series cluster controllers to provide SNA communication capability. This would allow non-IBM DTE access to the SNA communication network. Possible scenarios for implementation of such a capability are shown in Figure 19.3. Depending upon the location of the terminal adaptor in the network, it could be packaged in a stand-alone version to support the non-IBM DTE, or packaged for inclusion in a PC. A terminal adaptor port expansion capability may also be required to connect to the multiple number of terminals which normally are supported by a cluster controller. Protocol conversion from SNA to X.25 may also be required for interworking to the existing packet network.

The SNA and X.25 capabilities of an ISDN terminal adaptor can be applied in PC CO-LAN (Central Office – Local Area Network) applications, as shown in Figure 19.4. With the LU 6.2 SNA capability, the terminal adaptor can support the higher layer peer-to-peer functions of IBM's Advanced-Program-to-Program-Communication (APPC) and Document Interchange Architecture (DIA).

For these computer host/terminal networking applications, terminal adaptor call set-up could be accomplished via external keypad, autocall programming activation or access to nailed-up connections through the central office.

Integrated voice and data requirements

To address the integrated voice and data market requirements additional terminal adaptor functionality must be provided to facilitate the voice access. This can be accomplished via handset/speaker jack connection and via provisions for analogue tip/ring access. The tip/ring access also can be used for connection of group 2 and 3 facsimile equipment and answering machines.

Addition of the PC in-slot ISDN interface with handset capability to the IBM compatible PC provides for a very effective way to integrate voice and data capabilities

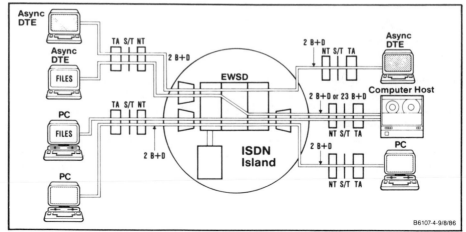

TA Application Scenario: Modem Replacement

Figure 19.1

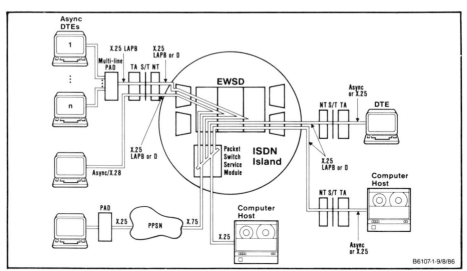

**TA Application Scenario:
Modem Replacement via X.25 Packet**

Figure 19.2

NETWORKS FOR THE 1990s

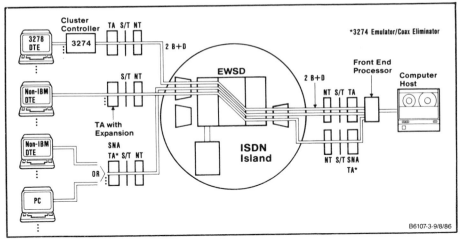

**TA Application Scenario:
Computer Host/Terminal Networking**

Figure 19.3

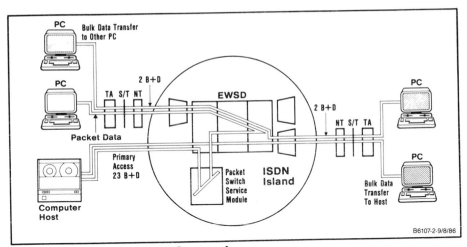

**TA Application Scenario:
PC CO-LAN Functionality**

Figure 19.4

ISDN Terminal Evolution

Figure 19.5

through ISDN access. The voice capability, in conjunction with the widespread distribution, application programs, processing capacity and peripheral capabilities of the PC, provide what we believe is the optimum and most economical introduction strategy for an ISDN integrated workstation. This concept is shown in Figure 19.5.

ISDN terminal adaptor technical considerations

For two non-ISDN terminal devices to communicate over an ISDN facility each device requires a compatible terminal adaptor to access the network. For the terminal adaptors to permit transparent attachment of two devices via the ISDN facility, they must have compatible implementations in the areas of ISDN channel selection, call establishment, conversion to the ISDN D channel signalling protocol, error checking and correcting, and rate adaption of the DCE interface data rate to the ISDN B or D channel rate. At present there is no single clear standard in these areas. For this reason the design implementation must provide the flexibility to be configured in such a way so as to select the appropriate call establishment and rate adaption procedures required by the terminal and communication environment. Some of these applicable procedures are summarised in Tables 1 and 2.

The market application studies summarised previously in this paper pointed out very strongly the need for two separate hardware implementations of the terminal adaptor, one PC in-slot based and the other stand-alone. Hardware design flexibility will be discussed separately for both of these implementations.

PC in-slot based ISDN terminal adaptor implementation

With the open bus architecture of the IBM PC system family, and the compatible systems,

166

```
┌─────────────────────────────────────────────────────────────┐
│              Call Establishment Procedures                    │
│                                                               │
│   Hayes AT Command Set Emulation                              │
│   Manual Call Set-up                                          │
│              via External Keypad                              │
│              via Autocall Set-up                              │
│              via PC Touch-Tone Keypad Emulation               │
│   Access to Nailed-Up Connection                              │
│   PC MS-DOS                                                   │
│                                                               │
└─────────────────────────────────────────────────────────────┘
```

Table 1

```
┌─────────────────────────────────────────────────────────────┐
│                 Rate Adaption Procedures                      │
│                                                               │
│   X.31  Flag Stuffing                                         │
│         For X.25 HDLC and SNA SDLC ≤ 19.2kbps                 │
│                                                               │
│   V.110                                                       │
│         For X.25 HDLC, SNA SDLC and IBM BSC > 19.2kbps        │
│                                                               │
│   Combination X.31/V.110                                      │
│         For 56kbps Open Networks                              │
│                                                               │
│   DMI Mode 2                                                  │
│         For Async, Isochronous, and IBM BSC ≤ 19.2kbps        │
│                                                               │
└─────────────────────────────────────────────────────────────┘
```

Table 2

it is possible to consider the integration of an external terminal adaptor ISDN S bus function onto a PC I/O slot feature board. This approach has several obvious advantages in the PC environment.

An interface to the ISDN S bus can be less expensive than an external adaptor approach. An in–slot approach can share the power and packaging of the host PC.

The adaptor does not require a ROM or EPROM design, since it can be loaded from the PC's diskette or disc. This allows significantly greater flexibility in tailoring the function of the adaptor to meet new application requirements.

New applications have an unconstrained access to the adaptor via a PC bus interface. The external adaptor approach only permits access to the S bus via established serial interfaces. These may be inappropriate for new applications.

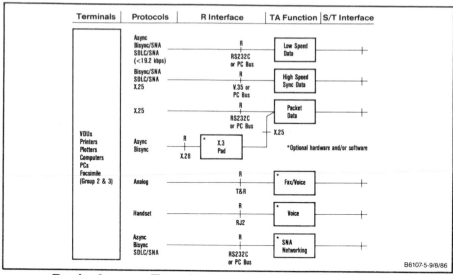

Terminals	Protocols	R Interface	TA Function	S/T Interface

Basic Access Terminal Adaptor Functionality

Figure 19.6

The source of user data could be either the PC bus, the output of one of the PC in–slot communication cards, or an external terminal. By using the PC bus as the source of the data, the existing PC in–slot asynchronous communication card functions could be incorporated in and replaced by the ISDN PC in–slot board. This has the advantage of saving a PC slot.

This approach permits existing asynchronous data communications and networking applications to use the ISDN network in a transparent manner. Applications that now utilise asynchronous D. C. Hayes compatible modems for access to the switched and leased lines will be able to make use of the ISDN networks without modification. This is important since the initial use of the ISDN network will be to support existing PC data communications applications.

Additional PC application areas are those that can take maximum advantage of the capabilities of the ISDN environment. This application category makes use of the high data rates provided by the B channels, the capability to integrate voice and data, and the ability to have simultaneous connections over the 2B + D channels of the S bus. The design implementation chosen should also provide the flexibility to be able to expand the adaptor capability through development and use of additional PC application programs.

Stand-alone ISDN terminal adaptor implementation

The stand–alone adaptor's basic application is to permit existing DTEs (terminals, PCs, and hosts), to connect to the S reference point basic access interface of the ISDN facilities. The stand–alone TA may be viewed as an ISDN compatible modem. As a modem converts a DCE/DTE interface, such as RS-232C, to an analogue telephone network compatible interface, the TA converts the same DCE/DTE interfaces to an all digital ISDN 2B + D S bus interface.

Since the ISDN S bus supports two 64 Kbits/s B channels and a 16 Kbits/s D channel, it is possible to attach multiple devices to the stand-alone adaptor. The 2B + D interface supports the simultaneous attachment of three devices, one device on each of the B channels and a device sharing the D channel with call set-up signalling. Thus, the adaptor can support simultaneous connection of one to three devices to the ISDN facilities. If sub-channel multiplexing is provided external to the TA, with a concentrator, the adaptor could provide an attachment service for multiple concentrated devices to the ISDN network. The adaptor must interface to existing DTEs, emulating a DCE interface so that the attaching DTE is unaware that it is actually interfacing to the ISDN facility. This involves presenting a compatible electrical interface and proper timing and control of interface signalling leads between the DTE and DCE. The DCE interface emulation function must also interface to the link level and network layer protocols, that is variations of asynchronous, synchronous and isochronous protocols. Once the call is established the adaptor must allow these existing protocols to work transparently on an end-to-end basis.

The stand-alone adaptor's major design objectives are support of:

high modularity with the ability to add features to increase or change the type and number of DTEs and devices attached to the S bus via the TA.

maximum data rates on the DTE interfaces as allowed by the limitations of the 2B + D S bus.

simultaneous use of the 2B + D channels.

To meet these design objectives, a base level of functionality is defined for the stand-alone adaptor. To this base level, a set of featurable options is permitted.

Unlike the PC in-slot adaptor which can provide for its functional flexibility via loads from the PC disk, these selectable options and capabilities should be provided via replaceable ROM cartridge implementations. In addition to the optional call establishment and rate adaption procedures summarised in Tables 1 and 2, other ROM selectable features to be considered are:

LAPB to LAPD protocol conversion, to support X.25 DTE.

asynchronous to X.25 protocol conversion via X.3 PAD.

IBM SNA 3274 emulation and coax elimination.

Other optional feature offerings which necessitate additional hardware and software can be implemented via a hardware modular plug-in, including:

voice capability, for addition of a handset, headset, or speaker.

tip and ring interface, for interface to Group 2 and 3 facsimile, analogue phones and answering machines.

multiple DCE port applications.

Terminal adaptor functionality is summarised in Figure 19.6. Selection of the specific adaptor capabilities could be by hardware/software feature offerings, or by menu set-up mechanisms where applicable. Menu set-up could be via factory/distributor preprogramming, or via local terminal session. In the future remote programming of the adaptor from a centralised location via B channel or D channel access is a possibility. This mechanism could also be used for centralised maintenance and troubleshooting.

20

EDI & Inter-Enterprise Systems

DR KAROL SZLICHCINSKI,
NIGEL FENTON, AND BOB HOLMES

Introduction

This is a composite paper based on three separate presentations given by the authors at the 1987 Electronic Data Interchange Conference held in London.

The first part, by Karol Szlichcinski of Butler Cox and Partners, starts from the premise that many organisations expect cost savings from EDI, but little more. However the experience of companies which have implemented EDI is that EDI can be critical in winning business, and brings a range of other management benefits. Potential users need to direct more management attention to EDI.

The second part, by Nigel Fenton of the UK Article Number Association, reviews the progress towards the data formatting standards and network services that are necessary prerequisites in making EDI a reality, and the role of the ANA in achieving this.

The final part, by Bob Holmes of Cunard, provides a case study of the evolution towards paperless trading in shipping and associated industries.

I: BENEFITS OF EDI – THEORY AND PRACTICE

The market for EDI is developing rapidly. Many large companies now use EDI in at least one major application, usually a financial one. Existing EDI users are planning new applications, and many non-users are considering an initial implementation. We have reached the stage of market development where it is vital for users and suppliers alike to look at the experience of early users for the answers to the basic questions about the commercial application of EDI:

what benefits does EDI bring?

do benefits achieved in practice match users' expectations?

what are the implications for users and suppliers?

This analysis is based on a programme of research on EDI carried out for a Butler Cox Foundation research report. The research included a survey of some 250 major European organisations, and an extensive programme of interviews and case studies with leading edge users of EDI in the UK, the rest of Europe and elsewhere.

For the purposes of research EDI is defined as the transfer of structured information in electronic form between computer systems in separate organisations. EDI is developing in a number of separate forms:

trade data interchange, the exchange of information relating to business transactions, typically in batch mode.

electronic funds transfer.

interactive applications, eg information and reservation services.

the exchange of graphics and other design information.

Not all such communications currently take place on-line. The exchange of magnetic tapes is preferred for some applications.

Users expect EDI to bring cost reductions

The survey showed that organisations expect the following benefits from EDI:

cost savings, arising in particular from less paper, reduced data entry, fewer errors.

the ability to offer better service to their customers, in particular through speedier transmission of information.

better and more controlled cash flow.

It is apparent that many organisations expect cost savings, but little more, from EDI. In addition the potential savings are often seen as unspectacular, and their achievement uncertain. It is, therefore, not surprising that EDI sometimes rates low in management priorities. Study of current EDI applications showed, however, that EDI can have more fundamental impacts on businesses.

EDI can win or lose you business

In some sectors, particularly those where it is well established, EDI is already a prerequisite for doing business. For example, one bank interviewed has found that many of the banks it does business with overseas insist on the use of SWIFT, the international financial messaging system, as an essential condition of business. The electronic exchange of seat reservation information and bookings has been an essential capability for airlines for a number of years.

In other sectors, in particular retailing and the motor industry, major organisations are beginning to enforce the use of EDI on organisations dependant on them, (whether suppliers or distributors), or discriminate in favour of those with EDI capability.

One large UK retailer is converting all its suppliers, in order of importance, to accepting orders via EDI.

One car manufacturer now insists that all significant suppliers accept orders via EDI.

Two car manufacturers have recently told all their UK dealers to install PCs for inputting orders to the company headquarters.

One European aircraft manufacturer selects suppliers for minor components on a points classification system, on which EDI capability is one criterion.

Market forces have brought about the same effect in other situations, where the introduction of EDI has led to substantial shifts in market share. This has occurred in particular where customer service, as opposed to price or product design, is the main basis for competition in a market.

> One consumer product is supplied to supermarkets by three major suppliers: the adoption of EDI for the receipt of orders by two of the three led to a considerable shift in market share in their favour.

> The engineering industry in the UK's West Midlands is served by five major toolmakers. After the introduction of EDI for the receipt of orders by two of them, a third experienced a 24 per cent downturn in business. Now all five accept orders via EDI.

In project–oriented areas of business EDI capability can win contracts, or at least get a company on the shortlist.

> One company in the construction industry won a contract because of its ability to accept in electronic form large volumes of plant drawings produced on a CAD system.

> The ability to exchange CAD outputs in electronic form is now an essential condition of participation in most aerospace consortia. Much of the exchange uses magnetic tape, but on–line systems are being piloted.

EDI brings a range of management benefits as well as cost savings

Electronic receipt of orders enables companies to offer better service to their customers, by allowing orders to be transmitted and acted on more quickly and accurately. This is how EDI brings about changes in market share, and why some organisations insist on it in their trading partners. EDI can also bring a range of other management benefits.

> *Better cashflow.* One UK company found that on average it had 30 per cent of invoices to its major customer outstanding at any one time because of real or suspected inaccuracies. The introduction of EDI for order placement and invoice transmission reduced this proportion to less than 5 per cent. Better cashflow for one side of a trading ralationship necessarily means worse cashflow for the other. Both sides benefit, however, from the greatly increased predictability of the timing of payments.

> *Improved stock control.* One US retailer has estimated that EDI for purchase orders saved it from carrying two weeks' worth of inventory. A European car manufacturer has been able to move from weekly to daily ordering *(the case is described in more detail below)*.

> *Better management information and control.* A supermarket chain in Europe runs a very decentralised operation, and uses EDI for direct ordering from individual stores to suppliers: they find EDI permits tighter management control over distribution. A UK firm, which has implemented EDI for the receipt of purchase orders from and dispatch of invoices to its major client, has found the more accurate information and rapid feedback when mistakes occur permits far more effective management of the relevant functions.

In addition, EDI can help overcome operational problems with existing methods of exchanging information with trading partners.

> An Italian supermarket chain had major problems in ordering from its suppliers because of the slowness and unreliability of the Italian postal system. It now places orders by automatic telex generation, but sees EDI as its ultimate objective. It now no longer has to carry inventory to cover postal delays (at least a week) and unreliability, and can sell fresher goods.

> A European car manufacturer used to place orders with its suppliers by telex, a process it found increasingly unsatisfactory: the final straw came when it had to send a telex 45 metres long to a supplier. EDI enables it to place orders daily rather than weekly.

Cost savings specifically related to document processing can indeed be achieved. One UK retailer has eliminated the rekeying of over 10,000 invoices a day. A US company is reported as having reduced the cost of processing a document by between $40 and $60. Electronic capture of credit card transaction data has enabled retailers to avoid the labour requirements of paper slip handling and reconciliation, and to negotiate reduced charges with the credit card companies. Cost savings on document processing are not, however, achieved easily or overnight. They require a high proportion of the relevant documents to be sent via EDI, and they may initially be offset by the capital investment required to implement the new system.

Implications for users and suppliers

A number of messages for users and for suppliers emerge from this review of the benefits of EDI:

> users should direct more management attention to EDI. It could offer a company – or its competitors – an advantage in the marketplace.

> in may cases EDI offers users benefits which are more important, and easier to achieve, than cost savings specifically related to document processing.

> suppliers need to educate potential users about the broader benefits of EDI, and tune their services to deliver them.

EDI, however, is not all plain sailing: there are a number of significant barriers which may need to be overcome, and in some cases substantial costs may need to be incurred. The benefits can, however, make it worth the management effort required to address these problems.

II: PRACTICAL STANDARDS FOR ELECTRONIC DATA EXCHANGE

An initiative to develop a standard for electronic trading data communications was taken in 1980 by the Article Number Association (ANA). The ANA, whose principal role is the administration of the international article numbering and barcoding system (EAN) in the UK, was a suitable centre for this work, since it has a large membership of manufacturers, retailers, and wholesalers from a very wide range of trades and industries. Furthermore, an interest in standardisation of data communications followed logically from the Association's concern with standard product numbering.

A Working Party was established to address the issue of defining one set of data communications standards that could be used in a wide of range of trade applications. The project was called Trading Data Communications, TRADACOMS. The task involved designing widely acceptable electronic file designs or formats for a range of common business transactions.

The Working Party based its standards on an established system of electronic data syntax rules. The syntax rules chosen were those developed by the Simplification of International Trade Procedures Board (SITPRO), a Government-sponsored body which, as part of the UN Economic Commission for Europe, has done much work internationally in the area of data exchange via computer media. The SITPRO syntax is now in fact subsumed by the widely supported United Nations Trade Data Interchange System (UNTDI).

The UNTDI syntax rules have the following advantages:

they are independent of machine, media or systems,

they do not affect the existing structure of data processing within users' in-house systems,

they are not affected by use of different communication protocols,

they offer maximum flexibility through the use of variable length data and conditional fields.

The outcome of this bringing together of the UNTDI syntax rules and the Working Party's file designs was a manual of standards for electronic data exchange. The publication of this manual (entitled *Trading Data Communications: Standards for Electronic Data Exchange*) in November 1982 cleared that first hurdle in the path to achieving direct data exchange.

One additional development which made this advance possible was the agreement by HM Customs and Excise that paper documents could be replaced for VAT purposes by computer transactions on electronic media. The TRADACOMS Standards have been fully agreed with HM Customs and Excise for electronic invoicing and, indeed, ANA was actively involved in the amendments to the 1980 Finance Act which allowed electronic invoicing for the first time in the UK.

TRADACOMS in practice

Since their publication in 1982, the TRADACOMS Standards have been adopted by over six hundred companies in the UK, in many industries – food, pharmaceuticals, retailing, wholesaling, consumer durables, shoes, carriers etc. They are now THE *de facto* standard for electronic exchange of common transactions in mainstream UK industry. They are also now the adopted standards of some international groups for use in inter-divisional electronic data exchange.

Quite recently, a series of new standard files has been designed specifically for, and with the input of, the distribution and transport sector. These files, including uplift notes, delivery confirmation and stock adjustments, will allow most of the most common transactions involved in the movement of goods between suppliers, warehouses, wholesalers and retailers to be conducted electronically.

It is a relatively simple and prompt process for the TRADACOMS Working Party to adapt the standards to ensure their continued relevance to the evolving needs of different industries. This may involve changing the sizes of a few fields or amending or adding certain data elements. Changes are only made after careful consideration with intending users since in many instances, business practices in industries can be improved by adopting the TRADACOMS Standards as they are. The TRADACOMS Standards were developed specifically with electronic communication in mind and are designed to free users from the relics and inefficiencies of paperwork systems.

The TRADACOMS Standards are straightforward to implement, although companies do need to be sure that inaccuracies and inconsistencies which could be ignored or re-interpreted in paperwork systems are not carried through into electronic communications. Because the Standards are intended to bridge, rather than to replace, in-house computer systems and file structures, users must make arrangements to convert data from one format to the other. A syntax conversion package, INTERBRIDGE, is available for this purpose from SITPRO. Users can also write their own software if they prefer.

Substantial benefits can be derived from these standards through the elimination of paperwork which is slow and expensive to process, and prone to errors in handling. Costs are reduced and there is a significant improvement in the speed of processing inter-company transactions. For example, matching invoices received from a supplier on a magnetic tape, with a priced delivery note in a retailer's or wholesaler's system, saves time, errors and handling costs.

The standards act as a bridge, linking users' different systems with a common language for data structure. They represent the best of business practice embodied in electronic message designs. The TRADACOMS Standards Group meets regularly to review the standards, taking account of user comments and requests for change or expansion, to ensure that they continue to meet current business requirements.

The need for a network

Many companies currently using the TRADACOMS Standards employ magnetic tapes and diskettes as the principal medium for exchange. This works well, and the larger users in the UK such as Boots, W H Smith, and Woolworth have developed streamlined procedures for the despatch, receipt and processing of tapes.

However, it has been recognised for some time that there are even greater benefits to be gained from the exchange of data in TRADACOMS format using direct telecommunications between computers. These benefits include increased speeds of data transfer, reduction in control problems associated with physical media such as magnetic tapes and floppy discs, and flexibility for intercommunication with future systems.

The existing TRADACOMS Standards allow for one-to-one transmission between companies and, indeed, several partners are already exchanging data using telecommunications. However, there are practical difficulties to overcome before such direct telecommunications exchange can take place between large numbers of companies.

The first prerequisite is for common telecommunications protocols. Different types of computer hardware tend to support or emulate different *de facto* communication standards (eg 2780, SNA, CO3). Consequently, users wishing to link their computers must decide upon a mutually convenient (or mutually least inconvenient) protocol, often involving the expense of installing protocol converters.

A further problem is the difficulty of scheduling transmissions between trading partners who have different data processing time tables. Bulk volume trading data often has relatively low intrinsic value, and companies do not normally need, nor can they afford, to have direct on-line real-time connections with each other; consequently users must again seek mutually acceptable schedules for transmissions to be exchanged.

These two obstacles were inhibiting the growth of data exchange using telecommunications. ANA, therefore, set about tackling the problem in order to allow wider and more effective use of the TRADACOMS Standards.

The solution was seen to be a low cost, store and retrieve network service, providing comprehensive protocol conversion to support all prevalent requirements. In 1983 the AANA drew up specifications for such a service that has developed into the TRADANET service of the late 1980s.

Each company needs only to establish one link to the service, which may be dial-up, or leased line (ranging from 2.4 Kbits/s to 64 Kbits/s), using any one of the wide range of protocols supported by the service. The service can also support communication via many types of computer, from mainframe to micro. Software support packages are provided where required to ease the process of communication for particular computers or protocols.

Each user has access to its own electronic postbox from which its TRADACOMS messages go for sorting and forwarding to the electronic mailboxes of its trading partners. Companies can see which of their messages have been received and withdrawn for processing by recipients within an hour or two of despatch. At off-peak times, trading messages can be available to business partners in a matter of minutes.

The practical benefits of using EDI supported by an efficient network include administrative savings, reduced errors, faster turnaround and improved cash flow, genuine progress to 'just-in-time' supply techniques, plus a simpler and more convenient approach to inter-enterprise business systems. Companies which recognise the potential of these advances and which are prepared to gear their operations to this electronic era can gain substantial competitive advantages.

Inter-industry initiatives

During the last few years, the general interest in electronic communications among user communities has grown rapidly. Some communities, because of their specialised trading requirements, have commenced the development of specific standards to meet their own communication needs. This is happening in the European motor industry's ODETTE project, and the UK shipping industry's DISH project.

ANA is playing a key role in ensuring the maximum cooperation and harmonisation between such groups through its Inter Industry Forum, which brings together interested parties in the standards arena to exchange news and views. The aim is to restrict divergence in the standards being produced. No industry trades in isolation, and fundamental compatibility between standards is essential for cross-industry communications.

There is no merit in pretending to the business community that two or more overlapping sets of standards are not going to cost more money than one set. Overlapping standards cost more to implement, maintain and enhance. They cost more money to support, and networks offering 'conversion' from one standard to another (even if this could be achieved without introducing ambiguity) must charge relatively higher prices.

A major step forward has already been taken with the development of and widespread support of UNTDI as the basis for standards construction. By providing a common set of syntax rules, with the flexibility for user community-driven message construction, UNTDI provides a system which enables practical electronic data exchange to be implemented within a useful timescale.

At an international level, there is reason to hope that initiatives underway to seek a convergence of mainstream standards may prove fruitful. The Joint Electronic Data Interchange task force (JEDI) initiated in the USA has already brought together users of UNTDI based standards (eg ODETTE and TRADACOMS) with proponents of the ANSI X12 standards. Differences and similarities between these two major systems have been identified. Moves towards an alignment of these standards, both in terms of the syntax, message design methodology and choice of data elements are underway. A new file specifically designed for export invoice exchange has been developed with major input from the UK. Further international formats will follow, to complement national standards like TRADACOMS. In recognition of the need for improved European cooperation a new hierarchy of inter-related working groups has been established bringing together SITPRO UK and its European counterparts with UN and JEDI, with EEC support.

III: PAPERLESS TRADING IN SHIPPING: A CASE STUDY

Shipping, like many other industries, was once more labour intensive than it is today. Desks groaned under the weight of paper and typewriters could be heard outside in the streets. Most shipping offices had a Manifest Department to which stacks of bills of lading were sent, to be typed again, this time on the ship's manifest. The completed manifest was put on board ship or mailed to ports of discharge. Deadlines had to be met. Office canteens served tea until late at night. Shipping notes and numerous other documents were also handled manually.

At Cunard Brocklebank in the late 1960s – comparatively early in the development of computer-based documentation systems – bills of lading were coded by documentation clerks and a specially trained squad of operators produced punched cards. A computer read the cards and transferred the data to the port at Southampton using privately leased telephone lines. The data was then sent to the USA and Canada, again via private telephone lines. Manifests were printed locally, by computer, as required.

The system has been updated and refined over the last 20 years. From the inception of container shipping, the potential of electronic data processing was recognised as an essential tool for equipment control, documentation and accounts. Apart from efficiency in administration and operation, an underlying consideration has been the provision of maximum services to exporters and importers. Thus evolved the system known as SPEED. SPEED enables Cunard Brocklebank to carry out the booking, documentation, equipment control, transport, marine operations and freight accounting functions quickly and efficiently.

The central system is duplicated in separate buildings, cross-connected by fibre optic links, giving a high degree of back-up in the event of major computer failure. High speed telecommunications links connect the head office at Liverpool with offices around the UK which have access to the system from colour VDUs and PCs. Printed output is provided via high speed mainframe printers or by personal matrix printers.

The typewriters are silent ... but the desks still groan under the weight of paper. The old type of form was usually designed for a specific purpose and was often of manageable size. The modern computer printout is bulky even when it contains only a small amount of information. The demand is now for *paperless* documentation via Electronic Data Interchange.

EDI technology is already available and the momentum for change is growing as more and more companies become concerned about the cost of paper documentation. Studies by international trade bodies estimate that documentation costs in the EEC are as much as £7 billion per annum. The estimate for the USA is similar.

Trade documentation is particularly well suited to EDI. Most of the data in trade documents is unchanged from the start of a transaction to its conclusion. In a single transaction up to 40 documents may be used, which share a common core of data that is typed or entered into computers at different stages by different people in different places. Using EDI this common data is entered into a computer once only; unnecessary work is saved and the possibility of error is reduced. The electronic interchange of documents within the transaction chain is much faster than conventional mail or courier services.

Pilot projects ... and beyond.

Two major pilots were started in the industry in 1986: DISH and SHIPNET to prove the feasibility and cost-effectiveness of EDI. During these trials, message formats were defined and all participants exchanged live data.

The messages for Booking, Shipping Instructions, Bills of Lading and Waybills, Invoices, Statements and Schedule Changes were based on internationally agreed standards. The recently agreed UNJEDI syntax rules should be used for the future.

As the trials drew to an end it became obvious that there was a requirement for a single EDI Users Association for the shipping and transport industry with the aim of extending the experience already gained, to develop EDI in other areas of the industry and to liaise with similar groups in Short Sea, Road Transport, Air Cargo, Ports, Banking, and Insurance. In short, all industries interested in the movement of goods.

Similarly, it became apparent that national and international data exchange systems should not be restricted in, or by, the choice of network and that it was essential for dialogue with network suppliers to press for links between networks.

The advantages of EDI in shipping

Reduced paperwork bringing administration savings through less handling of documents, less filing, copying and mailing. The duplication and transcription of data is reduced when staff have access to a common database. At least seven per cent of the cost of exporting goods is attributable to paperwork and the percentage rises quickly when specialised goods are involved.

Elimination of data entry overheads for the receiving system and the cost of re-keying data into the data processing system.

Accuracy improved by eliminating many keying errors, reducing error tracing and correction procedures.

Timeliness of information receipt is more certain and fast, achieving savings through lower stock holding by industry, quicker clearance by Customs and the speedier production of statistics by Government.

Accelerated invoice/payment cycle achieved with benefits to the seller of goods, providing opportunity to reduce borrowings and interest payment on monies borrowed to finance movement of goods – improved cashflow.

Greater control of transportation through speedier advices, with reduction in delays and consequent economies.

Common type of data transfer which would otherwise be subject to many conversions.

Speedier more efficient customer service through EDI updating of customer data bases.

More stable relationships between organisations should lead to mutually more favourable terms of trading.

How a paperless transaction in handled

Cunard Brocklebank, as a participant in the DISH trials, has already carried out completely paperless transactions. The concept is still in its infancy but rapid progress is being made. This is how DISH transactions are being processed.

1   The customer telephones the Shipping Line's Booking Department and is given a booking reference number.

2   The Line's Booking Clerk issues a booking and enters skeleton details of the consignment into the data base to await the transmission of full booking details from the customer via the value added network. Messages coming in on the network are held on a transitional data base. On receipt of the booking details, the data is checked and then transmitted to the permanent data base. The booking is now in the system: it looks just like any other computer booking but it arrived differently.

3   The Cunard Brocklebank booking system automatically requests transport from the Transport Department. The necessary containers are positioned at the shipper's premises.

4   Building on information given at the time of booking the shipper prepares an Export Consignment Shipping Instruction within the computer and transmits it to the Line.

5   The Line's Documentation Clerks receive the shipping instructions, again on the transitional data base. The information provided by the shipper is checked and processed and transferred to the permanent data base. The Bill of Lading number, freight charge details, container number, seal number and any superimposed special clauses are added.

6   Immediately loading to the vessel is confirmed, the Bill of Lading/Waybill and Freight Invoice are transmitted to the shipper across the third party network.

7   The Bill of Lading/Waybill and Invoice are received by the shipper. Action by shippers varies but, in the case of one major exporter, the electronic documents transmitted by the Line are linked to the commercial invoice and transmitted electronically to the USA.

8   The shipper is able to monitor the sailing of the vessel by interrogating a
facility designed to advise details of any changes in the sailing dates/times of
vessels on which electronic bookings have been made.

It should be noted that DISH transactions are being carried out using Data Freight
Receipts or Liner Waybills. The forms are purely electronic and although shippers have
the ability to print out as hard copy from their computer, they do not require a paper
form from the Shipping Line. A negotiable Bill of Lading can be handled electronically,
speeding up the transfer of information but the Shipping Line is obliged to issue a paper
form for use later on in the transaction chain.

Customs procedures and Direct Trader Input

The 'manual' system of clearing goods through Customs by lodging paper forms is
gradually being replaced by Direct Trader Input (DTI).

DTI is a system which allows the transmission of customs entries electronically from the
Forwarding Agents or Shipping Line's computer systems to the H M Customs' computer
at Hardmondsworth. The H M Customs' system for handling these electronic entries is
called Departmental Entry Processing System (DEPS). DEPS will be replaced within the
next few years by Customs Handling of Import and Export Freight (CHIEF).

The development of CHIEF is part of a wider project called Customs 88. This will
introduce a single internationally agreed commodity classification replacing, as far as the
UK is concerned, the Brussels Nomenclature – this is known as the Harmonised System
(HS). The EEC is using the introduction of HS to launch an integrated tariff which has
been given the French acronym TARIC, or Tarif Integre Communautaire. Another
feature of Customs 88 is the introduction of the Single Administrative Document (SAD) a
form said to replace 70 or so documents currently in use in community trade.

'Manual' system

Customs entries are typed on the appropriate form and taken by hand to the Custom
House. After lodging with H M Customs the entries are processed by H M Customs'
computer which is programmed to reject on the first error. H M Customs then issue a
form requesting clarification. This form has to be collected, completed and returned to the
House. The entry is then examined further. If a second error is found the procedure is
repeated, and so on until the entry is accepted. This is very time consuming.

Having accepted the entry H M Customs could call for (A) Document check (B)
Physical check before releasing the goods. Once the entry has been cleared H M Customs
issue an out of charge note to go to the Dock where Customs release the goods from their
control.

The main disadvantages are:

time wasted walking to and from the Customs House,

time wasted clearing up errors.

Direct Trader Input

DTI users are connected to DEPS by terminals within their offices. Entries are transmitted
electronically to DEPS. Errors are automatically notified to the user by H M Customs and
can be overwritten on the VDU screen and transmitted back to DEPS. Although a hard

copy entry is still required, this can be printed from the computer. It is error free and immediately acceptable at the Customs House. At the same time notification of document check/physical examination, if required, is given, H M Customs issue the out of charge note as in the manual system.

The main advantages of DTI are:

cuts down leg work to and from the Customs House,

as errors can be overwritten and corrections transmitted to DEPS, Customs clearance is much quicker,

all paper entries from the DTI software are error free when handed to the Customs,

the requirements for document and physical checks is known earlier and delays in the delivery of goods are mimimised,

DTI also offers a very valuable facility for export entries.

DEPS offers other facilities:

converts currency

converts quantity (eg pounds to kilos)

calculates *ad valorem* charges (duty)

holds VAT rates

gives information about EEC quotes

holds the Customs tariff

gives details of new Customs notices (procedures)

holds details of Agent's accounts

holds details of entry input and clearance details

DTI is now spreading to many UK ports. Felixstowe, Ipswich, Harwich, Southampton, Ramsgate, Medway Port, London, Manchester, Grimsby, Immingham and Hull are some of the ports using the system. DTI is an excellent example of electronic data interchange and its potential is enormous, especially if an interface with the facilities of a UK EDI User Association could be achieved.

Future

The use of electronic data interchange across the complete transaction chain of exporters, banks, ports, air lines, insurance companies, shipping lines, importers, freight forwarders, H M Customs, ferry operators and road hauliers is achievable. The number of EDI Users is growing at the phenomenal rate of 100 per cent per annum. The benefits are tangible, the technology is proven, paperless shipping documentation and electronic customs clearance have been achieved. There is still much work to be done in the shipping and transport industry but as potential EDI Users join forces in a mutually beneficial association, further practical and cost effective systems improvements will surely follow. *It is time for at least the major part of the paper mountain to be obliterated.*

21

X.400 Implementation for International Communications

HIROSHI KURIHARA & KATSUSHI SATO

Introduction

Office Automation (or OA) has become a very popular term for the new office facilities such as personal computers, word processors and copy machines, that are now commonly used in the office environment. Most of these facilities, however, are currently used as stand-alone devices. The new demand is for OA networks by which they can communicate with each other independently of their media types. From the Open Systems Interconnection (OSI) point of view, these OA networks will provide not only network layer service but also application layer service by means of such special functions as media-conversion and mailbox.

In 1981, CCITT started a study on the standardisation of message handling systems (MHS) which have the special functions mentioned above. In 1984, eight new X.400 series recommendations were completed for MHS.

KDD, the international telecommunication carrier of Japan, set up a project in 1981 to develop a new message handling system, and in March 1985 successfully completed the prototype system (called the KDD-MHS hereafter) plus the interconnection test with the Canadian EAN messaging system by using the standardised protocols for MHS. The developed system has high potential for international messaging services. The KDD-MHS not only has the functions defined by the X.400 series recommendations but also has the functions for conventional message store-and-forward systems. Hence KDD has been studying the ways to apply the technology acquired from the development to the international messaging services such as mail box service provided on a commercial basis. This paper outlines both the development of the KDD-MHS and KDD's plan for future international messaging services based on MHS.

MHS model and implementation

System model

The CCITT MHS model defined in the X.400 Recommendation consists of message transfer agents (MTAs) and user agents (UAs). There are several possibilities in mapping MTAs and UAs into a physical system. The KDD-MHS includes many UAs and one MTA. UAs in the KDD-MHS are categorised into three types, according to the types of terminals to be attached to them: TTY-UA (teleprinter-UA), TTX-UA (teletex-UA), and FAX-UA (G3 facsimile-UA). The functional view of the KDD-MHS in the CCITT MHS model is shown in Figure 21.1.

The KDD-MHS supports the following two forms of originator/recipient names (O/R names) described in X.400:

Form 1
Country Name + Administration Domain Name + Personal
Name + [Organisation Name] + [Organisational Unit Name(s)]

Form 2
X.121 address

Form 1 O/R names will be used most commonly in a messaging community to indicate originator and recipient, because each element is presented in a user-friendly form. For Form 1, Organisation Name and Organisational Unit Name(s) can be omitted when the UA is uniquely identified in the KDD-MHS by other elements.

Form 2 O/R names will be used also to indicate terminals such as teletex terminals that are connected directly to the network.

Physical network configuration

The type of physical network, such as packet switched data network (PSDN) or circuit switched data network (CSDN), to be used for the MHS is left to the implementor's decision. KDD selected PSDN as the physical network for KDD-MHS, because the packet switched public data network (PSPDN), one of PSDN, is presently the most widely available public data network in the world.

When a messaging system is connected to a PSDN, PAD facilities have to be installed between the PSDN and any terminal that does not have an X.25 interface. The physical network configuration for the KDD-MHS is shown in Figure 21.2. For teleprinter terminals and G3 facsimile terminals, the standardised X.28 PAD and the FPAD, respectively, are used to access the KDD-MHS. The FPAD protocol specially designed by KDD is performed between the FPAD and the KDD-MHS in Layer 4 (above the network layer).

Messaging service elements implemented

Most of the message transfer service (MT service) elements and many of the inter-personal messaging service (IPM service) elements defined in X.400 can be provided by the KDD-MHS. In addition to these elements, the KDD-MHS can provide non-CCITT-standardised service elements, such as serial numbering of messages, message re-transmission and hold for receipt, based on the conventional private message store-and-forward services that have been provided by KDD for international communications.

Features of the KDD-MHS

Terminal Interfaces

As already briefly described, the KDD-MHS can communicate with three types of terminals: teleprinter, G3 facsimile and teletex. These terminals are summarised in Figure 21.3. Although the KDD-MHS cannot handle Telex terminals, they are considered to be important for commercial services, and KDD installed the telex interface for commercial systems based upon the KDD-MHS.

Teleprinters will be widely used as telecommunication terminals for the foreseeable

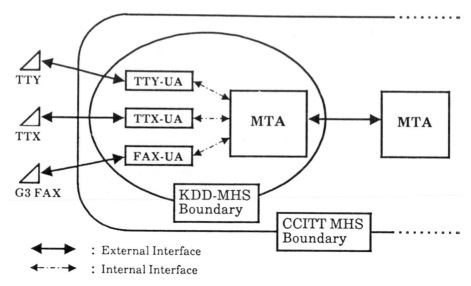

Figure 21.1

Functional View of the KDD-MHS

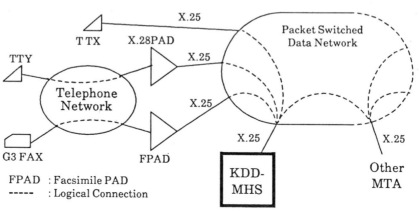

Figure 21.2

Physical Network Configuration for the KDD-MHS

future because of a wide variety of characters they offer and their lower cost. Personal computers and communicating word processors will be categorised as teleprinters.

Facsimile is very useful for the transmission of a visual image that cannot be adequately represented by characters. In today's market, there are four types of standardised facsimiles (G1, G2, G3 and G4) with the G3 facsimile being the most popular.

Teletex is regarded as a sophisticated telex. The telex terminals currently in use around the world are expected to be replaced by terminals similar to those used for teletext in the near future.

Media–conversion

Media–conversion, or encoded information type conversion, is one of the most important functions required for the KDD-MHS, because the KDD-MHS has not only to handle three types of terminals but also to enable these terminals to communicate with each other. This conversion function will enable a user to reduce the number of terminals in his office. Moreover, it will allow more users (a wider variety of terminal types) to participate in the same messaging community. The cases in which the media conversion function is used in the KDD-MHS are shown in Figure 21.4. An example of multi-media communication through the KDD-MHS by means of this function is shown in Figure 21.5.

Message files

Some messaging services are provided to users by the KDD-MHS through the use of message files located in the UAs and an MTA. The message flow through these files is shown in Figure 21.6.

Each UA in the KDD-MHS has the following three message files. Based on the recommendations, these files are located in the local part of UA.

UA message files

The mailbox file (MF) stores the user messages delivered from the MTA, until the recipient user reads them out.

The retrieval file (RF) automatically stores all user messages that were output to the user terminal, for a certain period of time. This file is used by the recipient to re-read out messages, or to forward (reissue) received messages to a third party.

The user file (UF) permanently stores any user messages that were prepared to be sent and/or copied from the retrieval file.

MTA message file

The MTA of the KDD-MHS has a deferred delivery file (DF), which is used to provide the deferred delivery service.

Interconnection with other messaging systems

A function to interconnect with other messaging systems is also essential to the KDD-MHS. The KDD-MHS uses the seven-layer OSI Reference Model from the Physical Layer up to the Application Layer according to the X.400 series recommendations for this

Characteristics of Supported Terminals

Terminal Type	Speed	Basic Features of Message	Notes
TTY (Teleprinter)	50-300bps 1200bps	- unlimited length (lines) - 72char./line upon conversion	IA No.5
TTX (Teletex)	2400bps	- paginated document - 72char./line, 55lines/page - A4 size	T.60, T.61
G3 FAX (G3 facsimile)	2400bps 4800bps 7200bps 9600bps	- paginated document - A4/B4 width - fine/normal resolution	T.4

Figure 21.3

Use of Media-Conversion

FROM \ TO	TTY	TTX	G3 FAX
TTY	○	●	●
TTX	●	○	●
G3 FAX	✕	✕	◎

where; ● : Conversion function is always used.
        ◎ : Conversion function is used if necessary.
        ○ : Conversion function is unnecessary.
        ✕ : It is not possible to communicate in this direction at present.

Figure 21.4

function. The specifications for the KDD–MHS interconnection function are shown in Figure 21.7.

In March 1985, KDD successfully completed an interconnection test, using this function to link with the EAN system of the University of British Columbia (UBC) in Canada.

Application to international commercial services

KDD has been planning to apply the technology acquired from the development of the KDD–MHS to the following commercial messaging services.

Public mail box service

A world–wide mailbox network could be formed by interconnecting all message systems that conform to the X.400 recommendations. In order to make conventional terminals also able to access such a messaging network, KDD developed the interface system for telex terminals accessing the commercial systems based on the KDD–MHS.

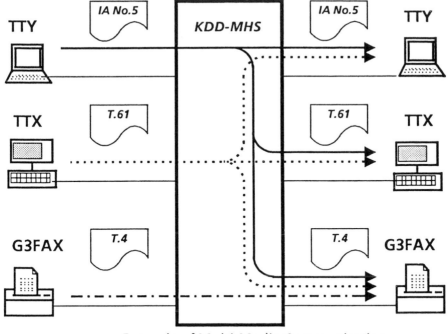

Example of Multi-Media Communication

Figure 21.5

Public facsimile message store-and-forward service

International G3 facsimile communication through public switched telephone network (PSTN) is growing rapidly. One of the problems is that the cost of this communication is expensive, due to the large volume of traffic. The KDD-MHS will be able to help somewhat by offering the deferred delivery service and the multi-destination service provided by MTAs, as well as reliable message transmission between MTAs.

Furthermore, G4 facsimiles will soon become popular in the market place. There will necessarily be a transition period during which both G3 and G4 facsimiles will be used. Hence, the KDD-MHS is now being updated to support G4 facsimile and to enable G4 facsimile and G3 facsimile to communicate with each other. This G4 access to MHS is now also being studied by the CCITT.

Private messaging network service

KDD had been providing the private store-and-forward services for international messages to such users as trading companies. In this service, only messages represented by characters could be handled; users, however, are now also requesting the ability to handle other media such as facsimile. In order to satisfy these requests, KDD is constructing the new commercial message handling systems based on the KDD-MHS. The first commercial system was completed at the end of 1985.

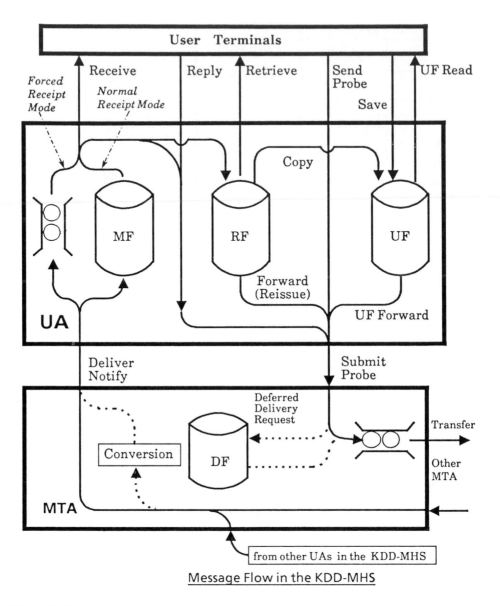

Message Flow in the KDD-MHS

Figure 21.6

Specifications for Interconnection Function

OSI Layer	Protocol		Remarks
Application	P2	X.420	· Multi-part body messages are not acceptable except in the case of Forwarded IP messages.
	P1	X.411	- P1 protocol was designed to be independent of message media type.
Presentation	X.409 & X.410		- The transfer syntax defined in X.409 is employed.
Sesssion	X.225		- Basic Activity Subset (BAS) is selected. - Connections are controlled as One-Way Communication (OWC). - 1SPDU = 1SSDU = 1APDU(MPDU)
Transport	X.214		- The class 0 (the simplest class) transport protocol is selected.
Network	X.25 (Level 3)		- Max Packet size = 128, 256, 512, 1024 octets (negotiable) - The protocol ID in each Incoming Call packet is used to determine the layer 4 protocol.
Data Link	X.25 (Level 2)		- LAPB - SLP
Physical	X.25 (Level 1)		- Speed = 2.4K, 4.8K, 9.6K, 48K bps (depend on modems and PSDN)

Figure 21.7

Concluding remarks

The development of the KDD-MHS based on the X.400 series recommendations and its commercial applications have been discussed in this paper. The interconnection of different messaging systems was proven to be viable based on the standardised messaging services and protocols. The new world–wide messaging community is envisaged in the 1990s, in which messages represented by a wide variety of media will be handled and directory functions will be provided, in accordance with the current CCITT X.400 series recommendations and those of the 1988 version. KDD is going to be one of the builders of such a community.

22

Applications for facsimile

LESTER DAVIS

An introduction to facsimile

As an introduction to facsimile, consider two people on a telephone call, one in London and one in New York. One person has a business document, drawing, accounts sheet, publication layout or printer's proof and is explaining to the other in order to have a discussion for comment or approval. What he needs is to give the other person a copy immediately. That is what facsimile does. A remote copy can be provided, usually at well under a minute a page with current G3 machines, on the same telephone line on which they have been speaking.

In practice the telephone conversation is often not necessary; suitably annotated, the document may be sufficient itself to elicit a suitable response. Simple operation of equipment combined with automatic reception and acknowledgement of reception, encourages such communication. Time zones and staff busy at meetings all day are no problem to providing the documents for later study.

The principle of facsimile has been around since Alexander Bain in 1842. More recently the standardisation agreed within CCITT has resulted in four groups of document facsimile being developed.

Group 1
Standardised in 1972 and providing A4 transmission in 6 minutes. Limited resolution copy using frequency modulation for transmission on the PSTN. Superseded by G2 and now by G3.

Group 2
Standardised in 1976 and providing A4 transmission in 3 minutes with the same resolution as G1. A combination of amplitude and phase modulation used for trasmission on the PSTN. Superseded by G3.

Group 3
Current standard for PSTN facsimile agreed by CCITT in 1980. It provides A4 transmission in 1 minute or less using a combination of data and bandwidth compression on the PSTN. G3 has improved resolution over G1 & G2, to give acceptable office-quality copy.

Group 4
Current standard for digital network facsimile agreed by CCITT in 1984. In its current class 1 facsimile mode it provides A4 transmission in a few seconds at 64 Kbits/s, with standardised resolutions higher than G3 to provide office-copier type quality.

The practical use of facsimile really started to expand with the improved performance of G3. From the launch of these digital machines, sales have approximately doubled each year in the UK.

Machines installed

1982	2824
1983	5593
1984	8080
1985	19269
1986	49521
1987	75000 budget figure

Figures from British Facsimile Industry Consultative Committee (BFICC)

At the end of 1986 there were 82,000 compatible facsimile machines in the UK and of the order of 2.5 million machines worldwide. The 100,000 machine population has already been passed in the UK during 1987, and there is no sign of a change in this rapid rate of growth. The UK outlook could well be for 200,000 machines installed during the year 1990 with a national population then of 1/2 million compatible terminals.

Facsimile growth has not occurred as a result of a development of any particular network, but rather through customer awareness of a product, mainly by using the PSTN, which has evolved into a quality business communications tool, reliable and acceptable for use in the office environment. Facsimile currently provides communication of graphics, handwritten and already-existing documents, and the opportunity for higher performance on ISDN will follow the networks' availability. A higher speed correctly priced transmission network with adequate coverage will attract new types of facsimile terminals to it providing that inter-operation with the existing facsimile population can be provided where required.

Types of facsimile equipment

Through years of specialised requirements, a number of different types of facsimile equipments have evolved. These are used for dedicated purposes and currently operate on particular selected networks. The availability of a new network in ISDN could generate new and enlivened interest in these products.

Facsimile equipment can be classified into four types.

Document communication machines
These comprise over 90 per cent of all facsimile machines. They are produced as transceivers, allowing transmission or reception from the terminal. They are designed to CCITT recommendations where currently the Group 3 PSTN machine predominates, but where Group 4 will emerge as ISDN appears. This far sighted appreciation of the need for communication and equipment standards has contributed to the rapid growth of facsimile to the customer's benefit.

Photofax transmission equipment
These machines normally produced as separate transmit and receive units are used for the transmission of full tone photographs, of a size less than A4. Often the received picture is printed on photographic paper. This equipment

is also produced to a CCITT recommendation which currently requires an analogue transmission medium and normally uses PSTN, speech band private circuits, high frequency (HF) or long wave radio. They may be used for one transmitter to one receiver communication or in broadcast network use for wirephoto services. There has been some activity in past years to digitise the transmission with some success, but it lacks both a transmission medium at a suitable rate and an agreed international standard. The wide availability of a digital network could provide the necessary incentive to agree a new standard, possibly very close to a grey-scale version of Group 4.

Weatherfax equipment
These machines are produced as separate transmit and receive units and usually operate on a broadcast basis with private circuits or a radio network. They provide a basically black and white reception of weather maps, of a size between A1 & A2, and in some cases limited grey scale reception of satellite cloud-cover images. The transmission is an analogue speech-band signal giving a limited speed of operation. Attempts to increase the speed and to improve the resolution have been thwarted by the limitations of the existing equipments and networks. The current standards were set by the World Meteorological Organisation and are well overdue for upgrade to a data-compressed transmission on the digital principles of Group 3 or on Group 4 for the higher transmission rates.

Pressfax equipment
These machines have more sophisticated scanning mechanisms using higher resolutions and, of necessity, higher scanning speeds, and they therefore require high data-rate networks. The transmission is of the whole newspaper page and the units are separate transmitter and receiver equipments. The full-size received copy of the whole page (including headlines, text, graphics, and half tone photographs) is used to produce printing plates for local printing prior to the subsequent distribution of the newspaper.

The specifications for these equipments are set by the individual manufacturers, compatibility not being necessary. The transmission requirements of 48 Kbits/s or higher are selected to suit the networks available and commercial considerations could in due course cause a shift towards operation on ISDN.

Constituent parts of a facsimile machine

To appreciate the inter-operation possibilities of facsimile equipment and the opportunities for developing the product into an integrated communication facilities consider its parts:

    document scanner
    output printer
    processor
    operator interface
    – selector switches (keyboard)

- display panel (CRT)
data memory
modem or line driver
network interface
power supplies

In principle this list is based on the current Group 3 machine. The keyboard and CRT items quoted in brackets as part of the operator interface are additional features starting to appear for G3 but are essential for the highest class of G4.

The development of products using these facilities with word processor and soft options, and with the capability to transmit documents in mixed character and graphics mode, will be in response to market forces.

For facsimile products to continue the market expansion achieved in Group 3 it was essential that at least the basic standards preceded the customer demand for the new Group 4 products. This was well appreciated and engineers working within the CCITT framework have developed and are continuing to refine standards for equipment which awaits the availability of a switched digital network.

CCITT Group 4 Recommendation

The CCITT statement for G4 facsimile apparatus contained in recommendation T.O is:

> 'Apparatus which incorporates means for reducing the redundant information in the document signal prior to transmission mainly via public data networks. The apparatus will utilise procedures applicable to the PDN and will assure an essentially error-free reception of the document. The apparatus may also be used on the public telephone network where an appropriate modulation process will be utilised.'

The characteristics of the facsimile apparatus are basically contained in CCITT recommendations T.5 and T.6. T.5 contains details of the breakdown of the requirement into three classes, and the relationship with teletex and mixed mode, it also details page sizes and the standard scanning resolutions. T.6 contains the recommendations for the facsimile coding scheme.

The three classes of Group 4 facsimile terminals as defined by CCITT Study Group 1 are,

Class I
Minimum requirement is a terminal able to send and receive documents containing facsimile encoded information.

Class II
Minimum requirement is a terminal able to transmit documents which are facsimile encoded. In addition, the terminal must be capable of receiving documents which are facsimile coded, teletex coded and also mixed-mode documents.

Class III
Minimum requirement is a terminal which is capable of generating, transmitting and receiving facsimile coded documents, teletex coded documents and mixed-mode documents.

Some of the key characteristics of G4 are as follows

The specified data rates for international operation are 2.4 Kbits/s, 4.8 Kbits/s, 9.6 Kbits/s and 48 Kbits/s. Additional rates may be used nationally.

The page is the basis of the facsimile message. A4, North American, B4 and A3 sizes having been considered.

Pel (Picture element) transmission densities are mandatory: 200 pels per inch for Class I and 200 and 300 pels per inch for Classes II & III. Optional densities 240, 300 (for class I) and 400 pels per inch are included.

The coding scheme is a refinement of the Modified Read two-dimensional method used in G3. In G4 because the transmission is essentially error free there is no need to repeat reference lines during transmission, and the K factor is raised to infinity so that each line is coded with reference to the previous line.

Fill bits and end-of-line codes used with G3 encoded data are not required in G4 allowing a saving in the data to be transmitted.

Areas left for further study include: other page sizes; other data rates; modem standard for PSTN; other coding schemes (for black and white images, for grey scale images, for colour images); access to services offered by message handling facilities. This should leave sufficient scope to cover all conceivable user requirements as or when required.

Group 3 to Group 4 inter-operation

Facsimile manufacturers have shown responsibility to their existing user bases in making new machines downwards compatible by one Group. The earliest machines were G1 6-minute machines, when G2 the 3-minute version was introduced the machines produced included both the G2 and G1 modes. Similarly with the G3 introduction these machines have the G2 mode for operation with that user base. The new Group 4 equipment will need Group 3 operation to address the million-plus machines now addressible through the PSTN.

Of the possible methods of achieving this G3 to G4 inter-operation, the present approach is to leave the initiative with the manufacturer to include this facility in the terminal, rather than considering conversion in the network itself. At the terminal there seem to be two possibilities:

providing the terminal with 2 ports, the digital G4 port and a separate analogue port through which the G3 PSTN transmission would be made.

digitising the PSTN destined analogue transmission at the terminal, or at the terminating equipment, then transmitting it across the digital network for speech type digital to analogue conversion at the ISDN-PSTN interface point.

At present these discussions continue with the first approach having already been implemented in one equipment.

A current G4 facsimile machine

The NEFAX D35 facsimile transceiver, for instance, provides single touch document transmission at 3 seconds per page. The receive copy is printed on plain paper using the latest in laser technology. Protocol conversion provides inter-operation with G3/G2 equipment.

Copy quality
High resolution 200 and 400 pels per inch in both directions.
Plain paper recording using cut sheets.
Halftone transmission and reception with 16 levels.
A3, B4 and A4 scanning

Speed
High data rates, digital mode to 54 Kbits/s giving 3 second per page transmission in MR (T6) coding.
High speed scanning and printing, 7 pages per minute.
G3/G2 operation on PSTN. G3 modem speeds to 9.6 Kbits/s with high speed control giving 12 sec per page transmission.
Protocol conversion between digital mode and G3/G2 provides facility for onward transmission.
Network connection by two ports.

Simplified operation
Single-touch dialling.
One touch group dialling to 10 groups.
Abbreviated dialling to 1000 destinations.
Automatic re-dial.
Automatic document feed, 50 pages.
Confidential reception.

Memory features.
Advanced store and forward capabilities.
10 or 20 Mbyte storage capacity.
Memory transmission and retransmission facility.
Serial/parallel broadcast.
Remote and relay broadcast.

Administrative features
ID indication.
Password functions
TSI/time/date/document/page number recording on received copies.
Journal printer.
Document status report.
Full sectionalised activity reports.

Conclusion

The scanning of facsimile documents for transmission produces a very large amount of data. The future requirements for higher resolution, better grey-scales and possibly for colour transmission, together with a requirement for the fastest practical transmission speed will lead to a real interest in 64 Kbits/s ISDN for facsimile use. The timescale for taking up this interest depends on the availability of a widespread network and on its cost. In the past facsimile equipment has developed to suit the available networks and this will be the same for ISDN. Recommendations and equipment are available for G4 document facsimile and will undoubtedly follow for other types for specialised facsimile requirements.

Facsimile communication products including facilities for text, memory and softcopy will continue to develop to meet customer requirements. These features can already be seen as new products appear in the marketplace which still demands performance, value and quality. On one hand there is a movement towards decentralised convenience facsimile on a one per desk basis and, on the other, a need for more sophisticated labour-saving routing and distribution facsimile for efficiency in communication.

The question of how mixed mode G4 class 3 facsimile inter-reacts with interfaces on computer workstations (and how these workstations communicate with existing facsimile installations) remains to be seen. Many of these features are technically possible, at a price; what is uncertain is the needs of the market where skilled operators may be required. In any case it is the economies of the transmission itself which affects its use. Higher capacity, reliable and economical networks will encourage data interchange in this information-hungry user environment and it is expected that full use will be made of evolving transmission systems.

23

A Token Ring Backbone Facility

NORMAN HOUSLEY

Introduction

Token rings, contrary to popular opinion, were not invented by IBM. In various forms, in a variety of countries, they have been implemented for both voice and/or data services for over fifteen years. Most notable have been the Cambridge (UK) initiatives, Pierce, Farmer and Newhall at Bell Labs, as well as the Distributed Computing Systems by Farber. IBM itself has implemented a number of ring architectures both for Series 1s and 8100s. The celebrated individual, Soderblom, continues to claim right of invention to the basic schemes and is vigorously defending his claims against all comers. Proteon Inc have been delivering 10 Mbits/s and 80 Mbits/s ring systems for a few years already. As is often the case, IBM has given the marketplace a new impetus. The gestation period for this product has been inordinately long; if it had been the product of a start-up entrepreneurial endeavour, the company would already be bankrupt. The initial announcements of the IBM cabling system – a necessary precursor to the token ring network, showed a professionally designed and built set of equipment tailored to an 'engineered wiring plan'. It appeared to be over-engineered and somewhat restrictive for the then–announced (hinted) token ring specifications. Users might be excused a certain reticence in using the cabling system since it was clearly expensive and designed for a product that did not exist. It was however much better than using point-to-point coaxial cable, the IBM solution of yesteryear.

All the above is now history. The token ring lives. As IBM has long insisted, it is a standard (IEE 802.5) and the technology is open for others to produce products. The cabling system continues to provide more flexible media options. The ring implementations have increasing functionality and connectivity features. An important element within the IBM design is that of network management support. This oft neglected function is an integral part of the ring environment, both for a stand–alone ring as well as one integrated within a mainframe SNA structure.

The specific focus of this paper is:

to identify decisions and events that have resulted in the, implementation of an IBM Token Ring Backbone at the University of Toronto,

to show the extent of the Backbone as at 1987,

to identify the important criteria for implementation,

to indicate future plans and evolution.

At the University, IBM token rings now co-exist with many other LAN technologies. Universities, unlike corporations, are a microcosm of the marketplace. Faculties, departments and individuals can and do make individual procurement decisions for information technologies, hence networks of networks will continue to exist. There are requirements to communicate across these networks. It is likely that the needs for gateways to satisfy this need will be provided by other than IBM. This will always be peripheral to IBM but a good niche market for other companies.

In addition to covering the specific items indicated above, this paper reviews the general background to planning and implementing campus-wide communication services.

General Background

Environment

The University is a multicampus, multibuilding institution. The main campus is located in the centre of Toronto; additional campuses are east and west approximately 25 Km from the city centre. The central campus is transversed by city streets. Fortunately some of the buildings are already connected by steam tunnels or duct banks. A great variety of computing facilities exists at the University, managed by individuals, departments or on behalf of the University as a whole. The computers range from micros to VAXs as well as medium-scale IBM systems and a CRAY X-MP.

Past communications era

The University had installed twisted pair and coaxial cable on an *ad hoc* basis for a number of years. Initially this began in the 1970s as a mechanism to transport analogue signals for centralised data acquisition and analysis. As IBM systems became more communications oriented, coaxial cables were also installed. These initial facilities were gradually expanded over the years. Bell local loops were also used since they have complete coverage of the campus.

New communications era

The increased penetration of computers, workstations and terminals throughout the University in the early 1980s highlighted the need for communications; as a result, a new vision of how communications should be planned and implemented evolved. A strong impetus developed to become master in one's own house. At the least this meant taking control of the physical facilities. Prior to this vision developing, Bell had been in primary control. The investment necessary to replace existing Bell facilities – which implies using the same 'old technology' of twisted pair and a centralised PBX – is many million dollars: this level of investment was not considered appropriate at this time. Hence selective investments were made, primarily (but not ignoring voice) for data communications. The University has come to view communications as a part of the physical fabric (infrastructure) of buildings, to be planned for in a similar manner as water and electrical facilities; very conscious efforts have been made to incorporate communications facilities in new buildings or during renovation.

This has manifested itself in the following manner:

conduits, cable tray in new buildings over and above that necessary for basic telephones (or sized to cover additional facilities).

extra duct banks in the ground specifically for communications as new construction or modification occurs.

cable tray in steam tunnel.

allocation of wiring closet space at building entry to facilitate interconnection of inter- and intra-building facilities.

identification of a central hub location on the campus for the termination of Bell facilities from the central office and new University facilities.

installation of new twisted pair and fibre optic cable in areas of high or potential traffic.

As of the summer of 1987, twisted pair facilities interconnect 30 buildings and fibre optic cable, 17. The cumulative installed length of fibre is over 7000 metres; the amount of twisted pairs is a minimum of 100 pairs normal telephone cable and up to 300 pairs in more heavily used locations. Twelve fibre, 50-micron, graded index, multimode cable was used initially as the physical optical medium. Mostly it is one cable but in some places it is more. The cable is from two vendors and of very different construction. The actual investment has been quite modest when compared to that associated with telephone facilities: the actual cost of fibre and twisted pair cable is about fifteen per cent of the total cost of approximately $400,000. A technology review in the first quarter of 1987 indicated the need for a change of fibre diameter to 62.5 microns. This diameter is optimally suited to the Fibre Distributed Data Interface (FDDI): 50-micron fibre would operate but it introduces different configuration limitations. It is of interest to note that the initial fibre size offered as a part of the IBM cabling systems was 100 microns. Notwithstanding the IBM Token Ring, FDDI may be the future standard.

Evolution of fibre backbone

Twisted pair facilities are a well-understood technology that can be used quite readily. Fibre-optic facilities do require much more thought. During the 1983 planning process, it was decided that fibre would become increasingly important as a communications medium. The University was examining various ways in which to enhance its data switching capability over and above the existing Gandalf PACX IV and decided to use Ethernet terminal server technology. Since this was to be an inter-building service, a decision was made to implement this approach using Codenoll equipment and fibre-optic cabling. The number of fibres, size and type of fibre were determined by performance, price and availability considerations. The ready availability of components, tools and instrumentation led us to the 50-micron choice. The feasibility and advantages of fibre have resulted in a motivation to invest more resources into this type of communications infrastructure. The optic environment has performed flawlessly since installation. Any difficulties have been with the end equipment.

The fibre is used for a variety of purposes today, which will expand very significantly over the next two years. Access to the CRAY X-MP is a factor in the increased demand. In particular, fibre carries the following traffic:

Ethernet with TCP/IP, DECNET, XNS protocols, the general purpose campus backbone.

IBM 3270 multiplexed point-to-point links.

IBM channel extender (Dataswitch 8044).

Gandalf P2K inter node and remote shelf, the circuit switched, workstation oriented backbone.

HUBNET, a 50 Mbits/s U of T development specifically for fibre.

IBM Token Ring Backbone.

Rather than being displaced, the PACX IV is now fully integrated with the new P2K forming an effective data switching facility whose functionality continues to grow. Wavelength Division Multiplexing is to be used on the fibre between P2K end equipment. This allows more efficient utilisation of the installed fibre with minimal investment.

Campus network architecture

Planning methodology

A number of elements encompass the planning for communications and establish the structure and shape of network developments. A primary factor in this regard is the decision to operate as a campus common carrier. This carrier model suggests that communications facilities should be catholic and have added value functions. Computing facilities are regarded as servers attached to a network environment. Both environments are planned autonomously but they are clearly linked by mutual interest. Planning is performed by examining the campus as a whole so that the features and facilities provided are an attribute of need rather than location. While there is an obvious tendency to implement facilities in those easy parts of the campus, for example where underground tunnels and ducts exist, a conscious effort is made to expand this aspect of physical infrastructure whenever possible.

The focus of activities is the implementation of an inter-building campus communications transport systems. The in-building networking environment is regarded as the domain of user departments, faculties or groups. The inter-building facilities connect with in-building networks not machines or workstations.

Hence, a network of networks exists. The inter-network interfaces circumscribe the campus carrier responsibilities. A set of facilities is implemented which it is believed will satisfy a substantial amount of the generic needs. Specific private (dedicated) use of inter-building facilities is permitted for both fibre and copper physical plant. Use of the fibre however is closely controlled, and primarily directed to overall campus needs since relatively little of it exists.

Funding for these initiatives has been obtained from a variety of sources; new capital injections as well as re-directed savings have been used. This funding has however been mostly *ad hoc*. The implementations have taken place over a few years and have been constrained by available fundings, so no 'grand campus' plan exists. As a consequence, implementation has tended to lag behind needs. The architectural approach has however, remained consistent. In retrospect, this limited funding approach, while painful at times to everyone, has forced innovative use of facilities and garnered continually increasing universal support. The basic facilities have given a high degree of flexibility to implement services as the demands have arisen.

Physical facilities

The fibre and copper plant constitute the physical media facilities. They are in many ways, the campus backbone. Any type of network and protocol can potentially be used for inter-building transmission. The copper facilities are the most flexible and are used for both private (dedicated) as well as shared use. The services that are provided on the fibre are oriented to national and international standards. As was indicated earlier, this backbone is utilised to provide a variety of communications services. By the support of these specific technologies and standards the University has encouraged procurement for communications and computer activities to occur from a defined set of possibilities.

The use of these physical fibre facilities is mediated by nodal processors, and these vary as a function of the type of backbone. Since there are currently three backbones, there are three types of nodal processors:

the Token Ring Backbone uses IBM AT Personal Computers as bridges.

the Ethernet General Purpose Backbone uses microVAX processors.

the P2K Terminal Switching Backbone uses P2K Subscriber shelves.

These nodal processors were selected on the basis of function, cost and performance. The microVAXs were initially microVAX Is in order that a project deadline could be met in 1985. MicroVAX IIs quickly displaced the Is. The ATs satisfy the capacity requirements at this early stage of the Token Ring Backbone. Since these nodal processors are developed and maintained by the campus carrier some consistency and reasonable lifetime is necessary. There is however no magic about these systems. It is the function and the performance that are important. All types of nodal processors are continually under review. Just as the fibre diameter has been changed, the nodal processors will go through a technological evolution. It is expected that nodal processors can be re-used as needs evolve and technology changes. In the cases of the general purpose backbone, general purpose processors (microVAX II) were chosen, allowing for backbone technology changes without corresponding disruption to departmental environments. The general purpose backbone could be changed today to an 80 Mbits/s Proteon token ring for an extremely modest investment. The emergence of FDDI can potentially be handled with the same ease since DEC is very involved with the standard development activity.

Network domains

There are currently three primary computing large scale domains at the campus:

UNIX systems, ULTRIX, BSD and ATT Version 7 operating systems.

DEC VMS systems.

IBM, MVS and VM environments (within an SNA structure).

The fact that these domains exist (and a desire for specific performance levels) has given rise to the need for the three backbone technologies identified previously. The computing domains impose protocol limitations at various levels of the ISO model. 'Gatewaying' between the domains, in the absence of full ISO standards, is an exercise in ingenuity. It can be done but usually some constraints are involved. At the highest levels, for example, the barriers are substantially diminished, for example, mail can be moved almost anywhere.

The General Purpose Backbone was chosen particularly for its universality and marketplace acceptance. In this case the nodal processors and the various protocols

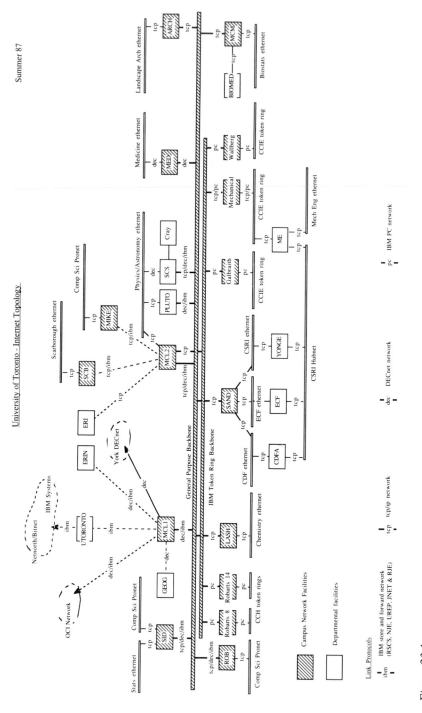

Figure 23.1

combine to form a Campus Internet, Figure 23.1. This internet architecture has resulted in an extremely robust environment which continues to evolve over time. The nodal processors handle various protocols in the ISO model hierarchy or its reasonable analogues in the TCP/IP, DNA and XNS architectures. A 'pure' nodal processor (which just provides an in-building network-to-backbone connection) operates up to the Network (IP) level of the hierarchy. Sometimes a nodal processor will provide other services such as printer support and file transfer facilities. These processors operate at all levels of the ISO hierarchy.

The IBM Token Ring Backbone has a similar schematic architecture as the General Purpose Backbone. It has nodal processors which mediate access to a transmission medium and connect departmental or group networks to a backbone. The function of these nodal processors is substantially different than the microVAX IIs in that they only operate at the Data Link level of the ISO model. Since the rings operate at this level, they integrate fully with the existing SNA hierarchy. The mechanisms which allow the integration can either be via emulation of existing Logical/Physical units or, where independent initiation of peer sessions is desired, implementation of LU 6.2 and PU 2.1.

The Terminal Switching backbone is protocol independent. It operates in a virtual circuit mode only. Its nodal processors are, in fact, primarily concentrators operating in a Time Division Multiplexing mode to funnel traffic onto the fibre. All switching is performed at the central node. However, a multi-switching node can be established so that traffic can be isolated to particular geographic areas. It is expected that this will occur as the needs for this architectural solution grow.

While it would certainly be more simple to develop, operate and manage a homogeneous network, such a solution could not satisfy the functional, capacity and geographic requirements. The multi-backbone approach is not unlike the national carrier's service evolution over the last decade in which more and more added value functions have been provided while utilising pieces of backbone facilities as appropiate. As a result packet switching and some end-to-end digital services have been developed well in advance of ISDN implementation.

The token ring backbone

Planning and rationale

Consideration of a token ring backbone on the campus occured in 1985. This arose due to the technical limitations of the Ethernet General Purpose Backbone (GPB) constraining its scope. The rationale for this activity is the known advantage of a token ring over a CSMA/CD media access protocol, as well as geographic coverage and the availability of higher capacity implementations. The geographic coverage of the GPB can now be extended by Link Level bridges. The impact on performance by their use is relatively minimal if judiciously used. At this time capacity is not a primary driving force, the existing GPB is not at a capacity constraint. However, constraints will occur as inter-building traffic grows. Mail and access to the Cray X-MP as well as more distributed computing will generate enough volume. The growth of traffic has been somewhat slower than anticipated: one reason for this is Paretto's principle (more activity is generated within groups than across groups); another is the rate of expansion of backbone facilities. If there is no backbone access, there will be no traffic. Thus the initial growth of traffic would be slower. The GPB is now of a size and function that traffic will grow

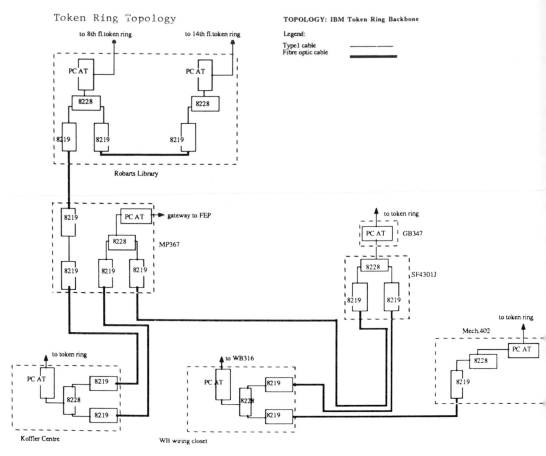

Figure 23.2 Token Ring Topology

substantially over the next couple of years. As it does, FDDI implementations will probably be available as a possible solution.

It may be deduced from the preceeding paragraph that the rationale for implementing an IBM Token Ring Backbone (ITB) is not capacity or geographic coverage. The area of coverage is greater than the GPB but the capacity is somewhat less. The requirement for an ITB is based on these premises:

local IBM Token Rings (ITRs) exist and they are being installed in significant numbers.

an ITB will optimally provide connectivity for the evolving SNA campus domain.

two University IBM partnerships – The Centre for Computer Integrated Engineering (CCIE) and the Centre for Computing in the Humanities (CCH) – have been initiated.

These two partnerships have a variety of computing equipment distributed within the campus. They also both require access to centrally based services and connectivity between each other. Since the partnerships do involve ITRs the most effective method for interconnection is the ITB. As has occurred with the other backbones, this one will grow as the need and funding dictate.

Coverage and scale

There exist about twelve ITRs on the campus at this time. In addition to the rings, a number of System 36s and many 3270 style workstations are in place. Of the twelve rings that do exist, seven utilise the ITB. The remainder are not in the proximity of the backbone or they currently use ring software which is incompatible with ITB. A few rings may never be near enough to the ITB for direct connection via the appropriate IBM Cabling System type cable. The ITB does however, add another dimension to connectivity options for workstations and hosts. It is expected that higher bandwidth connections will always be possible as a consequence of the ITB presence.

The actual topology of the network is as shown in Figure 23.2. It is designed with the existing requirements in mind, so modifications to this topology will no doubt occur over the next two years as the requirements for access increase. As the area of coverage expands, it is possible for the backbone itself to become a series of rings. The particular topology chosen as the network grows will trade off a number of factors including:

   use of fibre strands.

   contraints implied by Mbits/s operation.

   maintainability and operability.

   fibre flux budget.

The simplest structure that will satisfy the design constraints and capacity needs will be implemented.

During 1987 the ITB will connect a number of buildings but there are ITRs that exist today which are not in proximity to the backbone. In some cases, the rings are only a short distance away but they are on the 'wrong side of the street.' This highlights one of the most difficult aspects of communications planning at the University, dealing with the civic nature of the in–city campus. This fact alone dramatically affects the cost of provisioning basic physical facilities to campus buildings: rewiring the campus in order to provide universal facilities will cost many millions of dollars. If it is done at all, it will only be in the context of a change in the telephone service. Facilities are added whenever and wherever possible but these will never permeate each office, classroom or residence.

Technical factors

In the ITB environment there are three primary subsystems considerations:

   the fibre–optic environment.

   bridges interconnecting ring facilities.

   gateways to facilitate access to machine resources.

The fibre–optic environment for a token ring is signficantly easier to engineer than the existing GPB. Changes to the fibre environment of the GPB can dramatically affect its operability. This can be avoided by re-design and additional expenditure. The coverage of the GPB has been stretched to the limitations imposed by the basic specifications. Re-engineering the GPB can be done at some expense and possibly reduction in capacity by using Link Level bridges. It will however, never be as easy to design as a token ring environment.

IBM recommend the use of two fibre paths, hence four fibres. This is to ensure continued operability in the event of a failure in the fibre system connectivity. A decision has been made to use only one forward and return path at this time. When an abundance of fibre and enough space diversity exists two paths may be feasible; it is however, questionable that this requirement is necessary. While the ITB is quite large in the context of a LAN, it is quite quick and easy to get to any part of it to make repairs and, to date, the fibre environment has been the most reliable portion of network technology.

As indicated previously, the fibre backbone is composed of 62.5/125 and 50/125 micron graded index strands. The two factors which affect the ring length are attenuation and dispersion. *Attenuation* is influenced by fibre type, connectors and joints. The maximum possible attenuation between Multi Station Access Units (MSAUs) is a specified design criterion by IBM. Actual loss can be compensated for, by the use of repeaters to boost the signal level. *Dispersion*, which primarily determines bandwidth, is a characteristic of fibre type, manufacturing process and diameter. The smaller the diameter, the more difficult it is to inject optical power, hence compounding the attenuation characteristics. Any of the standard fibre sizes – 50/125, 62.5/125, 85/125, 100/140 – have sufficient bandwidth to operate at more than 16 Mbits/s with the signalling method used by IBM. These parameters, attenuation and dispersion, do not change appreciably with age. Hence, a correctly engineered fibre environment should remain so in the absence of change.

The maximum possible length of a token ring is limited only by the maximum acceptable delay around the ring. While this is somewhat dependent on the actual application, rings in general can exceed tens of kilometres.

The bridges which interconnect rings to the ITB can be any of the IBM Personal Computers. At this time we have chosen AT-based machines. This was a conservative choice, in that it was the fastest IBM Personal Computer. While a simple IBM PC should be able to perform satisfactorily in these early days, the safety margin implied by greater processing capability was required. In actual fact, these machines are on loan and a firm decision as to which nodal processor to use is required before the end of the year, since the existing machines are to be returned. One potential option is the IBM RT PC. In addition to having greater processing capacity than an AT, it can also handle Token Ring and Ethernet type traffic. It can therefore be used as a nodal processor for both the ITB and GPB and is, in general, more flexible than any of the standard PCs. This particular machine is being provided with increased functionality monthly. A decision as to the optimal solution is expected by calendar year end, when enough experience will have been gained as to the particular operating, functional and capacity characteristics of the various machines.

A wider set of options are available to connect token rings to IBM hosts. These can be either communications based (for example an AT with an SDLC link to a 3705) or channel based (for example 372X, 3174). These options are differentiated by cost, capacity and functionality. Of the options, the 3725 is the most capable and, if the 3725 is already installed, the most cost effective. In the absence of a 3725, a 3174 offers the optimal method of connection. In particular the model L, with a local channel attachment feature and the Token Ring 3270 Gateway, provides for up to 140 token ring attached devices to communicate with an IBM Host. The host will deal with the devices as PU 2.0 nodes. It is expected that all of these options will be used over the next two years to phase cost levels with capacity needs. The eventual solution will be direct TRB to a Front End Processor.

Management and diagnosis

Just as the Token Ring fits into the SNA hierarchy, it integrates with IBM's network management philosophy. The new management system is termed Netview. This replaces (although it is actually partially composed of) previous SNA network management software packages. The ring portion of an SNA network is supervised by Netview PC, a software package for an IBM PC. This package performs what has come to be expected (and more) in supervisory systems. Data collection, analysis and diagnostics are provided. In a multi-ring environment, supervision can be carried out by one PC or many and be disjointed or integrated together. All in all, IBM have delivered a professional, comprehensive package of function at a relatively inexpensive level of cost. This compares very favourably with available Ethernet diagnostic tools. Netview is becoming a more general-purpose communications management tool. It can be used with voice and data networks as well as with non-IBM products. As with many IBM facilities, Netview may become a *de facto* standard.

At this time the ITB uses Netview PC only. Very few of the old host-based management tools are used. In our particular environment the cost and utility are not in alignment. However with the ITB, it is mandatory that the monitoring and diagnostic tools be in place. They will grow more comprehensive as needs dictate.

Conclusions

The ITB adds yet another high capacity communications system to the University infrastructure. This has been achieved at relatively low cost due to leverage obtained from earlier physical facility investments. The choice to use optical-fibre technology for local networking back in 1983 has proved to be fortuitous. This initiative has provided for a flexible evolving environment, which caters to the distributed nature of the institution itself and its computing systems.

24

Primary Rate LAN Interconnection for Office Applications

PETER CLARK

The Unison Project

The four-year, £2 million, Unison Project was established to investigate the interconnection and interworking of Local Area Network (LAN) based multi-media office systems. It is a collaborative research project within the Alvey Programme under their Infrastructure and Communications Director, Keith Bartlett. (*See NOTE at end of this chapter*).

The collaborators are, with their locations:

Logica, London (who are providing the management)

Acorn Computers Limited, Cambridge

The University of Cambridge Computer Laboratory

Loughborough University of Technology

SERC Rutherford Appleton Laboratory, Didcot

The formal objectives of the project are as follows:

To investigate the efficacy of LAN-based office systems for inter-site working and to provide services such as document preparation, electronic mail and interactive working (conferencing).

To develop techniques for such systems to handle multi-media information: text, graphics and voice.

To investigate the use of 'agent services' in a new approach to transport services.

To develop an experimental fast local switch based on the Cambridge Fast Ring.

Clearly the project could never investigate at reasonable depth all of the aspects of the objectives, and the identification of a suitable subset is included in the project plan as a necessary activity.

Unison, as its name implies, has its origins in a previous collaboration – 'Project Universe'. This project successfully established satellite links between a number of LANs and performed some research on the network that this supported.[1]

Unison used many of the ideas, and some of the hardware and software developed by

Universe, and identified a programme of research based on terrestrial high speed links between LANs for office applications.

The Alvey High Speed Network: a primary rate ISDN

The high speed terrestrial links required by Unison were quickly identified to be circuits with bit rates similar to those encountered on existing LANs. Most Unison sites were equipped with Cambridge Ring LANs operating with effective data rates of over one Megabit per second (1 Mbits/s): the 2.048 Mbits/s offered by BT MegaStream or the equivalent from Mercury Communications Ltd were suitable candidates for the links.

However, the possibility of providing a switched network of these links to support Unison and other Alvey projects, based on the emerging I-Series Recommendations of the CCITT, was being considered by the Alvey Directorate. This was particularly attractive to Unison as it would offer hands-on experience of a prototype primary rate ISDN, with flexible circuit switching between sites rather than a fixed topology.

The Alvey High Speed Network was agreed and has been developed to provide Unison access to just such a network. The network meets the basic requirement of providing a circuit-switched bearer service at bit rates of $n \times 64$ Kbits/s for $1 < n \leqslant 30$ based on CCITT Recommendation I.421. Time slot 0 is used for synchronisation and alarm patterns, time slot 16 carries the common-channel message-based user signalling.

At the heart of the system is an automatic cross-connection equipment (ACE) with added controls which fulfill the necessary slot switching and manipulation to enable circuits to be established in response to D-channel requests.

The total topology of the Alvey High Speed Network is shown in Figure 24.1. It should be noted that whilst only one ACE is used, the system design is generalised rather than based on a simple star, such that the concept of routing rather than point-to-point connection has been incorporated in the design. It is as representative of a real ISDN as possible in that, by using loop-backs, the one ACE can produce realistic framing slip or skew.

At each user site the Unison equipment has had to terminate the network, the function that would normally be performed by the network terminating equipment (NTE) to support a choice of I-series interfaces, terminal adaptors and an operator console. This is illustrated in Figure 24.2.

The Unison project uses a subset of the facilities provided by the Alvey High Speed Network and can be regarded as a closed user group for simplicity. At each site it uses a single I.421 primary rate interface and provides its own terminal adaptor, which is described in detail later.

Unison needed to use the network before its development was complete. To this end an interim phased network was made available to Unison, comprising initially fixed (plug-patchable) 2 Mbits/s wide circuits and then slotted $n \times 64$ Kbits/s circuits individually switched by an operator at a central console attached to an ACE. Interim NTEs took the form of drop and insert multiplexers used as barrier and signal conditioning devices only.

Figure 24.3 shows the final network provision for Unison. Also shown is the additional high speed link between the two collaborators in Cambridge and the alternative Mercury limb of the network which provides a link between Cambridge University and the other ACE. These extra links have enabled a number of interesting network architecture/performance experiments to be devised.

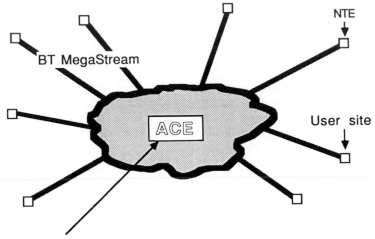

Central Switch at BT, Gower Street, London

The Alvey High Speed Network Topology

Figure 24.1

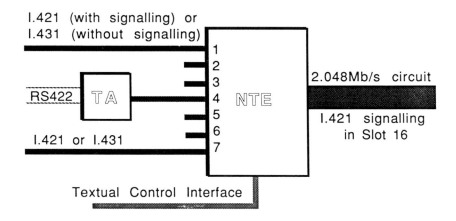

The NTE showing Interfaces supported

Figure 24.2

The high speed switch or exchange

At each Unison site, the terminal adaptor (TA) was developed by Unison rather than provided as part of an NTE. It takes the form of a high speed switch or 'exchange' comprising a Cambridge Fast Ring (CFR) implemented within an equipment rack. This CFR is based on the chip design work of the University of Cambridge Computer Laboratory and Acorn Computers Ltd which was made available to the project. Working chip prototypes have been made of this 50 Mbits/s second generation, version of the well known Cambridge Ring.

The CFR provides a data path between the incoming I.421 link and one or more LANs, other management devices and even other I.421 links.

A terminology has been developed (*Figure 24.4*) for the component parts of the *exchange architecture*. The *portal* is the hardware and software that sits between LAN and CFR, and different portals service different types of LAN. The *ramp* is that interface between high speed link and CFR. It has considerable buffering, the ability to handle signals of n × 64 Kbits/s slotted format, and the ability to generate d-channel signalling requests and responses. Finally the *management* fulfills the CFR management role which includes that of a directory service.

The purpose of the exchange architecture is primarily to support communications between peer portals on different LANs by allowing them to exchange CFR packets with each other over circuits across the network. The long haul circuits established over the ISDN are made transparent to the peer portals.

Office applications

Given the above communications architecture, which can be seen to be generalised rather than application specific, the Unison Project has to apply it within the context of multi-media office systems. This leads directly to the need to define an office and understand the sort of communications traffic encountered in a multi-media office.

The traditional understanding of an office is a *place* in which clerical, administrative and/or intellectual work is performed. Work involving the manipulation or processing of materials is not done in an office. The introduction of the flow of *materials* immediately creates a factory, shop, bank or other enterprise. Similarly a flow of pupils creates a schoolroom although pupils can exist as trainee clerical staff.

In general, the more non-deterministic an office becomes, the more it can benefit from having multi-media communications readily available. By contrast, the tasks performed in a strictly routine, input-driven office can often be reduced to sufficient simplicity that communications are strictly confined to the one most appropriate medium. In all offices the work usually includes two major components, the manipulation of data or ideas and communication. Communication includes all activities using telephones, mail, photo-copying, and talking to other people in the course of work.

With the coming of LANs and ISDN the office can now be geographically distributed, and movable with the individual.

The Unison definition of an office is:

> 'Anywhere where human work is performed involving the use of communication and/or the manipulation or processing of data or ideas, but excluding anywhere whose primary function is to process materials or living things'.

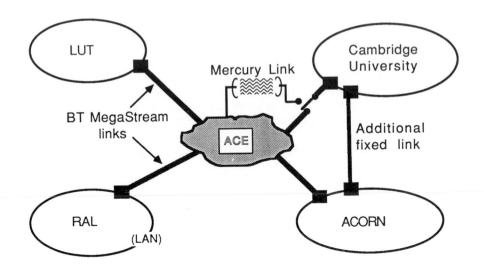

Unison's use of the Alvey High Speed Network

Figure 24.3

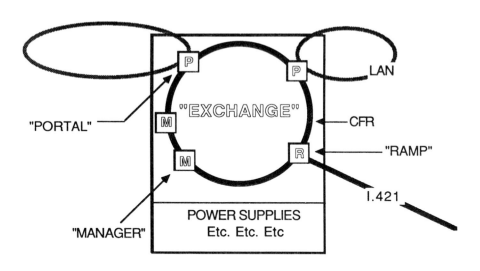

The Unison Exchange Architecture

Figure 24.4

In the context of the OSI Reference Model, the definition of a Multi-Media Office Application is:

> 'That function resident at the Application Layer, 7, of the Model, that uses the integrated services provided by the lower layers, to directly serve the end-user of multi-media information in the office'.

Office communications traffic

The multi-media office system is by nature diverse and makes a broad range of demands on its supportive communications system. The first obvious demand is that of real time speech (telephone) and real time conferencing (speech to more than one destination and/or video or graphics). A toll quality voice channel uses, say, 64 Kbits/s but places onerous demands on availability and delay. The user may notice an echo of only 40 milliseconds and be irritated by a delay of half a second. A slow scan head-and-shoulders colour image of perhaps 500 pixels square can be refreshed, say, every half-second over LANs + ISDN at rates of typically 500 Kbits/s peaking to twice that during rapid movement, but lip-movement will be lost. With codecs moving faster refresh can be achieved.

The second obvious category of demand is that of the multi-media document. This may be simply an electronic manifestation of text with format information and monochome graphics, but it could include multiple voice annotations, correction histories, colour images, etc. Existing and emerging document standards begin to tackle some of the problems of document definition but further research is needed to understand mechanisms for handling multi-media documents and their editing on heterogeneous workstations connected to LANs.

An important factor, in viewing and manipulating a document remotely rather than within a local store, is the ability to scroll through that document quickly. In the Unison environment scrolling of textual documents is unlikely to be constrained by the speed of communications. An 80 column page with full 16-bit characters will scroll at 60 lines per second at 64 Kbits/s. However a graphics image, such as the monochrome fax image of an A4 page (8 pixels per mm by 7.7 lines per mm), would scroll through in 59 seconds at 64 Kbits/s (without compression but assuming no protocol overhead), but in just 4 seconds at 1 Mbit/s.

The bulk transfer of data across LANs and ISDNs such as large database files, also occurs in an office environment but can sometimes be reduced by the use of 'agents' or applications that perform tasks on those databases *in situ* rather than move them to the user. In the LAN/ISDN distributed office environment, the ownership of data and application software may influence the access to and movement of data.

Other problems to avoid occur when downline loading of software over networks. The ten-past-nine problem arises when many users on a network want to start work in the morning by loading many kilobytes of code into their personal workstations, quickly congesting the system for others who may be scrolling through files.

Collaborative research plan

The Unison research plan has been divided into four phases, the first of which was to establish the communications architecture described above. Each phase includes a planning activity for identifying and planning the applications research of the subsequent phase.

The first phase included the development of the architecture, including implementation of the CFR, the use of Inmos Transputers in the ramps, and the development and replication of Unison Exchanges (VME based). Early tests showed that the interim Alvey High Speed Network sustained an error-rate over links of better than 1 in 5×10^9 when connected in a loop through all the sites.

Further research has begun to incorporate aspects of agents which may be categorised into:

  those agents associated with or performing a task for an application program,

  those associated with a user (person) to give that user freedom of movement around sites,

  the type of agent concerned with holding multi-media information together or assembling it when required from diverse storage locations into a single multi-media document or presentation.

Other current research work includes the optimisation of video images over the network for conferencing, and the development of the 'electronic blackboard or overhead projector' enabling conference participants at any site to add their own electronic chalkmarks to a display which is seen simultaneously on all sites.

NOTE: *The Alvey Programme* of advanced information technology (IT) research is a joint venture between three UK Government Departments – the Department of Trade and Industry, The Ministry of Defence, and the Department of Education and Science (acting through the Science and Engineering Research Council) – and British industry and academia. It is a five-year programme, begun in 1983 and costing £350 million, of which £200 million comes from public funds and £150 million from industry. Its objective is to stimulate British IT research through a programme of collaborative, pre-competitive projects which fit into overall strategies which have been developed for the key technologies of Intelligent Knowledge Based Systems (IKBS), the Man–Machine Interface (MMI), Software Engineering (SE), Very Large Scale Integration (VLSI) and Computing Architectures.[3]

In addition, a limited programme of research has been identified within an overall Infrastructure and Communications (IC) strategy. The two complementary communications research projects within this category are Unison and Admiral and both make use of the Alvey High Speed Network.

MANAGEMENT &
OPERATIONS

25

Management & Organisational Issues

RAY REARDON

Telecommunications: critical to success

In many companies, telecommunications is already a major expense area, and growing. Leading–edge companies today spend five per cent or more of their total revenue on information systems[1]. Often networking and telecommunications costs account for a third of this. In the 1990s these figures, and higher, will increasingly become more common.

Quite apart from the issues relating to technology, architecture and application, there are equally important issues relating to the management and operation of networks, several of which are covered in the papers that follow. In addition there are three major areas worth considering further in the light of the increasingly critical dependency on telecommunications:

> alignment with overall business goals;
> the need for a single organisational focus;
> network management for high performance.

Alignment with corporate goals

Any serious planning for networks has to start with an understanding of the overall corporate goals and strategies. What are they, and what part do telecommunications play in their achievement?

The need for networking is driven by the business strategies of the various functional divisions within the company, a significant proportion of which assume new information systems solutions, which in turn are generally telecommunications based.

Telecommunications–based systems have now become an essential prerequisite for the development and evolution of new business process systems. Moreover they are key determinants behind productivity and quality improvement strategies as well as enhanced management control and decision making. Similary, as companies look to information systems solutions to generate additional competitive edge, they tend to look to telecommunications based information systems. In short, telecommunications is becoming more than just important. It is becoming a key strategic asset in its own right and a critical success factor in the achievement of corporate goals.

Critical success factors (CSF's) are those key areas in which things must go right in order to achieve the goals and objectives of the business[2]. They are those areas which are important enough to demand regular review by the senior management team of the corporation. They are also those areas deserving very clear direction and policy setting by senior management.

Having recognised telecommunications as a critical success factor, management must then formally give it the '4 Ms',

Mission

Manpower

Money

Machines

in keeping with its specific contribution to the achievement of business goals and strategies, both in the (tactical) mid-term and the (strategic) longer term.

Fròm this flows the structure, goals, and objectives of the Network and Telecommunications organisation itself, which in turn will have its own strategies and CSFs. These should then lead to clearly articulated and visible service commitments with dates, volumes, and performance criteria (in keeping with the resources allocated of course) which can be related back and aligned with the achievement of overall corporate goals.

The key words are 'visibility' and 'alignment'. Without such a visible and aligned network management system, there is the danger that senior management will underestimate the dependency on telecommunications, allocate to it the wrong level of authority and resource, and only become involved when things have gone wrong.

Single organisational focus

Managing corporate networking and telecommunications involves a wide range of disciplines and many leading-edge companies are establishing a single organisational focus responsible for all aspects, as summarised in Figure 25.1[3].

This mission can no longer be seen as part of 'Building Services', for instance, or part of 'Computing Services Technical Support'. It needs its own senior executive, reporting directly to the chief information officer of the company[4].

Five major groupings of activity have been identified within information systems organisations generally.[5] These can be extended to the telecommunications environment:

Strategic:	planning & control.
Tactical:	resource management.
Engineering:	design & implementation.
Operational:	service delivery & user support.
Administration:	procedural & financial.

The organisation of the networking and telecommunications group could well reflect this, although not necessarily parallel it exactly. The structure needs to consider the following.

Managing the Service as a 'Business within a Business'

There needs to be clear responsibility for the overall cost-effectiveness of the service and its capabilities aligned with overall business goals. This should include formal responsibility

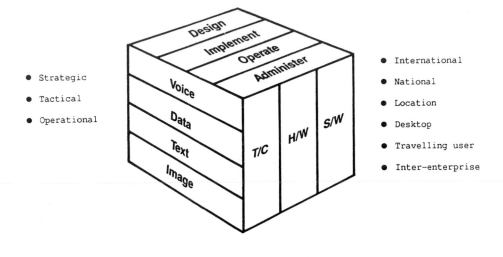

The Telecomms Mission

Figure 25.1

for gathering and projecting requirements, for building the strategic plan, and for identifying the resources required in both the short and long term. There needs to be a clearly-articulated strategic plan document as well as published service level commitments that general management, the users, and the service organisation itself can relate to unequivocally.

Architecture and Design

This area needs to understand technology and product capabilities, both current and future, and to select the technical path forward. It takes the requirements in terms of function required, volumes, and service level criteria and specifies the overall technical solution. This will include the architectural decisions, component product selection, network topography, and perfomance criteria to be achieved. The desired level of network operability, security, resilience and disaster recovery capability is designed in at this stage. The output will be reasonably detailed specifications of actual projects to be implemented in the coming months. The planning horizon will typically stretch over two to five years.

Implementation and Integrity

This area takes the project specifications and desired dates and converts them into reality. As part of this, it produces and publishes the overall implementation plan at a detailed level both for the immediate period and, in somewhat less detail, for a one-to-two-year horizon. It may well do part of the project 'build' itself but will also 'sub-contract' activities to other groups both within and outside the company. Regardless of who carries out the actual work, this organisation must maintain ultimate responsibility for meeting specifications, achieving dates and, most important of all, ensuring that the technical integrity of the existing and future service is maintained and not compromised. The management of change is a prime responsibility of this area.

Production Service

This has the prime responsibility of running the existing service and for formally accepting new facilities into service (or for rejecting them if they do not meet the specification or they affect performance stability). There will be no doubt as to the objectives since these should be clearly spelled out in published Service Level Agreements. Ideally the network should not need 'operating' in the same way as traditional data processing systems. Nevertheless problems will occur and there will be potential problems to be identified and avoided. It is essential that it is provided with the necessary network management tools which allow it to monitor the service and to take corrective or preventative action. Another prime activity to be considered is the provision of a 'service line' which end-users can call for speedy resolution of individual problems.

Administration and Control

In some ways this is a catch-all category but it is important to recognise from the outset that the administration behind networks and telecommunications services is not trivial. Orders will need to be placed and bills to be paid. Equipment and other resources will need to be owned and tracked. Agreements will be needed with other service suppliers and sub-contracted activities. User identities and levels of authorisation need to be recorded and reflected in systems profiles and tables. Actual performance against Service Level Agreements need to be measured, reported and tracked. Whether these activies are large enough to warrant a dedicated organisational entity, or whether they are embedded in other departments, depends on the size and complexity of the network. The important thing is that the activities need to be identified and resourced and not ignored.

Managing for performance

In the early 1970s, end user availability of on-line systems of around 90 per cent was typical and accepted. By the end of the 1970s it was around 95 per cent. Today, with well chosen configurations and effective change management, above 99 per cent in prime shift is commonplace.

However nights and weekends are more difficult. New releases, 'sys-gens', and general housekeeping all have to be managed. In the 1990s, end users will demand and expect '24/7/100' (100 per cent availability, 24 hours a day, seven days a week) for critical applications. This leaves very little scope for the network to lose anything at all!

This will imply the ability to make non-disruptive changes to network components, software, and tables. It may also require 'staging systems' to facilitate the addition of new function and major change without impacting the stability of the existing services. It will certainly imply in-built resilience, dynamic alternate routing, and overall continuity of operations and disaster fallback capability. It will also require powerful network management facilities that can oversee all elements contributing to the network service.

It is accepted that voice networks are best served by a dedicated processor or switch known as a PBX or switchboard. More recently the concept of the dedicated Communications Network Management (CNM) processor for data networks has also come to be accepted. It is not essential that a CNM is separate from host application processors, but it does work better that way.

The CNM provides a focal point for network management for the managed data network itself and also for other telecommunications components, as long as they can provide the necessary monitoring and control information within an overall network management architecture[6,7]. It will include the following functions:

Session establishment: setting up sessions between the workstation and host application across the communications network. This may also include access control and profile management as well as statistical reporting and accounting. Most importantly it should provide the user with a friendly access menu.

Alert monitoring: literally tens of thousands of events (or more) occur on a network of any size or complexity every day. Operational efficiency depends on the filtering out of trivial or automatically handleable event information and the audio/visual highlighting of more important events.
Once alerted the operator needs a comprehensive set of enquiry, visibility and manipulation tools available to enable him to take the necessary action.

Pro-active monitoring: obviously it is better to identify potential problems and queues before they become problems requiring recovery. Status monitoring facilities and automatic threshold alerts should also be part of the CNM.

Session monitoring: when an individual end-user or host application has a problem, and calls the 'service line' operator for help, it is important for the operator to be able to display all the components involved. Ideally this should include all the network route components in the session and even visibility into and across other interconnected networks.

Performance measurement and reporting: the network manager needs a whole range of facilities to be available to measure performance against Service Level Agreements and to provide the necessary statistical information to manage and plan the network. This will include traffic volumes and capacity utilisation as well as response time analysis over specific routes.

Problem management: once a non-transient problem is encountered it should be recorded so that all parties, including support organisations as well as operations, can reference, resolve, and update specific problems.

As these needs, and more, are becoming recognised and appreciated, the implementation of a cohesive suite of network management tools on a dedicated network management processor is becoming more commonplace and will be the norm by the early 1990s.

In conclusion

As the new decade gets underway, the job of the networking and telecommunications group will become one of the most important strategic roles in the whole organisation. What used to be seen as an expense item is becoming recognised as one of the most important determinants of competitive advantage and profit. What used to be seen as a straightforward technical support activity that could safely be buried within some convenient service department will justifiably become a major area of interest for the chief executive.

26

Creating the Communications Strategy

DAVID HONEY

Introduction

It doesn't take a crystal ball to predict that networks for the 1990s will need to cater for more traffic and a greater range of services than the 1980s vintage! A more difficult question to answer is: will this demand be met by a small number of value added networks, or a large number of private networks? Either way, the increased business dependency on communication services will mean they will feature as a vital part of any business plan or strategy.

The 1960s can be categorised by the growth in batch processing computer systems, the 1970s by the move to on-line systems, and the first half of the 1980s by the move to highly responsive transaction processing systems. Now we are nearing the end of the 1980s and a trend is perceptible which further enhances the criticality of communication services by extending what were previously internal services, to external users, namely the customers. In addition to the 'pull' coming from the users of communications services, rapidly falling costs and significantly increased bandwidths will produce a substantial 'push' – hopefully in the same direction. Clearly, unless these services are adequately planned and managed, opportunities will be missed and, even worse, disasters will occur.

What is a communications strategy?

Strategy is 'the art of conducting a campaign and manoeuvring an army'. For 'campaign' read 'meeting business objectives and fulfilling business requirements', and for 'army' read 'communication services'. What the communications strategy provides is a means to an end; it maps out the agreed route by which the business objectives will be achieved.

The strategy might map out more than one route, or devise new routes as part of a review and update process, but if at any time the army is not on one of the agreed routes then the whole object of the exercise is at risk.

Figure 26.1 illustrates the relationships between communications strategy, Information Technology (IT) strategy, and business objectives. A communications strategy can be created without an IT strategy being in place, but we have found that on such occasions the communications strategy ends up defining a minimum set of IT directives.

Why have a communications strategy?

It is generally accepted that any business, of whatever size, needs some form of strategy. Without the sense of direction provided by objectives or mission, a business is destined to wander aimlessly until acquired by a predator or collapses due to being uncompetitive.

Business Objectives

I.T. Strategy

Communications
Strategy

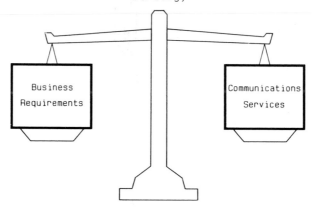

| Business Requirements | Communications Services |

Figure 26.1

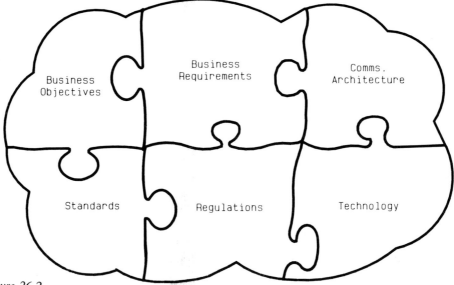

Business
Objectives

Business
Requirements

Comms.
Architecture

Standards

Regulations

Technology

Figure 26.2

Similarly, in order to provide compatible communication services that are consistent with the business strategy, a communications strategy is required.

In the face of rapidly changing technology, a dynamic regulatory environment, confusing and sometimes conflicting standards, and the need for flexible solutions to address long term business requirements, investing in communication services can be a very high risk. The element of risk can be reduced and the quality of solution enhanced, by formulating a communications strategy that addresses the key issues and forms an integral part of an overall business strategy.

What should a communications strategy cover?

By communications we are really talking about telecommunications, and the communication of information. Information comprises four generic types – data, text, image and voice – and communication services provide the mechanisms to convey and present information to the communicators.

What are the key areas that need to be considered when formulating a communications strategy? Experience at Deloitte Haskins and Sells shows that the headings in Figure 26.2 provide a good starting point. The relative importance and content of each area very much depends on particular circumstances. Each of these areas is presented in more detail below. Corporate networking is taken as a particular example of a communications service, which typically forms a major part of any corporate communications strategy.

Business objectives

Logically, a communications strategy is a subset of an overall business strategy. The business strategy should clearly define the business objectives, and the part communication services play in achieving those objectives.

This is not just an academic exercise; numerous communication projects have failed due to the lack of support and sense of direction provided by a business strategy. A communications strategy without a business strategy is like a house without foundations; it might stay up. A business strategy should typically look forward three to five years, and define the shape and direction of the business over that period. Unfortunately, it is highly unlikely that a business strategy will remain static over such a period of time, and it must be recognised that it is subject to change.

Continual change to a business strategy is very unwise, but refinements are usually beneficial in light of unpredictable internal and external business changes. Bearing in mind that even the most seemingly minor change to a business objective can have major implications to a company when implemented, these proposed changes must be regularly reviewed, and approved or rejected under formal change control procedures. Some organisations might review their business objectives once every six months, others once a month, the review period will depend on the nature of the business. Business factors which influence the decision to implement a communications network include the following.

> *Changing Corporate Organisation* Large companies can undergo significant change through mergers, acquisitions, and sell-offs. These changes can present completely new business opportunities for networking, or a network inherited through a minor acquisition can prove to be a major corporate asset if fully exploited.

In contrast to the opportunities presented by acquisitions or mergers, sell-offs of even small locations can have a significant impact on the viability of an existing network, if the locations sold happen to be major network nodes.

New Business Directions In addition to networking as a means of reducing communication costs and improving quality of service, corporate networking can produce competitive advantage and create business opportunities. Companies can move in new business directions by exploiting these opportunities.

Over the past two decades, banks and building societies have been investing in large data networks to serve Automatic Teller Machines (ATMs), and to provide financial services. Without fast and reliable networks these on-line services could not be provided. Financial services are no longer just the preserve of banks and building societies; other service sectors such as insurance and retailing are exploiting their current networks, or investing in new communications technology to compete in this marketplace.

Enhancing Effectiveness and Efficiency What is effectiveness? It means 'doing the right job' as opposed to 'doing the job right'. Many businesses suffer from the problem of resources; whilst doing a job very efficiently, staff are working ineffectively, through no fault of their own. This can be due to company organisation or internal procedures. A business objective could be to increase turnover, profit margin, market share, whatever, by improving the effectiveness and efficiency of specific company departments.

Business requirements

Once the business objectives have been defined and formally agreed, the task of identifying the business requirements associated with achieving the objectives can begin. Networking is about providing a service, and that service is to the users. When attempting to identify the business requirements, the users must be extensively consulted, and their inputs fully considered. In a large organisation the number of users will be too high for them all to be individually consulted, so user representatives must be appointed.

Once fully briefed and adequately prepared, these representatives should gather the inputs from their users, and then report back to the business requirements forum. Questionnaires and fact-finding interviews are techniques used during this user education and data collection phase.

During the requirements identification stage, management should be sensitive to user expectations, and not oversell the solutions. This stage should be considered an invaluable opportunity to build credibility with, and gain the confidence of the users.

Typical parameters, which could feature as part of the business requirements for a corporate wide area data network, include:

number and location of sites to be covered,

number and skill levels of users at each site,

numbers and types of terminal equipment,

numbers and types of application processors,

applications,

traffic profiles,

desired quality of service.

When considering such parameters current and projected figures would normally be determined.

When considering traffic and capacity planning, it is worth remembering a well known data-processing law which states 'information will expand to fill the space available'. This can be modified for communication services to read 'with any successful communications service, traffic will always increase to congest the bandwidth available unless restricted'. It is better to restrict traffic, than to have a useless congested network.

Large organisations can have many functional and geographical boundaries, these boundaries and areas of centralisation can have a major impact on the business requirements for a corporate communications network. Figure 26.3 shows an example of layering being used to help identify the requirements of a large organisation. The requirements for each functionally different part of the business should be addressed separately, even if they turn out to be the same.

Data networks can be required to provide connectivity for a wide range of application processors: from supercomputers to basic desktop personal computers. The demands made on a network to support such a diverse range of computer processing are stringent, and consequently the business requirements in terms of providing the required connectivity need to be accurately determined.

Overall the business requirements must be clear and unambiguous; once identified and agreed they will form the basis of the communications strategy. Just as the business strategy is subject to change via a formal review procedure, so are the business requirements.

Communications Architecture

The term, communications architecture, as presented in this paper, is used to describe the number of levels and form of application processors a data communications network is expected to support. This is not the same as data network architectures, such as Systems Network Architecture (SNA) or Open Systems Interconnection (OSI). By defining a communications architecture for an organisation, communication flows between application processors, and application processors and users can be determined.

A large corporate organisation could have a hierarchical communications architecture, with mainframes at the corporate headquarters and personal computers at the user level. It is possible for a communications architecture to have from one, to many levels; a possible five level architecture is shown below.

Level 5 – Centralised Network Management

Level 4 – Corporate Mainframes

Level 3 – Subsidiary Mainframes

Level 2 – Multi User Servers

Level 1 – Single User Workstations

A communications architecture supporting distributed processing has long been seen as a desirable objective, but its satisfactory implementation has proven elusive. A distributed processing system makes heavy demands on communication services, and many of the

Multi-National
National
Site or Division
Department
Work Group
Single User

Figure 26.3

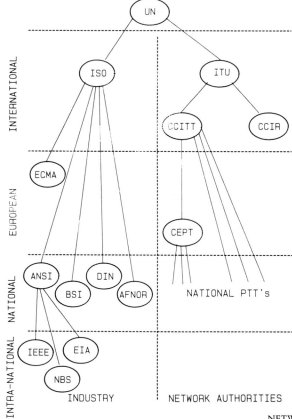

Figure 26.4

226

essential components, such as a truly networked operating system, are still not available.

The increasing bandwidth and falling cost of communication circuits means it will be technically feasible and economically viable to link processors together, making them perform as one virtual uniprocessor, irrespective of the geographical distances separating them. The network, in effect acting as the equivalent of a high speed bus, will allow processors and peripheral activities to be very closely coupled.

Unfortunately, whilst users will benefit from the increased transparency of the network (they won't need to know where data they require are stored, or which is the best processor to run their particular application on), maintaining the network service is likely to be harder. Management and support of a distributed processing system is much more difficult than with a traditional centralised processing system; the necessary network management tools are still very much in their infancy, and standards do not exist. The networking pioneers of the late 1980s and early 1990s are likely to be those trying to support truly distributed processing over wide area networks.

Whilst addressing communications architecture, policies and guidelines should be covered. Users of communication services, and indeed the service providers, need to be educated and trained as to the network uses to encourage, the abuses to discourage, and how the service will evolve. Even those services which are considered to have a short life will require development and modifications; it is not possible to determine all the likely changes to a service in advance of it being implemented, but a policy on how such changes will be handled can be determined. Such a policy is typically termed a 'migration policy'.

Standards

Conformance to internationally agreed standards can be considered as an indication of the 'openness' of communications equipment. This openness provides the ability for systems from different vendors to communicate meaningfully, and offer multiple sources of compatible equipment. Unfortunately, conformance to the same standard is seldom sufficient to guarantee interworking capability since many standards offer options, and the support of different options can mean interworking difficulties. The only way to guarantee interworking capability is actually to test the equipment under the desired conditions.

Certification centres have been set up to determine that equipment conforms to internationally agreed standards. Some centres are apparently considering the next logical step, which is the certification of the interworking capabilities between vendor specific equipment. Broadly speaking there are three categories of standards:

> international – from international standards
> organisations such as ISO, ECMA and CCITT;
>
> national – from national organisations such as BSI, ANSI and DIN;
>
> proprietary standards from vendors.

Figure 26.4 shows the major standards organisations involved in communication services, and their hierarchical relationships. Many proprietary standards, such as IBM's SNA, have become *de facto* or industry standards, due to their widespread influence and adoption. The most significant international standard that currently exists for computer networks is ISO's Open Systems Interconnection (OSI) Model, which provides a framework for open systems. Individual standards are either in place, or being written, for all seven layers of

TELECOMS REGULATION
AN INTERNATIONAL PERSPECTIVE

Country	Service/Equipment					
	Local Calls	Long Dist. Calls	Int. Calls	Value added Services	Private Equipment	Public Exch. Equipment
US	😠	😠	🙂	😊	🙂	😊
Japan	😠	😠	😠	😊	🙂	😐
UK	😠	😠	😠	😊	😊	😐
France	😠	😠	😠	😠	😊	😐
W. Germany	😠	😠	😠	😠	😠	😐

😠 Monopoly   😠 Duopoly   😐 Restricted Access   🙂 Competitive but dominant supplier   😊 Liberalised

Figure 26.5

Figure 26.6

the model. The major communications equipment manufacturers devote a substantial amount of time and money, attempting to influence international standards. Successful examples of this are Xerox, Intel and DEC promoting Ethernet as an international local area network standard (which was subsequently used as the basis for the IEEE 802.3 and ISO 8802.3 standards) and IBM promoting its token ring technology as another LAN standard (which formed the basis of the IEEE 802.5 and ISO 8802.5 standards).

Regulations

A factor that can have a major influence on the communication services that a business can exploit, is the telecommunications regulatory environment in which the business has to operate. Regulations vary considerably between countries; the US is relatively unregulated whilst Germany is highly regulated.

Figure 26.5 illustrates the current state of liberalisation in five major countries, based on research done by the *Financial Times* of the UK. Simple telephone services are shown under the headings of local, long distance and international calls; then value added services and finally equipment under the headings of private and public exchange. The countries at the top of the table are more liberalised than the ones lower down.

The global trend is one of increased liberalisation and value added services look as though they will be the first service in the table to be liberalised across the five countries. Prior to the Telecommunications Act of 1981, the UK was considered to be highly regulated. Since then, deregulation has been the name of the game, and the UK has been leading the world (outside the USA) in the speed with which it has liberalised the UK marketplace for telecommunications equipment and services. This deregulation is presenting unique business opportunities for organisations in a position to exploit the liberalisation, and to derive competive advantage from it.

Two licences from the Office of Telecommunications (OFTEL) – the *Branch Systems General Licence* (BSGL), and the *Value Added and Data Services* (VADS) licence – are likely to have significant impact on communication services in the UK. These permit greater freedom in the way telecommunications traffic is carried by private networks, and the way private and public networks interwork.

Value Added Networks Services (VANS) and Managed Data Networks (MDNs) are generic descriptions of services offered to third parties under the VADS Licence. A Managed Data Network offers a complete network service providing operation, support, maintenance, planning and facilities management.

The differences in regulations from one country to another can cause major difficulties for the providers of multinational private networks, or those multinational companies who wish to standardise on telecommunications equipment internationally. Obviously, regulations will form an important part of the communications strategy for these companies.

Technology

Formulating a communications strategy will involve evaluating technical solutions to determine the strategic direction.

The first part of the exercise is to evaluate generic solutions, rather than vendor-specific solutions. This will help to focus attention on the identified business requirements, rather than on the 'bells and whistles' which vendors sometimes use to distract and seduce potential customers.

Examples of generic solutions for a wide area data network in the UK are:

a private packet switched or circuit switched network eg based on X.25, X.21 technology,

a value added data network (VAN), eg Telecom Gold or Tradanet,

a managed data network (MDN), eg IBM's Managed Network Service or Travinet's (Midland Bank) Fastrak service.

Generic solutions for local area data networks are less tied up in regulatory issues than wide area networks. The solutions are dependent on technologies such as token rings, Carrier Sense Multiple Access with Collision Detection (CSMA/CD) buses, and even the more traditional data and message switches. A network's characteristics will largely be determined by the type of traffic (data, text, image or voice) it is to carry, and the required quality of service.

The quality of service offered by a network is fundamental to its success. A network provides a service to its users, and the quality of that service is how the users measure the network's performance. If the quality of service offered by a network is too low, then users will turn their backs on it; too high, and excessive sums of money will be spent which can undermine the network economics.

Once a generic technical solution has been selected, vendor specific implementations can be evaluated and a selection made. It is quite possible that the evaluation may be iterative, with a particular generic solution being rejected due to the poor quality of vendor implementations. Technology is the sixth and final area shown in Figure 26.2. However, it does not mark the end of the process; we still need to evaluate the implications of the selected course(s) of action.

Costs, Benefits and Risks

A costs, benefits and risks analysis of the selected solutions should be performed before a final selection is made, and defined as part of a communications strategy. The analysis can be done manually, but, the use of spreadsheet-type personal computer programs, or decision support tools, make this analysis easier and more dynamic. The analysis does not stop once the communications strategy is defined and agreed; the analysis continues as business objectives/requirements are reviewed and changes proposed. The analysis helps to determine the implications of any proposed changes, and should form part of the decision making process on whether or not changes should be accepted or rejected.

Summary and conclusions

This paper has argued the need for a communications strategy as a subset of an overall business strategy, and has described the key areas which should be addressed for a communications strategy covering corporate networking.

Experience indicates that a communications strategy is essential for any sizable organisation which is dependent on its communication services to conduct its business. The strategy will help to ensure that current and future communication services are consistent with, and optimal for, the business objectives and requirements.

In conclusion, it is worth noting that the arguments put forward to justify the creation of a communications strategy for scenarios in the 1980s, are likely to be even more persuasive for networks in the 1990s.

27

Network Management with NetView

DAVID FOSTER

The network manager's requirements

In all commercial organisations, whether large or small, the employees now need increasingly greater access to information services for successful completion of their normal, daily tasks. Such information services are made available to them through the organisation's information network. That does not imply that all the services are provided by the network, indeed, some of the services may well be provided by external organisations, and hence the network must provide gateways or bridges to such information sources. The network manager must be able to design and operate the network, as if it were a utility, giving high quality service to the users. IBM, through its Systems Network Architecture (SNA), enables its customers to build such utility networks. That architecture also defines where and how gateways to systems of other architectures can be incorporated including, for example, bridges based on OSI protocols.

The service provided will be measured in terms of its business value, for example by improving the productivity of those people now able to communicate electronically, or by increasing the competitive advantage gained through more timely or better informed decisions. In some cases members of the public will be users of the network services, as when using on-line cash dispensers, using home banking facilities, or gaining access via public data services, such as Prestel gateways. The service level agreement which the network manager has with users groups will be translated into a series of quantified criteria which can be used as the management controls of the network. Typically, these will define the services offered, the hours of operation, the level of interrupts which can be tolerated, the response time required by the users, and a value to be placed on the service so defined.

To manage the services offered, and to meet the defined service level objectives, requires that the network manager's staff are provided with the tools and instrumentation necessary to monitor both the components of the network, and the quality of the service delivered. Further, the managers of the network service organisation need summarised trend, exception, and service related reports. IBM has extensive experience of providing and enhancing such tools for use within SNA based networks. These tools can be used to manage networks of various sizes: those which are discrete and managed from a single control centre; those which may require the use of multiple control centres each having its own scope of responsibility; and those where separately owned and managed SNA networks are interconnected.

A paper which describes how IBM has implemented such organisations and used SNA to provide the IBM United Kingdom internal network, and IBM's value added network

```
UK NETWORK        *** INO SYSTEM PYD1 ***        TERMINAL= PYDS14C3
1 : HIGH USE SERVICES FOR UK        * USE FOR IBM BUSINESS ONLY *
STATUS OF SERVICES      19:39, TUESDAY  , MARCH  31, 1987
        SERVICE         |      SERVICE         |      SERVICE
===========================================================================
UKFSC    UP    06:15   | WARVM5  UP    06:15   | ICINFO * UP    06:15 I
CICS     UP    06:15 I | WARVM8  UP    06:15   |
IMSA     UP    07:13 I | LCCVM   UP    15:30   |
IMSB     UP    06:15 I | CERES   UP    06:15   |
TSOD     UP    06:15 I | EMDS    UP    06:15   |
TSOA     UP    06:15 I | HONE    UP    06:15 I |
TSONHC   UP    06:15 I | HON2    UP    06:15 I |
INFOMAN  UP    06:15 I | HON3    UP    06:15 I |
NHBVM1   UP    06:15   | HON4    UP    06:15 I |
NHBVM6   UP    06:15   | RETR    UP    06:15 I |
NHBVM9   UP    06:15   | RETU    UP    06:15 I |
UMIS     UP    06:15   | RETRD   UP    06:15 I |
UMIS1    UP    06:15   | RETUD   UP    06:15 I |
UMIS2    UP    06:15   | TSMA    UP    06:15 I |
===========================================================================
=> TYPE "VAMP/INFO" FOR HELP IN USING VAMP PANELS
=> TYPE SERVICE NAME AS SHOWN ABOVE TO LOGON

=>
```

Menu of applications: The user is able to see the status of applications and select the one which he/she wishes access.

Figure 27.1

```
N E T V I E W                        OPER1      03/30/87 15:27:44
NPDA-30A                  * ALERTS-DYNAMIC *
DOMAIN: CNM01

    DATE/TIME   TYPE RESNAME   ALERT DESCRIPTION:PROBABLE CAUSE
    03/30 10:43 CTRL SYAC112   TIMEOUT:DEVICE OFF/REMOTE MODEM OFF/COMM
    03/30 10:42 LAN  L22081    LOBE WIRE FAULT:RING ADAPTER CABLE
    03/30 10:11 CTRL PU47002   NEG SNA RESP:HOST PGM/HOST COMMUN PGM/DEVICE
    03/30 10:11 WKST*PU47002   SNA COMMUNICATION ERROR:SNA COMMUNICATIONS
    03/30 10:05 LINE LINE16    TIMEOUT:DEVICE/REMOTE MODEM OFF/COMMUNICATIONS
    03/30 08:50 CTRL PU47002   NEG SNA RESP:HOST PGM/HOST COMMUN PGM/DEVICE
    03/28 20:51 CTRL SYAC011   FORMAT EXCEPTION SDLC DISC:OH IF NORMAL/DEVICE
    03/28 20:50 CTRL PVM       TIMEOUT:DEVICE OFF/REMOTE MODEM OFF/COMM
    03/28 17:01 CTRL PU47002   NEG SNA RESP:HOST PGM/HOST COMMUN PGM/DEVICE
    03/27 08:50 LOOP*PU47002   LOOP OPEN:LOOP
    03/26 17:52 3380 DDEV420   SEEK CHECK:DASD DRIVE
    03/26 17:22 3420 TDEV241   DATA CHECK:TAPE DRIVE/MEDIA
    03/26 12:22 WKST*PU47002   PROGRAM CHECK:RESOURCE MANAGER PROGRAM
    03/26 12:22 CTRL PSVC01A   SWITCHED VC FAILURE:REMOTE X.25 ATTACHMENT

DEPRESS ENTER KEY TO VIEW ALERTS-STATIC

???
CMD==>
```

Monitoring of alerts: The operator's screen is updated each time a relevant event needs to be called to his/her attention.

Figure 27.2

offering, also reviews the developments in management within Open Systems Interconnection (OSI), comparing and contrasting the current capabilities of SNA network management products with the likely expectations from implementations of OSI management.[1] It concludes that managed intelligent networks will continue to require the greater level of function that is provided today by SNA based products. The next section of this paper summarises the facilities of NetView, IBM's principle network management product.

NetView

As was described earlier, the users of networks require access to a range of services. They may well be presented with a menu of applications such as that shown in Figure 27.1 which contains the applications menu offered to IBM employees in the United Kingdom.

The services offered are based on processors in any of three computing centres, on some local processors, or even outside IBM UK. The user of the network is not aware of this. The network must be monitored by the control centre staff. This monitoring can be achieved in two ways – both provided by NetView – alert and status monitoring.

Alert monitoring

The software and microcode in the components of an SNA network can generate 'alerts'. These are defined message formats which can be sent to NetView and stored. Based on a profile defined for the specific user, a selected subset of these alerts can be dynamically displayed on a monitor screen. The selection is achieved by filters, and permits concurrent monitoring of different subsets of the network by the assigned personnel. Whenever a new event is written to the monitor screen, an audible alarm is also sounded to attract the operator's attention.

Figure 27.2 shows an example of such a screen. Note that in addition to the alerts relating to connectivity, there are examples of CPU and attached processors creating alerts. It also shows an example of an error detected when using X.25 communications. If it is not obvious to the operator what recovery action is needed, then further screens are available to indicate the probable causes, to suggest recommended actions, to provide more detail of the specific incident, and to provide more generalised help to the user.

In this way, the control centre staff are able to detect incidents before the phone starts ringing when users have lost service. In a well designed network that should occur very infrequently. The network will have been designed with significant alternate routing and component redundancy. This makes it even more necessary that the control centre staff have monitor screens available to them in order to detect the first failure, rather than the second or third failure when catastrophic loss of service might occur.

Status monitoring

The second type of monitoring provided by NetView is shown in Figure 27.3 which provides a summary of the status of all the resources within the scope of NetView. The screen is refreshed at regular intervals and uses colour to indicate quickly and clearly the overall health of the network. For example the column headed *Active* is coloured green, and the *Inactive* column is coloured in red.

Attention should be drawn to the column headed *Monitor*. This shows how one of the functions provided by NetView helps automate network operation and recovery. Selected

```
STATMON.DSS                 DOMAIN STATUS SUMMARY                     15:27
HOST: HOST1        *0*      *1*      *2*      *3*      *4*
                  ACTIVE   PENDING   INACT    MONIT    NEVACT       OTHER
 ....2 NCP/CA MAJOR  ....2    .....    .....    .....    .....       .....
 ...68  LINES        ...53    .....    .....    .....    ...15       .....
 ..143  PUS/CLUSTERS ..113    ...21    .....    .....    ....9       .....
 ..471  LUS/TERMS    ..451    .....    ....8    .....    ...12       .....
 ....2 SWITCHED MAJ  ....2    .....    .....    .....    .....       .....
 ...43  SWITCHED PUS .....    .....    .....    .....    .....       ...43
 ...64  SWITCHED LUS .....    .....    .....    .....    .....       ...64
 ....1 LOCAL MAJ NDS ....1    .....    .....    .....    .....       .....
 ....1  PUS          ....1    .....    .....    .....    .....       .....
 ...35  LUS/TERMS    ...35    .....    .....    .....    .....       .....
 ...10 APPL MAJ NDS  ...10    .....    .....    .....    .....       .....
 ...79  APPLICATIONS ...76    .....    .....    .....    .....       ....3
                     _____                             _____
 ..919 TOTAL NODES   ..744    ...21    ....8    .....    ...36       ..110



CMD==>
1=HELP 2=END 3=RETURN 4=BROWSE LOG 6=ROLL            9=REFRESH
```

Status Monitoring: The operator's screen is updated at regular intervals to show the current status of the SNA resources

Figure 27.3

```
STATMON.DSD(ANALYSIS)      DOMAIN STATUS DETAIL (ANALYSIS)           15:28
HOST: HOST1        *0*      *1*      *2*      *3*      *4*  ELAPSED TIME 6:41
                  ACTIVE   PENDING   INACT    MONIT    NEVACT       OTHER
 ?..143  PUS/CLUSTERS ?...13   ?...21  ?.....   ?.....   ?..109     ?.....

DISPLAY:                      STATUS    ACTIVE  PENDING  INACTIVE   OTHER
  HIGHER NODE     NODE ID.    SINCE    COUNT % COUNT %  COUNT %   COUNT %
  ? SUMMARY     ? BNPAPU   A  8:47       1 100   0   0    0   0     0   0
  ? DETAIL      ? BL4P1    A  8:47       1 100   0   0    0   0     0   0
 THIS NODE      ? XP16     A  8:47       1 100   0   0    0   0     0   0
  ? SUMMARY     ? XP17     A  8:47       1 100   0   0    0   0     0   0
  ? DETAIL      ? XP18     A  8:47       1 100   0   0    0   0     0   0
                ? XP19     A  8:47       1 100   0   0    0   0     0   0
                ? PVM      A 10:49       3  99   3   0    1   1     0   0
 _____  ? L14P1    A  8:47       1 100   0   0    0   0     0   0
 DETAIL FORMAT: ? L15P1    A  8:47       1 100   0   0    0   0     0   0
  ? DESCRIPT    ? L16P6    A 10:13       1  79   3  16    2   5     0   0
                ? PU47002  A 10:09       2  99   1   0    1   1     0   0
                ? L32P1    A  8:47       1 100   0   0    0   0     0   0
                ? NPAPU    A  8:47       1 100   0   0    0   0     0   0


CMD==>
1=HELP 2=END 3=RETURN 4=BROWSE LOG 6=ROLL            10=VTAM 11=CLIST
```

Availability Summary: The operator is able to review the immediate past availability history of selected resources.

Figure 27.4

resources may be defined as eligible for monitoring. When NetView detects that such a resource has become inactive, NetView will regularly attempt to reactivate that resource unless, for example, the line to which it is attached is also inactive. In this latter case such recovery would be applied to the higher level resource(s) if they were defined as eligible for monitoring.

The status monitor screen in NetView also provides a set of indicators at the top of the screen. These will be turned on under programmed control, as defined by the user[2] and may indicate that a message of some significance has just been written to the log file. Each of the indicators can be assigned specific significance such as the degree of urgency with which an operator should view the message. From the screen shown in Figure 27.3, the operator can select the appropriate indicator which will cause the log file to be desplayed starting at the first message which caused the indicator to be set on, and which has not yet been viewed.

Also from the status monitor the operator can request the display of immediate history. In Figure 27.4 one can see the recent history of the selected set of resources indicating that it is equally significant to know the number of interruptions as well as the proportion of time that service has been offered.

Session monitoring

In an SNA network, the logical connection between two communicating entities is termed a session. For example, when a terminal user logs on to a database enquiry system, such as Information Management System/VS (IMS/VS), then a session is formed between the terminal and IMS/VS. That session will be routed across the network, probably traversing many components. If the user has a problem such as slow response time (or even worse, no response) then the control centre operator will need to be able to determine which components are used in the particular session path, and to display the response time history for this and other sessions. This is the role of the session monitor component in NetView.

Figure 27.5 shows a configuration diagram based on data recorded by NetView at the time the session was established. There is much detailed information provided, because experience shows that this is the type of information which the operators need to be able to diagnose quickly problems in today's networks. The operator can select further displays, and in the case of poor response time, can also call for the status of parts of a route. The response from NetView would be a display showing the amount of traffic moved in both directions over the section of the route, and indications of any congestion or slowdown in the communications controllers involved.

The operator may need to review the history of the response time perceived by the user. If the SNA terminal is capable of measuring this, then defined record formats are used for NetView to request the regular retrieval of this data which can then be displayed as shown in Figure 27.6.

Help for the NetView user

The operators of today's networks need to be highly skilled and well trained. NetView permits a group of such people to be located anywhere that they can gain access to NetView. Indeed they log on to it in the same way as any user logs on to applications. Acquiring the skill they need comes also from experience. Networks change and grow. New facilities are added. These require support and help to the user. NetView provides a

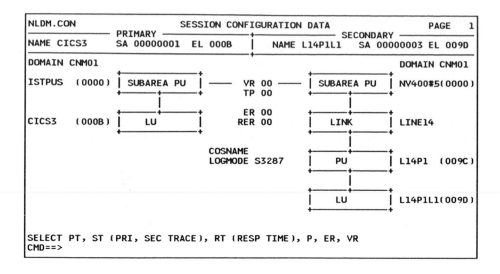

Display of Session Route: The operator is able to determine the network components traversed by a specific session.

Figure 27.5

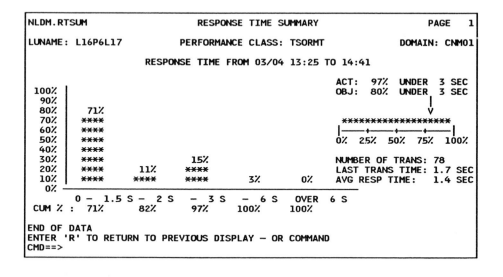

Response Time Measurement: The operator is able to review the recorded response time measurements for a user.

Figure 27.6

great deal of such on-line help which can be accessed from a series of menus – especially useful if using NetView in a training mode. Alternatively, the operator can call up help at any time when using NetView by keying in the *Help* command. There is also an index facility within NetView and which lists, in alphabetic sequence, topics for which information is available.

Customisation

Each customer's network has its own characteristics and unique requirements. NetView provides a comprehensive set of facilities to help manage the network service. It will usually be necessary to add or change some of the panels displayed and the design of NetView provides for this; most of the possible changes and additions are made by simple editing of source files. One typical example is the use of *CLISTs* which are sets of commands and logic statements, used to allow automated operation of a network to be enhanced in a way which meets the requirements of individual network managers. The facilities of NetView are also used to provide the means for automated and/or remote operation of processors attached to the SNA network.

Reporting facilities

So far this paper has described the presentation of information to operators at the level of discrete events or summaries of the recent history. The managers of a network need trend analysis data and control information for feedback into design or service reporting applications. This requirement is also satisfied by NetView as indicated in the following examples:

> *Alert reporting*
> The NetView operator, when reviewing events which have caused an alert to be presented, can request that the data be passed to a IBM problem management product, Information/Management[3]. The data passed will be used as the basis for tracking and analysis by other professionals and managers. NetView can be instructed to copy each event record to an external file for input to summary reporting such as that possible with IBM's Service Level Reporter, SLR[4].

> *Response time reporting*
> The same mechanism of writing to an external file enables the network manager to receive summary reports of response time achievements for selected sets of services. These are based on data recorded by NetView, from terminals which are able to support this function.

NetView summary

NetView has been shown to be a tool which provides many of the facilities needed to operate, control, diagnose, and measure the type of utility network which organisations are building today. It is based on SNA, and IBM's experience over the past decade from supplying products to build the network infrastructure, and from continually developing and enhancing the support within SNA for network management.

There is a need to extend the scope of the network management disciplines beyond those parts of the network which are explicitly addressable as SNA components.

Reference has already been made in this paper to the consideration within OSI of network management. IBM is on record as supporting and participating in the development of such extensions to OSI. However, as already indicated these is a need to extend the network management capabilities in the networks being installed today. For that reason, IBM published in 1986 a definition of its Network Management Architecture and announced a product, NetView/PC[5,6]. which enables the degree of control described in this paper to extend beyond the SNA components of a network. This is summarised in the following section of this paper.

The need for a network management architecture

Communications networks being installed today are typified by a number of characteristics including:

increasing bandwidth required to service each user's requirements;

the need to include equipment and systems from many suppliers in building an organisation's communications network;

the need to be able to take advantage of a variety of carrier services as they become available and economically justifiable for use in meeting the business requirements. An example of this is the use of 2 Mbits/s facilities to derive data and voice channels.

To build such networks requires that the network designer is able to select the various components and systems so that they can be made to work together in a coherent manner. That is the basic requirement which IBM met by publishing its network architectures. Network management is one of the major elements in the IBM network architectures.

IBM's open network management architecture

The IBM Network Management Architecture defines the roles of network components in providing and/or receiving network management data. These roles are mapped onto three elements – Focal Point, Entry Point, and Service Point. The architecture also documents the formats and protocols to be used for data interchange between these elements[5].

A *Focal Point* allows one to take a view of the whole network, or a significant subset of it. It is also the repository of data required for longer term analysis such as performance or problem related records. Further, a focal point could include the control functions required for distribution of software or other files. NetView, Information/Management and the Service Level Reporter referred to earlier in this paper can be seen to be examples of focal point implementations.

An *Entry Point* is itself addressable by the SNA network so that it can participate in the exchange of network management data with its focal point. In addition it also participates in the user's data flows. Examples of entry points are terminal controllers such as the IBM 3174 Subsystem Controller, and departmental processors such as the IBM S/36.

A *Service Point* has SNA addressability in the same way as an Entry Point, but it does not handle the data flow on behalf of the users. It is the point at which a transformation may be made between the defined and published SNA Network Management flows, and the control/reporting mechanisms of the non-SNA parts of the network.

NetView/PC as a service point

In September 1986 IBM announced NetView/PC, which became available in June 1987. This software, running on a suitably configured IBM PC/AT or IBM PC/XT, is an implementation of a service point. It can provide local control on non-SNA resources. It can also provide centralised monitoring and control through its interfaces with NetView. The controlled resources are monitored by software running under the control of NetView/PC via standard PC interfaces. A number of manufacturers have announced that they will develop software to use NetView/PC for integrating their products into the scope of a common network management system. They include manufacturers of multiplexer, local area network, and PBX products.

Summary

Managing the service delivered by the type of networks now used or being installed in many business enterprises requires investment in skill, management, and instrumentation. NetView is an IBM product designed to support the operators and managers of such networks. It is an implementation of the focal point concept defined in an open architecture, and is used extensively within IBM and in IBM customers' organisations. In association with NetView/PC, it can be used to extend the scope of network management beyond the boundaries of SNA Networks, and to ensure that network managers will have the required means of control that befits a valuable corporate asset – the telecommunications or information network.

28

Security in Open Systems

MICHAEL HARROP

Background

In late 1982, a proposal was made to Working Group 1 of ISO/TC97/SC16 (the working group which developed the OSI Reference Model 7498) that an OSI Security Architecture for the Reference Model should be produced[1]. This proposal resulted from:

Indications from various groups who foresaw a need for OSI standards which could be used in a secure environment;

The rapidly growing use of network systems which require some degree of protection for the information carried on the network;

The introduction of data protection legislation which requires suppliers to demonstrtate some degree of system security.

In February 1983, therefore, work officially began to define a security architecture for the OSI Reference Model[2].

Some general observations on EDP security

Before examining the proposed OSI security architecture in more detail, it is appropriate to say a few words about the factors which affect EDP security in general. Specifically, the following questions should be considered: 'what assets are we trying to protect?', 'what threats are we trying to counter?', and 'what mechanisms are available to provide the required protection?'.

In general terms the assets to be protected may be grouped into one of the following categories:

data and/or information contained in, or implied by, the data;

data processing services;

tangible assets such as computers and communication equipment.

The threats to be countered may be categorised as any unauthorised actions which result in, or are intended to result in, the destruction, disclosure, removal, loss, corruption or modification of any part of the assets, or which cause an interruption or denial of service. Threats may be further categorised as accidental or intentional, and passive or active[3]. (A passive threat is one in which no modification is made to any message or to the operation of the system. For example a wire tap may be regarded as a passive threat in those cases where the traffic on a channel is simply monitored. An active threat, on the other hand, involves some change to the system or to a message.)

The mechanisms used to counter threats may be classed as preventive, detective and recovery, although some mechanisms may fall into two or all three of these classes. Specific security mechanisms include: physical security, cryptographic techniques (including encipherment), trusted hardware and software, authentication techniques (eg passwords), modification detection techniques and codes, insertion of spurious traffic, audit trails, access control lists, and digital signature mechanisms.

The notion of 'trust' in hardware and software implies that appropriate care has been taken in the design and implementation of the system such that one can have confidence in the correct functioning of a system. Methods used for establishing trust include formal proof, and verification and validation techniques.

The OSI Security Architecture contains an annex entitled *Background Information on Security in OSI* which goes into more detail on each of these mechanisms.

Figure 28.1 gives an overview of the essentials of EDP security[4]. Clearly any measures taken to protect information within an OSI environment will represent but part of the total security picture. OSI security is concerned with protecting that portion of a communications path which enables end systems to exchange data. Comprehensive EDP security requirements will almost certainly demand that measures be in place to protect the information in the end systems themselves. In addition, and depending on the degree of protection required, measures which fall outside the OSI environment may well be required in order to support and/or ensure the effectiveness of the OSI security features.

The reason for touching on these more general security issues here is to emphasise that there is more to security than OSI security. However, for those OSI systems which require some degree of protection, the security architecture describes services and related mechanisms which can be provided within the framework of the Reference Model and indicates the placement of those services and mechanisms.

The development of a security architecture for OSI

In developing the security architecture, some guiding principles were established for the allocation of services and the placement of mechanisms. The principles themselves hint at some of the problems involved in trying to effect security in a layered architecture. The principles are as follows:

> that the number of alternative ways of providing a service should be minimised;
>
> that it is acceptable to build secure systems by providing security services in more than one layer;
>
> that additional functionality required for security should not unnecessarily
>
> duplicate the existing OSI functions;
>
> that violation of layer independence should be avoided;
>
> that the amount of trusted functionality should be minimised;
>
> that, wherever an entity is dependent on a security mechanism provided by an entity in a lower layer, any intermediate layers should be constructed in such a way that security violation is impracticable;

ESSENTIALS OF EDP SECURITY

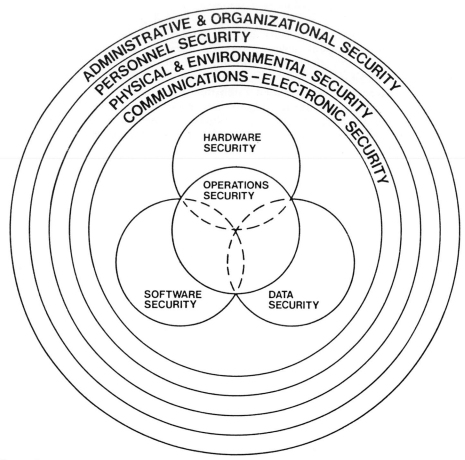

Figure 28.1

that, wherever possible, the additional security functions of a layer should be defined in such a way that implementation as a self-contained module or modules is not precluded;

that the security architecture as defined is assumed to apply to Open Systems consisting of end systems containing all seven layers, and to relay systems of less than seven layers.

Having agreed upon overall principles to guide the security architecture development, the process then became one of determining what security services were appropriate to OSI. What mechanisms could (and should) be used to provide those services? Where in the reference model should the services and mechanisms be located? How should the services be invoked?

OSI Security Services

The security services considered appropriate to OSI are as follows:

access control which protects against the unauthorised use of resources accessible through OSI;

data confidentiality which provides protection against unauthorised disclosure;

authentication which provides confirmation of the identity of the communicating peer entities or of the origin of data;

traffic flow confidentiality which provides protection of information which may be derived or inferred from traffic flow patterns;

data integrity which is available with and without recovery;

non-repudiation of both origin and delivery of data. This is intended to protect the sender and/or the receiver against a user who falsely denies receipt and/or delivery of the data.

OSI security mechanisms

The mechanisms considered appropriate to provide the OSI security services are as follows:

encipherment which is available in a number of forms and which can provide confidentiality of data or traffic flow information and can complement a number of the other mechanisms (note that the use of encipherment implies the use of a key management mechanism);

digital Signature Mechanisms which themselves imply the use of some cryptographic process as part of the signing process;

access Control Mechanisms which may use, for example, passwords, tokens, and access control information bases to determine and enforce access rights;

data Integrity Mechanisms which may involve, for example, block checking codes or cryptographic check functions (for single data units) plus some form of sequence checking and/or time stamping (for sequences of data units);

authentication Exchange Mechanisms which may consist of passwords, cryptographic techniques and handshaking techniques;

traffic Padding Mechanisms which provide protection against traffic analysis;

routing Control Mechanisms which are intended to ensure that only physically secure sub-networks, relays or links are chosen;

notarisation Mechanisms which will involve a trusted third party notary and trusted communication channels and which provide assurance of integrity, origin, time and/or destination of data.

Position of services and mechanisms in the Reference Model

One can visualise that it would be possible to provide many of the services, and to place

RELATIONSHIP OF LAYERS AND MECHANISMS

MECHANISM	1	2	3	4	5	6	7
ENCIPHERMENT	X	X	X	X	.	X	.
DIGITAL SIGNATURE	.	.	X	X	.	X	X
ACCESS CONTROL	.	.	X	X	.	.	X
DATA INTEGRITY	.	.	X	X	.	X	.
AUTHENTICATION EXCHANGE	.	.	X	X	.	.	.
TRAFFIC PADDING	.	.	X	.	.	.	X
ROUTING CONTROL	.	.	X	.	.	.	.
NOTARIZATION	.	.	.	.	.	X	X

(Table header: LAYER)

NOTE - APPLICATION LAYER (I.E. LAYER 7) SERVICES
WILL BE DEPENDENT UPON THE APPLICATION
PROCESS WHICH MAY PROVIDE ALL OF THE SERVICES
THEMSELVES USING THE SAME KINDS OF MECHANISMS
PLACED AT VARIOUS POINTS IN THE REFERENCE
MODEL. THIS IS OUTSIDE THE SCOPE OF OSI.

Figure 28.2

RELATIONSHIP OF LAYERS AND SERVICES

SERVICE	1	2	3	4	5	6	7
AUTHENTICATION	.	.	Y	Y	.	.	Y
ACCESS CONTROL	.	.	Y	Y	.	.	Y
CONFIDENTIALITY	Y	Y	Y	Y	.	Y	Y
INTEGRITY	.	.	Y	Y	.	.	Y
NON REPUDIATION	.	.	.	.	.	.	Y

(Table header: LAYER)

NOTE 1 - IN THE CASES OF CONFIDENTIALITY AND INTEGRITY,
THE ARCHITECTURE INDICATES A FURTHER REFINE-
MENT OF LAYER SERVICES DEPENDING ON THE
TYPE OF CONFIDENTIALITY OR INTEGRITY (E.G.
CONNECTION-ORIENTED VS CONNECTIONLESS AND
WITH/WITHOUT RECOVERY.)

NOTE 2 - IN THE CASE OF LAYER 7, THE APPLICATION
PROCESS MAY ITSELF PROVIDE SECURITY
SERVICES.

NOTE 3 - Y INDICATES THAT THE SERVICE SHOULD BE
INCORPORATED IN THE LAYER AS A PROVIDER
OPTION.

Figure 28.3

many of the mechanisms at several points in the Reference Model. However, one of the objectives in producing the Security Architecture was to minimise the number of places at which a service could be provided.

In considering the question of placement we are concerned with the services which could or should be provided to a particular Layer and the mechanisms which can provide those particular services at that particular Layer. For example, at the Physical Layer, the principle mechanism available is total encipherment of the data stream. This enables the services of connection confidentiality and traffic flow security to be provided but the protection is limited to passive threats.

In some cases a single mechanism will be sufficient and appropriate to provide the required service but in other cases a combination of mechanisms will be needed. For example, at the Transport Layer, the services provided are authentication, access control, confidentiality, and integrity. Peer entity authentication is provided by a combination of cryptographically-derived authentication exchanges, password exchanges and signature mechanisms. Integrity services may be provided by integrity mechanisms in conjunction with encipherment mechanisms.

Figure 28.2 indicates the mechanisms available at each of the Layers. Figure 28.3 shows the relationship between Layers and services, that is the Layers at which particular services can be provided.

Where a service is required at a particular Layer but is not available at the Layer, it may make use of services in lower Layers. However, such instances give rise to the requirement for trusted functionality in the intermediate Layers.

Pervasive security mechanisms

As noted above, for OSI security to be effective, a number of other non-OSI-specific security features may be required, particularly where a high degree of security is demanded. These measures, which are not specific to any one Layer are described in the Security Architecture as 'pervasive measures' and include trusted functionality (that is trusted hardware and software), error detection and error handling (logging and recovery), and security audit trail recording.

How the security services will be invoked

The Security Architecture permits the operation of both mandatory and discretionary security policies. Mandatory policies are those imposed by the 'owner' of the system; discretionary policies are those applied at the discretion of the user.

Requests for a particular level of protection will be made when a connection is established (in a connection-oriented environment) or at each instance of a UNITDATA request (if operating under a connectionless service). Each (N)-service request will be made by an (N + 1)-entity using the Quality of Service parameter to specify the particular security requirements. These will be checked against a security management information base which will contain information on the mandatory protection requirements of the (N + 1)-entity. The service request will be rejected if the level of sensitivity requested lies outside the range defined for that entity.

When the combined mandatory and discretionary security requirements have been established, the (N)-Layer will attempt to achieve the target level of protection, either by using mechanisms directly within the Layer or by requesting services from the Layer below. If the (N)-Layer is unable to achieve the level of protection requested, the service request will be rejected and no communication will take place.

Other issues

Security management

Security management is concerned with the control and distribution of information for use in providing security services or in reporting on security-related events. Identified security management functions include the maintenance of a security management information base, maintaining and distributing authentication and access control service information, key management (see below), and audit trail logging and error handling. Security management is being considered in conjunction with the work being done to develop an OSI Management Framework[5].

Key management

Any encipherment mechanism requires the use of some form of key management. This involves the generation, control, and distribution of keys in a secure manner.

Most of these functions are outside the OSI environment and are, in any case, operational rather than architectural functions. However, effective key management will be essential to effective security in an OSI environment.

Preferred placement of services and mechanisms

Looking at Figure 28.3, it is apparent that most of the services could be obtained at more than one Layer. There is a danger that this will lead to a proliferation of services or to different implementations offering the same service in different places of the architecture. While some degree of proliferation of services is almost certainly inevitable, it is felt that a statement of preferred placement of services will contribute significantly to limiting this proliferation. Annex C of the Security Architecture is a statement of preferred placement of encipherment functions. This recognises that most applications will require encipherment at only one Layer and outlines the placement recommended for encipherment according to the particular services required.

Follow-on work

A number of issues have been identified as being important to OSI security but which are outside the scope of the security architecture project. These areas include encipherment processes in general and key management in particular, the development of an access control framework, the provision of audit trail facilities over a communications medium, the specification and selection of security mechanisms, the interaction between mandatory and discretionary services, protocols to support management aspects of security, and the development of techniques for the establishment of trust. The application of encipherment techniques and some aspects of access control are now being considered by ISO. The remaining items will probably be addressed over the next few years.

Status of the work

The OSI Security Architecture has received approval as a Draft Proposal (DP). Comments received with the DP ballots have been incorporated and the document has been recommended for circulation as a Draft International Standard (DIS) which is the last stage of balloting prior to actually becoming an international standard. DIS balloting is expected to be completed in late 1987.

Summary

The OSI Security Architecture provides much needed architectural guidance for applications requiring security features in an open system environment. However, it should not be viewed in terms of providing total system security – other complementary measures will be required which lie outside of OSI. Nor should the Security Architecture be thought of as representing the totality of work which needs to be done to offer OSI security as much additional work will be required to resolve implementation issues.

29

Justification of E-Mail & Conferencing Systems

DR BENGT A OLSEN

Introduction

Human networks are people talking to each other, sharing ideas, information and resources. The important feature is the communication method that creates the link between people and groups of people.

Networks cut across an organisation or even a society by providing a cross-disciplinary approach to people and issues. Only in special cases do networks coincide with the hierarchical line organisation or with project groups in a matrix organisation. Networks are more complex, they are diagonal and three-dimensional in nature. People from different levels of the society can be involved. We are all influenced by the information overload which the present society generates. With the help of human networks we can select and get the information we need in time. In many successful companies a network style of management is being introduced[1].

The benefits of human networks are that communication will be rooted in informality and equality. Communication will not only be top down and possibly bottom up but also diagonal and lateral. The successful companies of the future will realise the power of networks where individuals nurture each other rather than climb over each other.

Whereas pure mail systems have a tendency to support mainly traditional hierarchical organisations, computer conferencing (group communication) systems have the benefit of being the medium for networks. Another difference is that in a pure mail system the sender supplies all the information whereas in a conferencing system the receiver has tools to select information thereby creating a method of coping with the possible information overload problem.

How cost-effective are new technologies in organisations? How will computer-based message systems benefit organisations? What are the associated costs of the new systems? What are the costs of the existing system be it manual or automated? Are the benefits of the new system worth the extra trouble and cost? In order to get answers to at least some of these questions a cost/benefit analysis has to be performed.

In this paper a cost/benefit analysis, in particular with regard to integrated computer mail and conferencing systems, is discussed. Most of the experience on which this paper is based stems from the use of the COM and PortaCOM services provided by the University of Stockholm Computing Center. (*See the Note at the end of the section for further information on these systems*).

PortaCOM is an international electronic mail and conferencing system. In addition to the facilities of a good electronic mail system, PortaCOM also has facilities to support group communication through 'computer conferences' or 'electronic meetings'.

In 1987 COM and PortaCOM supports a total community of more than 20,000 users in more than 30 countries and is growing at 50 per cent per annum.

Which are the areas of application of computer conferences?

Some of the areas of application listed below can be served by both mail and conferencing systems and some only by the latter[2].

Booking and control of facilities: facilities (publicly available resources) such as meeting rooms, conference rooms, overhead projectors, company cars, dictating machines, portable computers and expensive equipment; also a lost and found service can be organised.

Managing people: enables much closer contact between managers and their staff and allows managers to supervise more staff, enables the manager to delegate more tasks and to get, more easily and quicker, reports on work status, well-founded and better supported decisions. This allows organisations with less hierarchy and may change the role of middle management. Matrix management is often used in geographically dispersed companies and the staff reports to different managers. The use of computer conferencing keeps all managers fully informed. Computer conferencing cuts off bureaucratic overheads.

Joint working arrangements: computer conferencing can be used for joint document production such as for quotations, policies and reports and job sharing, for example, customer service and secretary pools. Project teams make faster progress at lower travel costs and less time is spent in meetings. A greater degree of participation is achieved and larger groups work better. Also the quality of work is improved.

Planning and progressing: activities involving several people such as monitoring of budgets, setting up agendas, distribution of minutes, reminders and policy issues and acceptance. Companies where the employees know and understand the main goal and policy are more successful than others.

Distributing information: regular distribution such as weekly and monthly reports, product changes and error reports. Staff feel more informed and working morale is improved. Computer conferencing reduces the amount of paper and provides quicker, cheaper and more effective distribution.

Meetings: all kinds of topics can be discussed in different kinds of meetings such as board meetings, committee meetings, conflict management meetings and Monday morning meetings. Prediscussion on positions and agreement to agenda, minutes are easily distributed, makes the face-to-face meeting shorter and more efficient; the actual problems are solved and not only discussed; issues can be dealt with as soon as they arise, instead of postponing them until the next scheduled meeting.

Communication with customers and suppliers: business correspondence and contact with user associations can be simplified. Links trading departments: order status, delivery details and complaints. Can be used to distribute urgent information for telex etc. Electronic messaging will be a key component for competitiveness. (If I send a mesage electronically it will take a couple of seconds. If the receiver responds within an hour we might have negotiated our business in a matter of hours rather than weeks, thereby accelerating commerce.)

Bringing like-minded people together: experiences in a particular area, perhaps among owners of a certain PC model; sharing valuable knowledge; 'universal brain' applications; discussion clubs. Computer conferencing opens new communication paths between people who do not know each other.

Buying and selling: small advertisements, delivery of information, agreement on transactions and arrangement of transfer of payments. For instance, yellow pages, postal mail order, software downloading. Expert help such as information brokers, information retrieval, translation services, financial and juridical help.

Electronic publishing: in traditional publishing there are months or years of delay. With electronic publishing you publish on an 'as a soon as it becomes available' basis. It takes a few days to reach most participants. The subscribers have a possibility to interact with the information supplier. Two media will merge into one.

Educational activities: enhances the communication between teachers and students, and students to students. Makes the Electronic University possible, that is training people in non-manual skills at times that fit. Courses that run over weeks, support regardless of location, cheaper than traditional communication.

Conference support: before the conference, planning organisation committees, communication with speakers, referees etc; during the conference, all participants are in the system upon arrival, communication between individuals, session electronic extension, information and arrangements, next conference planning; after the conference, panel discussions can be continued, follow up by organisers.

Which are the components of a cost/benefit analysis?

Efficiency versus effectiveness

In cost/benefit analysis efficiency as well as effectiveness is of importance. If we perform the same task in less time and at less cost we work more efficiently and increase our productivity. If we perform the same task using the same amount of time but with higher quality output we have improved our effectiveness. In some applications we improve the efficiency in others' effectiveness. These measures are thus closely related to quantity and quality respectively.

Tangible versus intangible benefits

A tangible benefit is one you can directly associate with hard dollars such as personnel savings, lower travel budget, increased output or increased income.

An intangible benefit can mainly be associated with soft dollars. You indirectly earn more by having the personnel better informed, you get better quality work done. There is no general way to estimate the value of, for example, a contract which you got thanks to improved efficiency and/or effectiveness.

Among intangible benefits can be mentioned:

improving the morale of the employees by simplifying certain tasks, eliminating certain monotonous tasks and stimulating creativity.

increasing productivity of the computer center as well as of the users by reducing time to finish certain tasks and reducing the need for extra personnel.

improving the image of data handling by offering better service to the users, a low threshold for inexperienced users and giving a positive image of data handling.

improving the quality of results of data handling.

Quality of medium

Several studies on computer-based message systems (CBMS) indicate that the computer-based system is better or worse than other media (for instance telephone, face-to-face meetings) as follows:

> better for routine messages where you do not interrupt the other person with a typical computerbased system.

> better in cases where the same message is sent to several people, some of whom need much time, others less time, to digest and understand the message (in a face-to-face meeting, the time is equal to all recipients).

> better in cases where the computer medium gives a faster communication than alternative media.

> not as good when you have to explain and discuss complicated issues, where many interactions back and forth are necessary to resolve the issue.

> less good where persuasion and the creation of a common spirit of unity and purpose is important[3].

Analysis of cost factors

In this paper we are not comparing different computer mediated communication solutions but rather computer conferencing systems with other media. In order to make a cost comparison one should perform a detailed feature analysis of each system and then rate the value of these features against the goals and objectives of the organisation. Such studies have rarely been made.

The primary cost factors for running a computer-based message system are:

> the wages and wage-related costs of the people in the organisation using the message system.

> the wages and wage-related costs of the people running and managing the message system.

> the cost of the computer usage on the central computer(s) handling message distribution including software costs.

> the cost of connecting to the computer, using internal or external terminal or computer networks.

> the cost of the user equipment, computer terminals or personal workstations.

The marginal costs of adding computer-based messaging to an existing organisation is very dependent on the existing computer infrastructure in the organisation. The marginal cost is much lower in an organisation which already has computers, computer networks, and terminals or workstations for many of the employees, purchased primarily for other computer applications in the organisation. This may be important, since this marginal cost may be decisive in whether to introduce and use a computer-based message system or not. Comparison of equipment and operating costs is only meaningful when the less expensive solution has all the capabilities offered by the more expensive system. In most of the examples below we assume that the user pays an hourly rate when using the CBMS, with access to a terminal at a marginal cost, say 25 per cent of the total annual rental cost.

Areas of application	Benefit features												
	1	2	3	4	5	6	7	8	9	10	11	12	13
Booking of facilities	2	3	3	3	–	–	3	2	1	1	3	–	3
Managing people	3	3	2	2	–	3	3	1	1	3	3	–	3
Joint working arrangements	3	1	2	2	3	3	2	2	2	2	3	–	3
Planning and progressing	3	2	3	2	3	3	2	–	1	2	3	–	3
Distribution of info	3	3	3	3	2	3	–	3	3	3	2	3	3
Support to ordinary meetings	3	2	2	2	3	3	3	1	2	3	1	3	3
Communication with customer	3	3	1	3	3	3	2	2	2	2	2	–	3
Bringing like-minded people together (Human networks)	3	3	2	3	1–3	2	3	3	–	3	3	–	3
Buying and selling	2	2	2	2	3	3	3	3	2	3	2	–	3
Electronic publishing	3	2	3	1	3	3	3	3	3	3	2	3	3
Educational activities	3	2	3	3	2	2	3	3	3	3	2	–	3
Support to (international) conferences	3	2	3	3	1	2	3	3	2	3	2	–	3

3) very important, 2) important, 1) less important, –) not applicable

Benefit features:

1 distance independence
2 better result due to more contacts
3 reduced time to complete a task, faster response etc

4 less cost, eg. less personnel, meeting cuts bureaucracy, travels, paperwork
5 more income
6 dealing with issue when they arise
7 distribution of info

8 new contacts
9 access to human networks

10 greater degree of participation
11 higher quality of information and of decisions
12 two way communication instead of one
13 enhancement of traditional media

Figure 29.1

Examples of cost/benefit analyses

Results from some cost/benefit studies are presented. They represent a wide spectrum and differ very much in scope and ambition. First follows a subjective classification of benefit components for various areas of application of computer conference systems (*Figure 29.1*). The scope is merely to show the spread of marks. The actual values are dependent on the special factors affecting the individual user.

In this analysis the costs of terminal, computer, network is assumed to be US$ per hour and the wage and wage-related costs US$ 20 per hour per person involved.

CBMS versus telephone

In Sweden, today, it is a fact that you reach the person you would like to talk to only in less than 25 per cent of the phone calls. This is mainly due to the fact that the person you would like to talk to is not available and rarely due to technical problems. The time to make the four calls which are needed to have one successful call is 22 minutes[4,5]. The cost of one telephone call lasting 4.5 minutes is a wage cost of US$ 7.30 plus a telephone charge cost of US$ 0.10–1.25 depending on the geographical distance. For the computer system, a writing time of 4.2 minutes and a reading time of 0.5 minutes per message are assumed.

Assuming that a group telephone call is not used, the cost of reaching people (*Figure 29.2*) shows that the computer is more beneficial for simple matters, requiring only one or a few messages to sort out, and when there is a need to reach more than one person. Apart from these tangible numbers you have the benefit of getting in touch with anyone in the group by sending an electronic message when it suits you.

Shorter face-to-face meetings – mainly local participants

Comparison with face-to-face meetings is similar, but for such meetings, travel may be an important additional cost factor. The wage and wage-related cost during the travel time must also be included. The result is that the total time for a group, of say 12 persons, is less with electronic than with spoken communication. There are also a number of psychological differences, many of them in favour of the electronic communication. The real costs vary very much, so the figures (*Figure 29.3*) in these examples should not be seen as more than examples.

The face-to-face meeting becomes ridiculously expensive for short meetings and for meetings with many participants. This is one typical example of a kind of communication which is so expensive without the computer that it hardly occurs. It is not surprising that work is usually organised to avoid this, by combining many points on the agenda for one face-to-face meeting, or arranging several meetings on the same journey, and by keeping groups small.

In addition, the figures show that the computer gets better cost/performance-ratios for matters which require a short time to discuss. Thus, the computer is especially suitable for the many small matters which occur in business work. Experience also shows that most of the communication in message systems refer to small matters which are finalised after two or three messages.

Additional benefits with computer conferencing are that all participants have equal opportunity to take part in the discussions, the information content is normally better, and the communication is documented.

Two-day face-to-face meeting – all participants travel

When many participants travel a long distance it is customary to organise two-day meetings, then travel cost, hotel and *per diem* cost add substantially to wages, etc. It is not possible to compare in a fair way the outcome of a face-to-face meeting among say 10 persons travelling to Brussels from all over Europe with the results of a discussion using a CBMS spread over a longer period among the same 10 persons. It is like comparing oranges and apples. Face-to-face meetings and electronic meetings are complementary to each other. But a superficial analysis gives some useful information. If then, for simplicity, we forget wages and take a hypothetical example, the average cost per person is US$ 1,050 (travel $800; two days *per diem* $100; hotel – one night $115; extras $35). This amount would pay for about one year's CBMS usage by an average user including network charges. The use of CBMS as a complement to travelling is both useful and cost efficient. This allows ordinary meetings be held at longer time intervals and the reduction of the travel budget can be set against the CBMS costs.

CBMS versus telex, letters and rapid delivery services

These costs again are very much dependent on the charges for the different services, distances etc. But for some instances CBMS has been found cheaper than telex (about half). Short CBMS letters are cheaper than ordinary mail but much faster and finally cost only about 10 per cent of rapid delivery services.

		1 person	2 persons	3 persons
Telephone call	US$	8.00	16.00	24.00
Computer message system				
– 1 message	US$	2.75	3.10	3.30
– 3 messages	US$	8.25	9.30	9.90
– 5 messages	US$	13.75	15.50	16.50

Figure 29.2

Group meeting cost/hour (US$)	5 people	12 people	33 people
Wage/wage-related costs	100	240	660
Travel costs assuming third of all participants travel an averahe of 150 x 2 kilometers, and that the meeting lasts 2 hours, including wage costs during travel	300	720	2000
Wage/wage-related costs	100	160	280
Computer costs	75	120	210
Face-to-face meeting			
– lasting 1 hour	700	1680	4660
– lasting 2 hours	400	960	2660
– lasting 3 hours	300	720	2000
– lasting 6 hours	200	480	1325
Computer conference	175	280	490

Figure 29.3

```
Savings:
50 persons x 1 hour x 220 days x $20          =$220,000

Costs for computertime, terminal and networks:
50 persons x 0.5 hour x 220 days x $15        = $82,000

Cost for software system                      =  $8,000

                          Saving: about US$130,000
```

Figure 29.4

Time savings in organisations

A high level user (about 30 minutes usage a day) saves one to two hours per day by reducing the number of and time in ordinary meetings, by eliminating work associated with preparing, sending and filing paper mail and memos, eliminating incomplete telephone calls and eliminating interruptions and restart[6]. Here only traditional communication is reduced. In addition new communication is added[5]. Figure 29.4 shows what this would mean for an organisation with 50 users.

The impact on human networks

In human networks there is a sort of more or less coordinated sharing of knowledge. We know from experience that this is very valuable.

An international example

The International Program Library (IPL) Computer Conference, was the first coordinated effort to share workload and expertise among academic institutions on an international scale using computer conferencing and computer networks. The particular area chosen was that of sharing information, experiences and advice about computer programs for computers ranging from personal to super computers.

Some of the most important motives for IPL are:

the total expertise necessary to cover a substantial amount of available software (10,000 codes) is formidable;

the duplication of work is unacceptably high;

all efforts to build centralised libraries of codes have failed because it has not been practically and economically feasible to gather and manage all expertise in one location;

there are many motivated users, the few thousand program librarians, the middle men and software experts, as well as the hundreds of thousands of end-users.

The long range goal is to have five hundred to two thousand program librarians and many thousand software experts and software houses to talk to and help each other via their terminals, normally connected to their local mail or conferencing system. In this way all expertise in the world would be inter-connected to each other. It is a formidable task to make this happen via a centralised system such as QZCOM, but when exchange of messages between many local CBMS is common using X.400 and more advanced protocols, this kind of application will flourish. Parallel conferences between experts on various software related subjects can then be held.

Value to the scientific community

It is extremely hard to estimate the value of the project. Let us assume that 500 librarians are cooperating and that each month there are 100 hits (where an end-user has been helped and found a program which would not have been found otherwise) and on average the end-user saves four months per hit by not reinventing programs and by obtaining higher quality and less faulty results. The direct value of this then exceeds

$$100 \times 12 \times 4/12 \times 45 \text{ k} = \text{US\$ } 18 \text{ million per/year.}$$

Total costs for running the IPL project

The cost for the time librarians spend with the project is not included in these total costs. The cost for personnel, computer time and network charges is estimated at

$$225 + 120 + 240 = \text{US\$ } 585,000.$$

A preliminary study of the outcome of a smaller pilot test with 100 librarians (about 40 active) from 18 countries during one year indicated that the above estimate is of the right order of magnitude.

A local example

At the Stockholm University Computing Center (QZ) we have about 150 conferences on internal matters. Typically a QZ employee is a member of 15 of them. These range from trade union matters, budget work, internal communication between members of different parts of the line organisation, projects, to information dissemination in general.

The use of electronic communication is an integrated part of their work. Many have terminals at home and do some of the work from home. A few are 'telecommuting' and many connect from 'any place in the world' while travelling. It thus allows a flexible work site. The manpower savings have not been studied in detail, but we estimate that we would need 5–10 per cent more people to perform what we are doing now if we had no access to computer conferencing. We have also experienced better communication between management and staff.

We also use this medium extensively to talk to our customers.

It simplifies contact with users.

It creates an environment of cooperation and togetherness.

It permits sharing of expertise and actual work among specialists in different computing centres.

The system connects many thousand specialists in Sweden as well as abroad, giving a wider knowledge base.

Very often other users answer questions before our specialists, and pay us for it!

Many thousand 'freeware' programs can be exchanged between users and downloaded.

We estimate that providing the equivalent service to our customers via traditional media would require at least another 10 staff.

Conclusion

A number of application areas for electronic messaging have been identified where users have reported the advantage to them of using electronic communication rather than (or as a complement to) conventional media. Some rather limited studies have been made of the cost/benefit of CBMS. The highest reduction in cost occurs for communication on simple matters, for communication in large groups, and where the alternative would have been to travel to face-to-face meetings.

There are however a number of questions to be answered. How do we measure quality improvements and how do we measure effectiveness? How about the information content? Is the exchanged information worth its price? How about sensitivity analyses? Do CBMS also have negative effects on the users and organisations? Without any doubt, for certain applications, a rationalisation of personnel is possible – but how far is it wise to go with respect to specialisation and vulnerability? Further research is needed to provide answers to these questions from behavioural and sociological as well as from the business economics point of view.

We are looking forward to the next few years with great expectations!

NOTES

COM was developed by the Defense Research Institute, FOA and the Stockholm University Computing Center, QZ. It was developed for DEC10 and 20 computers and has been used at about 20 installations starting 1979, the most well known being QZCOM in Sweden and EuroKOM at the University College Dublin which serves as the Information Exchange System, IES for ESPRIT. Usage increases 20 to 40 per cent per year at present installations. A portable version, PortaCOM, has been developed.

PortaCOM was initiated under the auspices of the joint European COST11 ter project. PartaCOM is a portable computer conference system written in Pascal, based on the specification of the COM system.

PortaCOM has been developed and ported by eight European institutes in Italy, Yugoslavia, Germany, Finland, Sweden, Norway and Denmark to a number of operating systems. The number of COM and PortaCOM systems in use in 1987 is about 50. This number is projected to double in each of the next few years!

30

The Seven Rules for Success

NEIL FARMER

Introduction: a sorry state of affairs

During the early-to-mid 1980s, the experiences of office automation were generally very disappointing. Looking back with the benefit of hindsight, we can see that few office automation installations have been either notable successes or dire failures — most installations have simply been non-events. These non-events usually have a reasonably high degree of user acceptance, together with claims for mainly qualitative benefits being achieved. Where quantified benefits exist, they are usually modest and even the qualitative benefits are not really convincing to an objective observer. As a rule of thumb, the office automation picture can be summarised as:

> 'About one in ten installations is a success ... One in ten is a failure ... and the remaining eight out of ten installations are non-events'.

The reasons for this sorry state of affairs are not that those responsible for installing office automation were not intelligent or motivated. In most cases they were. Nor is the situation primarily due to a lack of competence or professionalism. In most cases, well established procedures for equipment selection, project control, user involvement and management support have been invoked. The real problem lies in widespread and fundamental misunderstandings about the nature of office automation and the rules for success in this field.

From our research in more than 400 organisations over the last five years, we have identified seven rules for success in office automation.

Rule 1:
Install office automation systems for particular applications

We regard the field of office automation as being made up of applications that use three types of overlapping systems: traditional (mainstream) data processing systems; general-purpose office automation systems; and specially designed office automation systems. Although traditional data processing systems and general-purpose office automation systems (such as word processing and electronic messaging) are quite well understood, the middle ground between them is less clear. For example, office automation systems may be designed to meet particular requirements by combining traditional data processing systems, standard packages or general-purpose systems into hybrid systems.

Consider a sales information system which comprises sales staff visit reports (text), order information by customer (data), and trade press information (text), with access to the information being provided through a sophisticated electronic retrieval system. Such systems are increasingly being used to meet specific business requirements. Indeed these hybrid systems usually give much bigger paybacks than standard facilities, such as word processing or electronic mail. Hybrid systems have been used to create quotations and the associated correspondence for customers; to combine data processing information with spreadsheets and word processing; to route electronic documents in a particular sequence for authorisation or for comments associated with capital projects; and to allow customers to place orders electronically using a combination of external electronic messaging services, internal data processing and internal electronic messaging.

Because hybrid systems offer greater opportunities than those associated with general-purpose office automation systems, *Rule 1* states that organisations should plan for and implement hybrid systems as well as general-purpose systems. To do this effectively, end-user computing support staff (who support users with standard packages and system building tools such as spreadsheets, database management systems or APL) and office automation support staff (who support users with word processing, electronic messaging, etc) should be combined into a single user support group. If this is not done, there are considerable dangers that support staff (and users) will adopt a narrow 'blinkered' view, and that hybrid applications will be overlooked or put off to some distant future date.

The idea of hybrid office automation systems is fundamental to an understanding of how office automation will be used in future. We believe that it is essential to break away from the naïve ideas that were propounded in the early 1980s. Office automation is *not* just a number of general purpose facilities that can be scattered around the office to provide magically increased efficiency and much less paperwork. A move away from providing general-purpose facilities and towards providing hybrid systems to meet real business-related needs is essential for sustained success in office automation. Electronic messaging is a key technology in the development of hybrid systems since many such systems are built upon 'electronic mail with the appropriate hooks'.

Rule 2:
Clearly define and quantify objectives

This rule sounds obvious but it is not. Most organisations that install office automation systems produce a list of objectives that is extensive (typically 6–10 main objectives), woolly, unquantified and unrealistic. A typical list of such objectives might read something like:

to increase efficiency in the office over the next five year planning period;

to reduce the volume of paperwork handled;

to improve the quality and timeliness of information and so improve the quality of decision making at managerial levels;

to educate staff in the use of office automation facilities;

to re-evaluate the performance and potential for different types of office automation facility;

to improve internal communications;

to stay ahead of our competitors in the use of office automation;

to retain staff who might otherwise leave the organisation.

All these objectives might sound worthy, but woolly objectives such as these almost always lead to non-event type installations.

In contrast, however, organisations that clearly establish and quantify objectives for each main application area have a much better track record of success. Examples of reasonably clear and quantified objectives might be:

> to improve by 15 per cent the productivity of departments A, B, and E by the end of the next financial year;

> to reduce the volume of paper files so that by the end of 1988, internal stationery requirements are lowered by 50 per cent and 1,500 square feet of office space is released from 1986 levels;

> to improve our document image in terms of context, layout and print quality so that the customer marketing response is increased by 10 per cent and overdue debt situation is reduced by 20 per cent on 1986 levels.

The reason why clear and quantified objectives are one of the keys to success in office automation is that they force those responsible to face up to the actions that will be necessary to achieve the objectives. If a 15 per cent productivity increase is to be achieved, who has to go – and what will the new organisation look like? Or, in what logical stages are we going to cut back on our paper files? What problems will need to be overcome? Who will be responsible? And so on.

Rule 3:
Phasing the three different types of OA applications can give continuing high levels of quantitative justification.

It is important to recognise that there are three main types of office automation applications – strategically important applications, specific operational applications and general purpose applications.

Strategically important applications are those that have a direct impact on the main function of the organisation: that is, they affect in a significant way the 'customer' or the service provided. There are many examples of this type of application.

> Some companies have provided customers (or agents) with personal computers so that they can place electronic orders. In extreme cases, microcomputers on customers' premises have even been used to maintain stock records and for automatic reordering. In this way, the supplier may be able to increase market share considerably, particularly if competitors are slow in offering comparable facilities.

> Some life insurance companies have supplied sales staff with portable computers and sophisticated software that can be used to prepare quotations that are matched closely to individual customer requirements. This approach has often led to a significant increase in market share.

> Some pharmaceutical companies have, over a period of years, used wordprocessors linked to laboratory computers to build up the extensive regulatory documentation that is needed for approval of a new drug by the relevant government bodies (the CSM in the UK and the FDA in the USA). As a result, the companies are able to launch new drugs about one-to-two months earlier than would otherwise have been possible – an advantage that may be worth tens of millions of dollars over a five-year period.

And the sophisticated sales information system that we mentioned to illustrate *Rule 1* can have a significant positive effect on the market shares of companies that adopt this approach.

For any given market or service, there are typically only a few strategically important applications, but these applications are usually associated with very large financial benefits or (if things go wrong) losses (*Figure 30.1*). Strategically important applications often succeed or fail very quickly, usually within the first year after installation. There are a growing number of examples of successful strategically important applications.

In contrast, specific operational applications are installed to improve the operational procedures associated with a particular business function that is not strategically important. One example is a microcomputer-based system which was installed to prepare engineering quotations and correspondence more quickly. Other examples include an integrated purchasing system that produces orders and correspondence, and a spreadsheet-based budgeting system used by accountants. Interestingly, the use of wordprocessing by typists also falls into this category because it relates specifically to the typing function.

Specific operational applications usually produce only modest benefits or losses (*Figure 30.1*). But the benefits (or losses) are cumulative, and they can become significant over a period of time. There are many examples of moderately successful specific operational applications.

General-purpose applications do not fall into the first two categories, but instead aim to improve office efficiency by providing an electronic, rather than paper-based, environment. Various studies have predicted that general-purpose facilities – such as wordprocessing, electronic mail and electronic information retrieval – can improve office productivity by between 15 per cent and 30 per cent, depending on the mix of office staff and current productivity levels. These benefits, however, have been realised only in certain circumstances, usually in conjunction with reduced staff levels and reorganisations of managerial/professional staff or support staff. Experience has shown than an essential prerequisite to achieving quantified benefits from the installation of general-purpose applications is a determination (usually driven by the chief executive) to reorganise.

In the early 1980s, we predicted that the cost benefits from general-purpose applications would follow a cyclical pattern (*Figure 30.1*). This pattern would be characterised by modest initial cost benefits as the obvious applications, such as word processing in typing pools or inter-site electronic mail (to replace postal, telex and carrier costs), were implemented. Some 'dead wood' would also be shed to justify the initial purchase of equipment. As demand for office systems increased, and as educational and 'critical mass' barriers had to be overcome, the overall cost-benefit situation would fall. Many, if not most, large organisations are currently in this situation – some even managed to avoid the early obvious benefits! A few organisations, however, have begun to climb out of the cost-benefit trough shown in Figure 30.1 by a process of reorganisation driven by top management.

Clearly, phasing the implementation of different types of application will have a major effect on the cumulative pattern of cost and benefits achieved. A major early success with a strategically important application can provide cost-benefits for years. An ongoing programme of retrenchment and reorganisation can have a similar effect.

Rule 4:
Qualitative benefits are not a universal panacea, so concentrate on the important applications.

1. COST-BENEFIT COMPARISONS

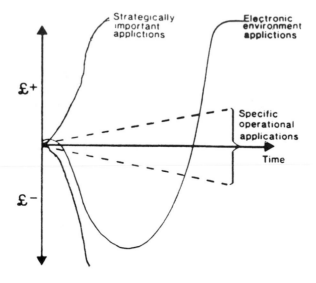

Figure 30.1

Many organisations are taking the 'soft option' by relying almost entirely on qualitative benefits to justify significant levels of investment in office automation. Unless this approach is very selective, however, we strongly believe it to be misguided. Two realities should be borne in mind when putting forward qualitative justifications for office automation. Firstly, there are certain key areas and people in the organisation for whom timely and high quality information can generate major benefits, even if the financial implications are difficult to estimate. For many others, the qualitative benefits are minimal or non-existent.

All qualitative benefits can and should be compared with quantitative benefits in terms of their value to the organisation. For example, a workshop of senior managers could be given the task of ranking potential applications in priority sequence. In this way, the arguments that inevitably arise between supporters of applications with predominantly quantified benefits and those with predominantly qualitative benefits can be resolved.

Many organisations claim to have achieved significant qualitative benefits from office automation, although very few have impressive arguments to justify these claims. When evaluating qualitative benefits, clear thinking and a lack of optimism are the most important prerequisites. Be wary of fancy formulas that claim to measure qualitative benefits. Concentrate on the small minority of qualitative benefits that are really important to the organisation. And do not assume that this approach necessarily means putting a terminal on the desks of key decision makers.

Rule 5:
User acceptance depends on at least one initial application being very relevant to the users job.

2.

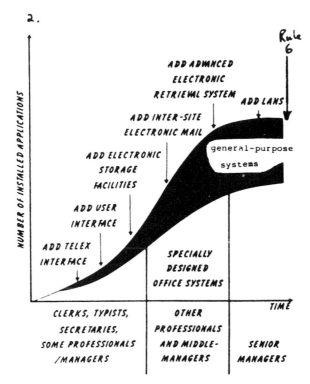

NUMBER OF INSTALLED APPLICATIONS (vertical axis)

Rule 6

ADD ADVANCED
ELECTRONIC
RETRIEVAL SYSTEM

ADD LANS

ADD INTER-SITE
ELECTRONIC MAIL

general-purpose
systems

ADD ELECTRONIC
STORAGE
FACILITIES

ADD USER
INTERFACE

ADD TELEX
INTERFACE

SPECIALLY
DESIGNED
OFFICE SYSTEMS

TIME

| CLERKS, TYPISTS, SECRETARIES, SOME PROFESSIONALS /MANAGERS | OTHER PROFESSIONALS AND MIDDLE-MANAGERS | SENIOR MANAGERS |

Measurement of changes due to office automation should only be used to confirm success

Figure 30.2

From our studies of leading-edge office automation users, particularly in the United States, we have discovered that widespread user acceptance has (knowingly or unknowingly) been based on this rule. The rule in full is made up of two parts, namely:

'The first application used by each new terminal user should be very relevant to that user's job. Other general purpose applications can be successfully added later.'

This rule sounds obvious but it is not. In practice, it means that many if not most, office automation programmes are fundamentally misguided. For example, it means that wordprocessing is a sound first application for typists, secretaries and text-oriented professionals, but is not a sound first application for most professionals (such as accountants, engineers or actuaries) or for senior managers. Electronic mail is very rarely suitable as a first application, except where the users are highly mobile (for example, sales staff).

Evidence from leading-edge users also strongly indicates that the traditional view of office automation, in which general-purpose applications are gradually built up to create an electronic environment is misguided. Organisations that rely on this approach tend to experience 'OA stagnation'.

In our research, over 80 per cent of leading-edge users who had achieved a very high terminal penetration (at least one terminal for every two office staff) had mainly built general-purpose systems as add-ons to other specific operational applications (such as wordprocessing for typists/secretaries, spreadsheets for accountants, and data processing applications for clerks and professional staff). Generally speaking in these organisations, the first users of office automation systems were typists, secretaries, numerate professionals (such as accountants) and clerks. Next, other middle managers and less numerate professionals began to use the systems, but senior managers were the last to use a terminal on their desks.

Among the remaining 20 per cent or so of leading-edge user organisations, the dominant reason for very high use of office automation systems was that a senior executive (normally the chief executive) personally 'drove' the OA programme. In this situation, user resistance or apathy had often been overcome, even though the first applications for new terminal users may have delivered only marginal benefits. Minority experiences of this kind have led many organisations to assume that this top-down approach is the most effective way to introduce office automation. In following this approach, many organisations have first installed office automation pilot trials for use by senior managers. However, our research strongly suggests that pilot trials designed to provide general-purpose systems for use by senior managers tend to fail. We also found that trials which aimed to meet senior management needs by providing systems tailored to their requirements often needed high levels of system support staff. If the level of support is reduced, the trial often fails.

We believe that *Rule 5* is a very sound approach regardless of whether the chief executive is driving the office automation programme or not.

Interestingly, if you follow the *Rule 5* approach to obtain the greatest user acceptance of office automation, quite high levels of cost benefit often result. For example, specific operational applications are often very relevant to the user's job and are quickly accepted. Furthermore, these applications usually result in modest but worthwhile cost benefits. In this way, the number of terminals installed can be built up, enabling general-purpose systems to be introduced later at a marginal cost. Similarly, by introducing strategically important applications at an early stage, large benefits can be achieved with high levels of user acceptance. Problems will not arise until it is necessary to carry out the fundamental reorganisations and significant staff reductions required to achieve the benefits of general-purpose applications. Thus, phasing different types of application to achieve real benefits while maintaining a high level of user acceptance is an important tactical consideration.

One potential problem with this approach is that while some applications (such as wordprocessing for secretaries and spreadsheets for accountants) can be installed very quickly, others that have to be specially designed can sometimes involve a considerable investigative or development effort. By mixing applications carefully, however, organisations can move relatively smoothly from the initial applications to a highly electronic office environment, while achieving both user acceptance and measurable cost benefits.

Rule 6:
Once an electronic office culture becomes established, *Rule 5* is no longer essential for widespread user acceptance.

Once an electronic culture is established in an organisation (typically when 30 per cent or more staff use terminals regularly for office automation), general-purpose facilities (particularly electronic mail and wordprocessing) become accepted as the first application by new terminal users. In other words, in an electronic culture, *Rule 5* tends to break down, although it is still a very sound approach. Figure 30.2 illustrates the relationship between *Rule 5* and *Rule 6*.

Rule 7:
Measurement of changes due to office automation should only be used to confirm success

A great deal of woolly thinking and pseudo-professionalism is associated with the measurement of the success or failure of office automation applications. All too often, the approach resembles that of a chemical experiment that is being carried out for the first time – everything conceivable is measured to see if anything has changed.

However, if clearly stated and quantified objectives have been established for each office automation installation, what needs to be measured should be blatantly obvious. For example, if the objective is to reduce staffing levels by 15 per cent, you take a headcount and you measure the before-and-after performance of the group concerned in terms of the main activities performed (examining lead times, number of errors, etc). If the objective is to save 1,000 square feet of office space, then you carry out a before-and-after comparison to see how the space is being used.

Office automation pilot trials, in particular, are a classic soft option. Often, they are carried out because the organisation is not sure what to do. In our view, most pilot trials are 'non-events' and actually delay progress towards successful office automation. Trials are only useful where meaningful benefits can be achieved and where the lessons are applicable to other areas of the organisation. Avoid trying to re-invent the wheel!

Conclusion

One final word of warning. Following all these rules does not guarantee success in office automation. A useful analogy is to think of horseracing. If you follow the rules, you are betting on the odds-on favourite and if you ignore them you are backing the 100–1 outsider. Far too many organisations are backing 100–1 outsiders.

Appendices

Appendix A
About the Authors

BEALE

Nicholas C L Beale is Vice Chairman of Beale International Technology Ltd, UK. He is Chairman of the EMUG Working Group 2 on Networking and of the Reconfiguration Group of IEEE 802.5, 802.8, ISA SP72, BSI OIS/6 WGI, and the EMUG Technical Committee.

CLARK

Peter Clark is Unison Project Manager, Logica Communications and Electronic Systems Ltd, UK. Since joining Logica in 1978 his responsibilities have included the management of several large office automation development programmes. Previously he worked for ICL on optical character recognition and then spent six years in developing advanced office equipment at Xerox Research UK / Rank Xerox.

CUSWORTH

Stewart D Cusworth holds a BSc in physics and an MSc in instrumentation. In 1986 he obtained a PhD for earlier work on a project concerned with optical-fibre sensors. Since 1985 he has been engaged as a research fellow in the Department of Electrical and Electronics Engineering at Manchester Polytechnic, UK, in the area of optical-fibre LANs.

DAVIS

Lester Davis is Product Manager with NEC Business Systems (Europe) Ltd. He has been involved in development and application of all types of facsimile equipment for almost 30 years. He currently has technical and marketing responsibilities for G3 and G4 products with particular emphasis on emerging requirements. He is Chairman of the UK consultative facsimile body, BFICC, and participant in CCITT meetings developing facsimile recommendations.

FARMER

Neil Farmer, is Office Systems Consultancy Manager with Butler Cox & Partners Ltd, UK. He is one of Europe's leading figures in the field of office systems. Before moving into consultancy five years ago, he was responsible for the office systems, O&M and OR activities of a large multinational pharmaceutical company. He is a sought-after speaker and presenter and has written many articles in the office systems field.

FENTON

Nigel Fenton is Executive Secretary of the Article Numbering Association, UK. He is responsible for the Association's EDI standards design work, and for its input to the international standards–making arena.

FOSTER

David Foster is a Consultant Systems Engineer with IBM UK. He read physics at the Queen's College Oxford from where he graduated in 1963. He joined IBM in 1973 as a systems engineer, primarily supporting customers in the finance industry. He is now a Consultant Systems Engineer in the Network Design and Management Group of the IBM UK Technical Support function which he joined in 1982.

FREUCK

Paul Freuck joined the Siemens Communication Systems Public Switching Division in 1985 as a member of the Technical Sales Support and Marketing Department. Mr Freuck is responsible for ISDN technical support. Prior to joining Siemens, he was with Stromberg-Carlson for five years and GTE for 13 years. He hold a BS degree in Electrical Engineering from the University of Wisconsin, USA.

GLEEN

Keith Gleen is a Head of Group with the Digital Networks Division of the Technology Applications Department of British Telecom Research Labs. His group was responsible for the connection of the IDA Pilot Service to InterStream Two. The group is currently developing network terminating equipment conforming to the CCITT I421 Recommendation for ISDN Primary Rate Access.

HARROP

Michael Harrop, a data communications advisor with the Treasury Board of Canada, has been involved in OSI work since 1978 and chairs the ISO/SC21 Group developing a security architecture. He is also immediate past president of the Network Users Association which is dedicated to increasing user participation in the standards process.

HERR

Thomas J Herr is Vice President, Network Systems Universal Information Services and Strategic Market Planning at AT&T Network Systems. In this capacity he is responsible for strategic market planning and technology services and development planning for network products and systems evolving to Universal Information Services. He joined Illinois Bell in 1967 and held supervisory positions in Illinois Bell and AT&T Bell Laboratories followed by Division Manager and General Manager roles in Illinois Bell. In 1981 he joined Bell Laboratories as Director, Operations Systems Planning and in 1983 became Network Market Planning and Management Vice President on AT&T Network Systems. He assumed his present position in 1986. Mr Herr received a BSEE and MSEE from the University of Wisconsin, USA.

HIELSCHER

S Joe Hielscher is a Product Manager with Wang Laboratories' OSI Research and Development Group in Lowell, Massachusetts, USA. He is responsible for TOP/MAP programmes and is closely involved with the future development of Wang communications architecture, and particularly with migration toward OSI. He is an active member of the NBS/OSINET, MAP/TOP, COS, and the NBS-OSI Implementors Workshops.

HOLMES

Bob Holmes is Customer Services Manager for Cunard Brocklebank Ltd, UK & Eire. He is responsible for the provision of documentation, booking, transport and equipment services to Atlantic Container Line and Gulf Container Line customers. As a member of the shipping industry's data interchange (DISH) Management Group he has experienced the introduction of paperless documentation in the UK. He is the Chairman of the Liverpool Steamship Owners Traffic Committee.

HONEY

David Honey is a senior consultant in the Business Communications Group at Deloitte Haskins & Sells Management Consultants, UK. He has an honours degree in communications and computing from the University of Essex, UK, and has spent a total of 16 years in the computing and telecommunications industries. He has extensive experience of local and wide area networking, and is currently involved in the application of communications technology to the global financial securities trading markets.

HOUSLEY

Norman Housley is Manager, Communications & Technical Support, University of Toronto Computing Services, Toronto, Canada. His responsibilities include all data networking facilities and the provisioning of computer systems for research, teaching and administration. From 1975–80 he was Assistant Director of Software, Remanco Systems. In 1981 he joined the University as Manager, Communications & Small Systems.

HUEBER

Dr Roland P O Hueber is currently Head of Division, Strategic Aspects of IT Integration for Advanced Applications, Commission of the European Communities. Trained as an engineer, physicist and biologist, his career led (after some time in academia) from work in aerospace long-term developments and systems engineering, to the assessment of technology potential and the definition of programmes and actions in the framework of the Community. The highlights of the work with the Commission include the development of program ESPRIT and, later, RACE and DELTA.

KAHL

Peter Kahl has been with the Deutsche Bundespost since 1968 and is currently head of the ISDN department in the FTZ, Darmstadt, Federal Republic of Germany.

KELLEY

T Michael Kelley is responsible for the marketing and sales of M/A-COM's VSAT product line in Canada, Mexico, and Latin America. Prior to joining M/A-COM, he worked for INTELSAT in both the Strategic Policy and Business Planning Offices, specialising in domestic leases. He is a graduate of Princeton University (BSEE) and George Washington University (MSEE).

KURIHARA

Hiroshi Kurihara is a Staff Director of the Group Business Strategy Department of Kokusai Denshin Denwa Co Ltd (KDD), Tokyo, Japan. He is engaged in data communication services including electronic mail services.

KUTNEY

John Kutney joined the Siemens Communications Systems Public Switching Division in 1985 as a staff engineer, Advanced Systems Group. Mr Kutney was the supervisor of the technical Marketing Customer Interaction Group and is currently Manager of Documentation. Prior to joining Siemens, he was with AT&T Bell Labs from 1979 to 1985 and with US Steel Corp from 1973 to 1979. Mr Kutney holds a BS degree from St Peter's College, an MS degree in Mathematics from Lehigh University, and an MBA in Marketing from the University of Chicago, USA.

MAIRS

Chris Mairs is a Director and Senior Consultant with Data Connection Ltd. He was the architect of their range of portable SNA and OSI software products and special developments, including SDLC secondary/primary, SNA secondary/primary, terminal emulation, file transfer, X.25, and an SNA-to-OSI gateway mapping between the SNA DFC and OSI Session Layers. He regularly provides communications consultancy for major computer manufacturers in the USA and Europe. Before joining Data Connection in 1981 he worked for IBM in Portsmouth, UK.

MEIJER

Anton Meijer is a widely respected independent consultant and international lecturer. He joined IBM Netherlands in 1968 and subsequently participated in the early stages of IBM's SNA while on assignment in the USA. From 1977–1981 he was a faculty member at IBM's European Systems Research Institute in La Hulpe, Belgium. From 1983–1984 he was consultant for James Martin Associates. Since 1985 he has been an independent consultant in the field of telematics as well as leading seminars on SNA, OSI and Telecommunications. He is co-author of *Computer Network Architecture*, the second edition of which was published in 1987.

OLSEN

Dr Bengt A Olsen is President, KOMunity Software AB, Stockholm, Sweden. He was formerly Director, Stockholm University Computing Center. Dr Olsen has been

Associate Professor of Computational Physics since 1968. He opened a computer conferencing service at QZ in 1975 using FORUM. Swedish representative in COST 11 since 1975, he intiated development of the joint European computer conferencing system PortaCOM.

PERNIN

Jean-Louis Pernin, graduated from the Ecole Nationale Superieure des Télécommunications in 1964. Since 1966, he has served ALCATEL as: engineer, project manager, Deputy Director in charge of Subscriber Loop and Distribution Systems, and Deputy Director of Marketing. Mr Pernin is currently Director of Corporate Planning, TELIC-ALCATEL, France. He is a Member of IEEE.

PLEVYAK

Thomas J Plevyak is Network Systems Manager at AT&T Network Systems. He started his career at AT&T Bell Laboratories in 1962 in the field of exploratory development of direct energy conversion devices. In 1970 he joined the AT&T General Departments where he planned and managed the introduction of new transmission technologies. In 1980, he became Network Planning Manager for the Western Electric Company. Mr Plevyak received a BSME from the University of Notre Dame in 1960, an MSME from the University of Connecticut in 1962, a certificate from the Bell Laboratories Communications Development Training Program in 1964, and an MS in Advanced Management from Pace University in 1976. He has published numerous technical papers and holds two US patents. He is Senior Technical Editor of IEEE Communications Systems Magazine and serves as Member of the IEEE Communications Systems Engineering Committee.

POO

Dr Gee-Swee Poo is an Associate Professor at the Department of Information Systems and Computer Science, National University of Singapore. After many years of telecommunication experience with the Standard Telecommunications Laboratory in England, he now specialises in local area network development, data communications, ISDN and network performance. His work has appeared in over 40 publications.

REARDON

Ray Reardon is one of the world's most experienced networking and telecommunications managers. He was first involved in telecommunications over 25 years ago as a teleprinter operator in the Royal Air Force. Subsequently he received his BSc (Econ) at the London School of Economics, during which time he made over 200 radio broadcasts for the BBC. He holds the Diploma of the London Institute of Bankers and is a member of the British Computer Society. As a systems engineer in the 1960s, he worked on the design and implementation of some of the earliest on-line banking systems. For the past 15 years he has been involved in the direction, design, development, implementation, operation and management of IBM's own networks in the UK and Europe, which are among the world's largest and most advanced international and national corporate networks. He is a frequent speaker at international conferences and regularly advises some of Europe's major companies in the area of networking and telecommunications.

RYLEY

Alan Ryley received a BSc in mathematics in 1964, an MSc in 1978 and a PhD in 1981. From 1964 to 1970 he worked as a research engineer at the Marconi Company. He is currently in the Department of Mathematics & Physics at the Manchester Polytechnic, UK, where his main research interest is in the performance of data link layer protocols.

SATO

Katsushi Sato is on the staff of the Engineering Department in the office of Corporate Strategy and Planning with Kokusai Denshin Denwa Co Ltd (KDD), Tokyo, Japan. He is engaged in the planning of a wide variety of network systems including value added network systems such as MHS.

SENIOR

John Senior holds an honours degree in physics and a masters degree in communication engineering. He has been employed as communication engineer with GEC Telecommunications and Plessey Office Systems. His present post is Principal Lecturer in Communication Engineering in the Department of Electrical and Electronic Engineering at Manchester Polytechnic. He is the author of a number of papers and a major text in the area of optical-fibre communications.

SCHWARTZ

Arthur J Schwartz was born in Brooklyn, NY, USA, in 1933 and graduated from the US Navy Electronics School in 1953. He has held a First-Class Radiotelephone License (FCC) since 1957, and is a Senior Member of the IEEE. From 1956–65 he was employed in field engineering and served as technical advisor in Rwanda. A technical writer since 1966, he served on the Apollo/Saturn programme, and was Editor of *Telecommunications* magazine from 1969–71. In 1971 he was named by ALCATEL to create and manage an English-language Technical Reports service, for which he produced over 160 documents, including 20 published articles. Since July 1987 he has been engaged in creating an English-language professional communications activity for an affiliate of the French National School of Telecommunications.

SPANIER

Steve Spanier is Manager of Technical Marketing at Excelan, Inc. His responsibilities include benchmarks, application notes, technical articles and presentations, customer training, and administration of Excelan's User Group. Prior to joining Excelan, he held technical support positions with Sun Microsystems and Tandem Computers. Steve holds a MSCS from West Coast University, USA.

SZLICHCINSKI

Dr Karol Szlichcinski is a Senior Consultant with Butler Cox and Partners Ltd, UK. He formerly headed a strategic marketing studies section in British Telecom. He led the research for a Butler Cox Foundation report on EDI published in 1987, and has extensive experience of studies of VANS markets.

VERVEST

Dr Peter Vervest has been working with Philips Telecommunications since 1979 where he has been Product Manager of New Telecommunication Services specialising in the field of electronic mail. In 1984 he was appointed Applications Project Manager at Philips International in Eindhoven as well as being elected to the faculty of the Technical Department of the Erasmus University Graduate School of Management in Rotterdam. In 1986 he was awarded the Doctor's degree in Technical Sciences *cum laude* from the Technische Hogeschool, Delft. In 1987 he became Group Manager Advanced and Interactive Media Systems of Philips Electronics UK, based in London. Dr Vervest has lectured throughout Europe and has written a number of reports and papers on the subject of electronic mail. He is the author of several books, including *Innovation in Electronic Mail* and another *Electronic Mail and Message Handling*, which has been translated into Japanese.

Appendix B
References

3   ISDN Evolution in France: The Will to Innovate

1   J L Pernin, T M Randall and A J Schwartz, *Integrating Subscribers into Evolving Digital Networks*. Proc. ICC 84, pp 204–208; Amsterdam, The Netherlands, 1984.

2   J A Le Guillou, J L Pernin and A J Schwartz, *Electronic Systems and Equipment for Evolving Loop Plant*. IEEE Trans. Commun. Vol 28, (7) pp 962–975, 1980.

3   J L Pernin, T M Randall, A J Schwartz, *op. cit.*

4   J L Pernin and A J Schwartz, *Economic Aspects of Multiservice Subscriber Loops in Telematics Networks*. IEEE Trans. Commun. Vol COM-30, (9), pp 2211–2214, 1982.

5   J L Pernin, *La Fibre Optique en Distribution: Pari économique raisonné ou illusion cartésienne*. (In French; includes extensive extracts and annotations in English); Proceedings of ISSLS 84; Nice, France, 1984.

6   M Trouvat, *RENAN project tests ISDN implementation in France*. Commutation et Transmission, N° 3, pp 5–14, 1985.

7   J Kotula, T M Randall and R Stone, *The E10-FIVE development: Status and Field results*. Proceedings of ISS 84 Vol 2 Paper 21A-5; Florence, Italy, 1984.

8   A Gresillon, A Terriez, and H Cournarie, *Customising Software for E10/MT Digital Switches*. Commutation et Transmission, N° 2, 1986.

5   The UK ISDN: Interworking Features

1   CCITT Red Book, Vol III – Fascicle III.3: *Digital Networks – transmission systems and multiplexing equipments*. Geneva 1985

2   CCITT Red Book, Vol III – Fascicle III.5: *Integrated Services Digital Network (ISDN)*, Geneva 1985

9   Wavelength Division Multiplexing in Optical Fibre LAN's

1   J M Senior, *Optical Fibre Communications: Principles and Practice*, Prentice/Hall International, 1985.

2   H Ishio, J Minowa and K Nosu *Review and status of wavelength-division-multiplexing technology and its application*. J. of Lightwave Technology, Vol 2 (4), pp 448–462, 1984.

3   E Rickard, *Wavelength division multiplexing: overview of the state of the art*. RADC-TR-81-47, 1981.

4   B D Metcalf and J F Providakes, *High capacity wavelength demultiplexer with large diameter GRIN rod lens.* Applied Optics, Vol 21, pp 794–796, 1982.

5   H D Hendricks, J L Spencer and C J Magee, *Fiber optics wavelength division multiplexing for data systems* Future Connections (NASA), Vol 1, pp 9–12, 1981.

6   G Winzer, H F Mahlein and A Reichelt, *Single-mode and multimode all-fiber directional couplers for WDM* Applied Optics, Vol 20, p 3128, 1981.

7   K Aiki, N Nakamura and J Umeda, *A frequency multiplexing light source with monolithically integrated distributed-feedback diode lasers.* IEEE J Quantum Electron, Vol 13, pp 220–223, 1977.

8   T Lee *LEDs and photodetectors for WDM lightwave systems.* Opt Laser Technol, pp 15–20, February 1982.

9   T Suhura, Y Handa, N Nishihara and J Koyama, *Monolithic integrated micrograting and photodiodes for wavelength demultiplexing.* Appl Phys Lett, Vol 40, pp 120–122, 1982.

10   G Winzer, *Wavelength multiplexing components – a review of single-mode devices and their applications.* J of Lightwave Technology, Vol 2 (4), pp 369–378, 1984.

11   H A Roberts, *Single mode fused wavelength division multiplexer* Proc. SPIE, 574, pp 100–104, 1985.

12   R M Metcalf and D R Boggs, *Ethernet: distributed packet switching for computer networks.* Commun Ass Comput Mach, Vol 19, pp 395–405, 1976.

13   M V Wilkes and D J Wheeler, *The Cambridge digital communication ring.* Proc Local Area Commun Network Symp (Boston), pp 47–61, 1979.

14   H Okada, Y Nomura and Y Nakaniski, *Multi-channel CSMA/CD method in broadband bus LANs.* IEEE Globecom '84 (Atlanta, CA, USA) pp 26–29, 1984.

15   A A Marsan and D Roffinella, *Multichannel local area network protocols.* IEEE J Selected Areas in Commun, Vol 1 (5), pp 885–897, 1983.

16   P C Wong and T S Yum, *A multichannel computer network with local and global transceiving media.* IEEE Infocom '85 (Washington DC, USA) pp 142–150, 1985.

17   F Ross, *FDDI – a tutorial.* IEEE Commun Mag, Vol 24 (5) pp 10–17, 1986.

18   S Oshima et al, *Small loss-deviation tapered fibre star coupler for LAN.* J of Lightwave Technology, Vol 3 (3), pp 556–560, 1985.

19   R V Schmidt et al, *Fibernet II: a fiber optic Ethernet.* IEEE J Selected Areas in Commun. Vol 1 (5), pp 702–710, 1983.

11   Message Handling as the Basis for Tele-Information Systems

1   An overview is given in: Uhlig, Farber and Bair, *The Office of the Future.* The International Council for Computer Communications, North-Holland Publishing Company: New York, 1979. See also: Vallee, *Computer Messaging Systems* McGraw-Hill, New York, 1984.

2   Proceedings of the *IFIP TC-6 International Symposium on Computer Message Systems*. Ottawa: Canada, 6–8 April, 1981

3   ISO/IS 7498, ISO/TC97/Sc16 (rev) *Information Processing Systems – Open Systems Interconnection – Basic Reference Model*. International Standards Organisation: Geneva, 1983

4   *CCITT, Recommendation X.400, Message Handling Systems: System Model – Service Elements*. Study Group VII, International Telecommunications Union: Geneva, 1984. See also *X.401, X.408, X.409, X.410, X.411, X.420, and X.430*.

5   A detail overview of the various mail and messaging systems is given in: Vervest et al, *Electronic Mail and Message Handling*. Frances Pinter Publishers: London, 1985.

6   Cf. Vervest, Visser, Van Aller, Wissema, *The Introduction of Electronic Mail – Perspectives for Telecommunications Managers – Results of the April/May 1985 Questionnaire for the International Communications Association (ICA)*, Dallas, EBURON: Delft, 1986.

7   Vervest, Wissema, *Electronic mail and Message Handling in the USA – Results of the May 1984 Study Tour*. Erasmus University: Rotterdam, October 1984. See also: Vervest, Wissema, *Electronic Mail and Message Handling in Japan – Results of the February, March 1985 Study Tour*. Erasmus University: Rotterdam, April 1985.

8   A standardisation-scenario analysis has been made in *Innovation in Electronic Mail*. North-Holland Publishing Company: Amsterdam, 1987.

12   FTAM: OSI File Transfer Access & Management

1   R desJardins, J S Foley, *Open Systems Interconnection: A Review and Status Report*. J of Telecommunications Networks, pp 194–209, Fall 1984.

2   W Rauch-Hindin, *Upper Layer OSI Protocols Near Completion*. Mini-Micro Systems, pp 53–66, July 1986.

3   P F Linington, *The Virtual Filestore Concept* North-Holland: Computer Networks 8, pp 13–16, 1984.

4   D Lewan, H G Long, *The OSI File Service* IEEE Proceedings, pp 1414–1419, December 1983.

5   *Demo Agreements Document Autofact '85, Version 4*. General Motors Corporation: Warren MI, 1985.

6   *MAP Specification, Version 2.1*. General Motors Corporation: Warren MI, 1985.

7   *TOP Specification, Version 1.0*, The Boeing Company: Seattle WA, 1985.

8   K Truoel, A Woodcock, *FTAM-SPAG Industrial Activity* ECMA/RARE Workshop Presentation: Copenhagen, May 1986.

9   MIL-STD-1780: *Military Standard File Transfer Protocol* Department of Defense: Washington D C, May 1984.

10   NBSIR-86-3385-1: *Implementation Agreements for Open Systems Interconnection*

Protocols Workshop for Implementors of OSI/NBS-ICST: Gaithersburg MD, July 1986.

11   ISO/TC97/SC21/DIS8571: *Information Processing Systems – Open Systems Interconnection – File Transfer, Access and Management – Part 1: General Introduction* Paris, February 1986.

12   ISO/TC97/SC21/DIS8571: *Information Processing Systems – Open Systems Interconnection – File Transfer, Access and Management – Part 2: The Virtual Filestore.* Paris, February 1986.

13   SNA Trends

1   A Meijer and P Peeters, *Computer Network Architectures.* Pitman: London, 1982.

2   *Systems Network Architecture: Concepts and Products.* IBM Corporation. Form Number GC30–3072.

3   *Systems Network Architecture: Technical Overview.* IBM Corporation, Form Number GC30–3072.

4   *Systems Network Architecture: Format and Protocol Reference Manual: Architecture Logic.* IBM Corporation, Form Number SC30–3112.

5   J D Atkins, *Path Control: the Transport Network of SNA.* IEEE Trans Commun, vol 28 (4), pp 527–538.

6   V Ahuja, *Routing and flow control in Systems Network Architecture.* IBM Syst. J, vol 18 (2) pp 298–314, 1979.

7   J H Benjamin, H L Hess, R A Weingarten, and W R Wheeler, *Interconnecting SNA Networks.* IBM Syst J, vol 22 (4), pp 344–366, 1983.

8   J P Gray, P J Hansen, P Homan, M A Lerner, and M Pozefsky, *Advanced Program-to-Program Communication is SNA.* IBM Syst J, vol 22 (4) pp 298–318, 1983.

9   *Systems Network Architecture – Transaction Programmer's Reference Manual for LU Type 6.2.* IBM Corporation, Form Number GC30–3084.

10   *Systems Network Architecture – Format and Protocol Reference Manual: Architecture Logic for LU Type 6.2.* IBM Corporation, Form Number SC30–3269.

11   T Schick and R F Brockish, *The Document Interchange Architecture: A Member of a Family of Architectures in the SNA environment* IBM Syst J, vol 21 (2), pp 220–244, 1982.

12   B C Housel and J C Scopinich, *SNA Distribution Services.* IBM Syst J, vol 22 (4), pp 319–343, 1983.

13   G A Deaton Jr, and R O Hippert Jr, *X.25 and related recommendations in IBM products.* IBM Syst J, vol 22 (1/2), pp 11–29, 1983.

14   E H Sussenguth, *Systems Network Architecture, A Perspective.* Proc 4th Int Conf Computer Commun, Kyoto, pp 353–358, 1978.

15   M Pozefsky and J P Gray, *A Perspective on Mixed System Networking*. Presentation to SHARE, February 1985.

16   A E Baratz, J P Gray, P E Green, J M Jaffe, and D P Pozefsky, *SNA Networks of Small Systems*. IEEE J on Selected Areas in Comm, Special Issue in Personal Computer Communications, May 1985.

15   The MAP/TOP Initiative

1   NRC 84: *Computer Integration of Design and Innovation: A National Opportunity*. US National Research Council p 17, 1984. This was based on experience from McDonnell Douglas Aircraft Co, Deere & Co, Westinghouse, GM, and Ingersoll Milling Machine Co.

2   SSA 86: *MAP TOP OSI Handbook* Ship Star Associates Inc (available from Beale International Technology Ltd.) These are the course notes for the Ship Star MAP/TOP seminars devised by RS Crowder.

16   The Emergence of TCP/IP

1   C Barney, *ISO Protocols Pose a Dilemma to Potential Users*. Electronics Week, May 13, 1985.

2   C C Cutler, et al, *Transport Protocols for Department of Defense Data Networks*. Report to the Department of Defense and the National Bureau of Standards. Committee on Computer-Computer Communications Protocols. National Academy Press: February 1985.

3   R Dalrymple, *LAN Standards Efforts Begin to Pay Off*. Mini-Micro Systems, March 1986.

4   J Estrin, W Carrico, *TCP/IP Protocols Address LAN Needs*. Mini-Micro Systems, May 1986.

5   E J Feinler, et al, *DDN Protocol Handbook*. Network Information Center, SRI International: Menlo Park, CA, December 1985.

6   J Haverty, G Tauss, *DoD Network Protocols: An Overview*. Government Data Systems, April/May 1986.

7   O Jacobsen, and F Perillo, editors, *TCP/IP Implementations and Vendors Guide* DDN Network Information Center, SRI International, February 1986.

8   E L Keller, *Feds Weighing OSI Compatibility In All Net Buys*. Computer Systems News, September 8, 1986.

9   D Ladermann, *For Now, Users Need Both SNA and TCP/IP* Information WEEK, May 19, 1986.

10   R A Moskowitz, *TCP/IP: Stairway to OSI*. Computer Decisions, April 22, 1986.

11   S Spanier, *Front-End vs. Kernel-Based Protocol Implementation: A Performance Comparison*. Excelan, Inc, San Jose, CA, January 1986.

12   Dr W Stallings, *The DOD Communication Protocol Standards.* Signal, April 1986.

17   Standards & Compatibility in LAN Integration

1   IEEE *Project 802, Local Network Standards.* Institute for Electrical and Electronic Engineers, 1983.

2   *The Ethernet: A local network-data link layer and physical layer specification, Version 1.0.* Digital, Intel and Xerox Corporations, UK, September 1980.

3   *Internet Datagram and Routing Information Protocol/Sequenced Packet Protocol.* Xerox Corporation, 1981.

4   *Military Standard Internet Protocol: MIL-STD-1777/Transmission Control Protocol: MIL-STD-1778.* Department of Defense, 1983.

5   ISO/IS 8073, *Information Processing Systems – Open Systems Interconnection Connection-oriented Transport Protocol.* International Standards Organization, 1984.

6   CCITT Red Book Vol VIII–Fascicle VIII.5, *Data communication networks: Open Systems Interconnection, system description techniques. Recommendations X.200-X.250.* ITU, Geneva, 1985.

7   *Manufacturing Automation Protocol (MAP) specification, version 2.1.* General Motors, 1985.

8   *Technical and Office Protocol (TOP) specification version 1.0.* Boeing, 1985.

21   X.400 Implementation for International Communications

1   CCITT Recommendations *X.400, X.401, X.408, X.409, X.410, X.411, X.420 and X.430.* 1984.

2   M Amano and K Kawaguchi, *X.400 services implementation for international communications.* Networks 85, pp 707–718, Online: London, June 1985.

3   H Ohmura, Y Kamiyama and H Kobayashi, *Development of a multimedia MHS based on CCITT X.400 Recommendations.* International Symposium on Computer Message Systems, Washington D C, Sept 1985.

4   K Kawaguchi, K Sato, R Sample, J Demco and B Hilpert, *Interconnecting Two X.400 Message Systems.* International symposium on Computer Message Systems, Washington D C, Sept 1985

24   Primary Rate LAN Interconnection for Office Applications

1   J W Burren, *Project Universe in Retrospect.* International Conference on Networks and Electronic Systems. IERE (No 63), 1985.

2   M V Wilkes, D J Wheeler, *The Cambridge Digital Computer Link* Proceedings of the Local Area Communication Network Symposium, May 1979. National Bureau of Standards Special Publication, 1979.

★   *Alvey Programme Annual Report 1985* IEE: Stevenage, 1985.

25 Management & Operational Issues

1   David P Norton, *The Economics of Computing in the Advanced Stages*. Nolan Norton & Co, 1984.

2   *Sloan Management Review*, Vol 24 (1), 1982.

3   Based on a diagram by Roger Mills, Internal Telecommunications Manager, IBM UK

4   Dr J Rockart, M I T Sloan School of Management. See Rockart, Ball, Bullen, & Harris, Computer Decisions. September 1983.

5   Edward A Van Schaik, *A Management System for the Information Business: Organisational Analysis*. Prentice Hall, 1985.

6   Charlie Blackshaw, *Experience with SNA Management Tools*. Networks '85 proceedings, Online, 1985.

7   David Foster, *Network Management with IBM's NetView*. Networks '87, Online, 1985. (Included in *Networks for the 1990s*.)

27 Network Management with NETVIEW

1   P Gibbon, J Willis and R Mills, *Managed intelligent networks – an IBM perspective*. Oxford Surveys in Information Technology, Volume 3 1986.

2   SC30–3346 *SNA Format and Protocols Reference Management Services*. IBM Systems Reference Library.

3   LY30–5586 *NetView Customization*. IBM Systems Reference Library.

4   SC30–3313 *NetView/PC Application Programming Interface Communication Services Reference*. IBM Systems Reference Library.

5   GH19–6529 *Service Level Reporter Version 3 General Information*. IBM Systems Reference Library.

6   GC34–4045 *Introducing the Information/Family*. IBM Systems Reference Library.

28 Security in Open Systems

1   ISO 7498 – *OSI Basic Reference Model*.

2   ISO 7498 Part II – *Security Architecture*.

3   DP7498/4 N1371 – *OSI Management Framework*.

4   RCMP/SIP1, *Security in the EDP Environment*. Jan 1979.

5   RCMP/SIP1, *EDP Threat Assessments, Concepts and Planning Guide*. Jan 1982.

29 Justification of E-Mail & Conference Systems

1   W Ulrich, Business Communication Company.

2   J Naisbitt, *Megatrends*. Future Publications. London, 1984.

3   J Palme, *Cost-benefit analysis of Computermediated message systems*. IFIP World Computer Congress, Dublin, 1986.

4   J Palme et al, *Report of a study of the utility of the COM computer conference system*. (in Swedish), 1980.

5   R P Uhlig et al, *The office of the future, communications and computers*. North Holland: 1979.

6   S R Hiltz and M Turoff, *The Network Nation: Human communication via computer*. Addison-Wesley Publishers, 1978.

7   P A Wilson, *Mailbox Message Systems*. National Computer Centre Publications. UK, 1983.

8   P A Wilson, (H T Smith editor), *Structures for Mailbox System Applications in Computer-Based Message Services*. North-Holland: 1985.

9   S R Hiltz and M Turoff, *Structuring Computer Mediated Communication Systems to Avoid Information Overload*. Comm ACM, July 1985.

Appendix C
Applicable CCITT & ISO Documents

DR PETER M H VERVEST

I: International Telegraph and Telephone Consultative Committee (CCITT) Recommendations

F. and T. Series

F.40x,y,z	Message Handling System Services (Draft Recommendations)
F.200	Teletex service
F.201	Interworking between the teletex service and the telex service
F.300	Videotex service
F.350	Provisions applying to the operation of an international public automatic message switching service for equipment utilising the International Telegraph Alphabet No.1
T.0	Classification of facsimile apparatus for document transmission over the public networks
T.2	Standardisation of Group 1 facsimile apparatus for document transmission
T.3	Standardisation of Group 2 facsimile apparatus for document transmission
T.4	Standardisation of Group 3 facsimile apparatus for document transmission
T.5	General aspects on Group 4 facsimile apparatus
T.50	International Alphabet No.5
T.51	Coded character sets for telematic services
T.60	Terminal equipment for use in the teletex service
T.61	Character repertoire and coded character set for the international teletex service
T.62	Control procedures for teletex and Group 4 facsimile services
T.63	Provisions for verification of teletex terminal compliance
T.70	Network-independent basic transport service for the telematic services
T.71	LAPB extended for half-duplex physical level service

T.72	Terminal capabilities for mixed-mode of operation
T.73	Document interchange protocol for the telematic services
T.90	Teletex requirements for interworking with the telex service
T.91	Teletex requirements for real-time interworking with the telex service in a packet switching network environment
T.100	International information exchange for interactive videotex
T.101	International interworking for videotex services

V. Series

V.21	300 bits per second duplex modem standardised for use in the general switched telephone network
V.22	1200 bits per second duplex modem standardised for use in the general switched telephone network and on point-to-point 2-wire leased telephone-type circuits
V.22bis	2400 bits per second duplex modem using the frequency division technique standardised for use in the general switched telephone network and on point-to-point 2-wire leased telephone-type circuits
V.23	600/1200 baud modem standardised for use in the general switched telephone network
V.24	List of definitions for interchange circuits between data terminal equipment and data circuit-terminating equipment
V.25	Automatic answering equipment and/or parallel automatic calling equipment on the general switched telephone network including procedures for disabling of echo control devices for both manually and automatically established calls
V.25bis	Automatic calling and/or answering equipment on the general switched telephone network (GSTN) using the 100-series interchange circuits
V.26bis	2400/1200 bits per second modem standardised for use in the general switched telephone network
V.26ter	2400 bits per second duplex modem using the echo cancellation technique standardised for use on the general switched telephone network and on point-to-point 2-wire leased telephone-type circuits
V.27ter	4800/2400 bits per second modem standardised for use in the general switched telephone network
V.32	A family of 2-wire, duplex modems operating at data signalling rates of up to 9600 bit/s for use on the general switched telephone networks and on leased telephone-type circuits
V.100	Interconnection between public data networks (PDNs) and the public switched telephone network (PSTN)

V.110	Support of data terminal equipments (DTEs) with V-series type interfaces by an integrated services digital network (ISDN)

X. Series

X.3	Packet assembly/disassembly facility (PAD) in a public data network
X.21	Interface between the data terminal equipment (DTE) and the data circuit-terminating equipment (DCE) for synchronous operation on public data networks
X.21bis	Use on public data networks of data terminal equipment (DTE) which is designed for interfacing to synchronous V-Series modems
X.22	Multiplex DTE/DCE interface for user classes 3–6
X.25	Interface between the data terminal equipment (DTE) for terminals operating in the packet mode and connected to public data networks by dedicated circuit
X.28	DTE/DCE interface for a start-stop mode data terminal equipment accessing the packet assembly/disassembly facility (PAD) in a public data network situated in the same country
X.29	Procedures for the exchange of control information and user data between a packet assembly/disassembly (PAD) facility and a packet mode DTE or another PAD
X.30	Support of X.21 and X.21bis based data terminal equipments (DTEs) by an integrated services digital network (ISDN)
X.31	Support of packet mode terminal equipment by an ISDN
X.32	Interface between data terminal equipment (DTE) and data circuit-terminating equipment (DCE) for terminals operating in the packet mode and accessing a packet switched public data network through a public switched telephone network or a circuit switched public data network
X.71	Decentralised terminal and transit control signalling system on international circuits between synchronous data networks
X.75	Terminal and transit call control procedures and data transfer system on international circuits between packet-switched data networks
X.200	Reference Model for Open Systems Interconnection for CCITT Applications
X.210	Open Systems Interconnection (OSI) Layer Service Definition Conventions
X.213	Network Service Definition for Open Systems Interconnection (OSI) for CCITT Applications
X.214	Transport Service Definition for Open Systems Interconnection (OSI) for CCITT Applications

X.215	Session Service Definition for Open Systems Interconnection (OSI) for CCITT Applications
X.244	Transport Protocol Specification for Open Systems Interconnection (OSI) for CCITT Applications
X.225	Session Protocol Specification for Open Systems Interconnection (OSI) for CCITT Applications
X.224	Procedure for the exchange of protocol identification during virtual Call Establishment on Packet Switched Public Data Networks
X.250	Formal description techniques for data communications protocols and services
X.300	General principles and arrangements for interworking between public data networks and other public networks
X.310	Procedures and arrangements for data terminal equipments accessing circuit switched digital data services through analogue telephone networks
X.400	Message handling systems: system model-service elements
X.401	Message handling systems basic service elements and optional user facilities
X.408	Message handling systems: encoded information type conversion rules
X.409	Message handling systems: presentation transfer syntax and notation
X.410	Message handling systems: remote operations and reliable transfer service
X.411	Message handling systems: message transfer layer
X.420	Message handling systems: interpersonal messaging user agent layer
X.430	Message handling systems: access protocol for Teletex terminals
X.ds1	Directory systems: model and service elements (Draft Recommendation January 1986)
X.ds2	Directory systems: information framework (Draft Recommendation January 1986)
X.ds3	Directory systems: protocols (Draft Recommendation January 1986)
X.ds4	Directory systems: standard attribute types (Draft Recommendation January 1986)
X.ds6	Directory systems: suggested naming practices (Draft Recommendation January 1986)
X.ds7	Directory systems: authentication framework (Draft Recommendation January 1986)

I. Series

I.120	Integrated Service Digital Networks (ISDNs)

I.210	Principles of telecommunication services supported by an ISDN
I.211	Bearer services supported by an ISDN
I.212	Teleservices supported by an ISDN
I.310	ISDN – Network functional principles
I.430	Basic user-network interface – Layer 1 specification
I.431	Primary rate user-network interface – Layer 1 specification
I.440	ISDN user-network interface data link layer – general aspects
I.441	ISDN user-network interface data link layer specification
I.450	ISDN user-network interface Layer 3 – general aspects
I.451	ISDN user-network interface Layer 3 specification

II International Standards Organisation (ISO) International Standards (IS), Draft International Standards (DIS) and Draft Proposals (DP)

IS 7498	Information processing systems – Open Systems Interconnection – Basic Reference Model (1984)
IS 1538	Programming languages – Algol 60 (1984)
IS 1539	Programming languages – Fortran (1980)
IS 1989	Programming languages – Cobol (1985)
IS 6160	Programming languages – PL/1 (1979)
IS 6373	Programming languages – Basic (1984)
IS 6937	Information processing – coded character sets for text communication (1983)
DIS 2110	Data communication – 25-pin DTE/DCE interface connector and pin assignment
DIS 7776	Information processing systems – data communications – high-level data link control procedures – description of the X.25 LAPB compatible DTE data link procedures
DIS 8072	Information processing systems – Open Systems Interconnection – transport service definition
DIS 8073	Information processing systems – Open Systems Interconnection – connection oriented transport protocol specification
DIS 8208	Data communication – X.25 packet level protocol for data terminal equipment

DIS 8326	Information processing systems – Open Systems Interconnection – basic connection oriented session service definition
DIS 8327	Information processing systems – Open Systems Interconnection – basic connection oriented session protocol specification
DIS 8348	Information processing systems – data communications – network service definition
DIS 8473	Information processing systems – data communications protocol for providing the connectionless-mode network service
DP 8485	Programming languages – APL
DP 8505	Information processing systems – text communication – functional description and service specification for message oriented text interchange system, (MOTIS)
DP 8509	Information processing systems – Open Systems Interconnection – service conventions
DP 8571	Open Systems Interconnection – file transfer, access and management (Parts 1, 2, 3, 4)
DIS 8602	Information processing systems – Open Systems Interconnection – protocol for providing the connectionless-mode transport service
DP 8613	Information processing systems – text preparation and interchange – document structures (Parts 1, 2, 3, 4)
DP 8632	Information processing systems – computer graphics metafile for transfer and storage of picture description information (Parts 1, 2, 3, 4)
DP 8648	Information processing systems – data communications – internal organisation of the network layer
DP 8649	Information processing – Open Systems Interconnection – definition of common application service elements (Parts 1, 2, 3)
DP 8650	Information processing – Open Systems Interconnection – specification of protocols for common application service elements (Parts 1, 2, 3)
DP 8651	Graphical Kernel System (GKS) language bindings (Part 1 – Fortran; part 2 – Pascal; part 3 – Ada)
DIS 8652	Programming languages – Ada
DP 8802/1	Local area networks – Part 1: general introduction
DP 8802/2	Information processing systems – local area networks – Part 2: logical link control
DP 8802/3	Information processing systems – local area networks – Part 3: carrier sense multiple access with collision detection

DP 8802/4	Information processing systems – local area networks – Part 4: token-passing bus access method and physical layer specification
DP 8802/5	Information processing systems – local area networks – Part 5: token ring access method and physical layer specification
DP 8802/6	Information processing systems – local area networks – Part 6: slotted ring access method and physical layer specification
DP 8822	Open Systems Interconnection – presentation service definition
DP 8823	Open Systems Interconnection – presentation protocol specification
DP 8824	Information processing – Open Systems Interconnection – specification of abstract syntax notation one (ASN.1)
DP 8825	Information processing – Open Systems Interconnection – specification of basic encoding rules for abstract syntax notation one (ASN.1)
DP 8831	Open Systems Interconnection – job transfer and manipulation concepts and services
DP 8832	Open Systems Interconnection – specification of the basic class protocol for job transfer and manipulation
DP 8878	Information processing systems – data communications – use of the X.25 to provide the open systems interconnection connection-oriented network service
DIS 8879	Information processing – text and office systems – Standard Generalised Markup Language (SGML)
DP 8886	Information processing systems – data communications – data link service definition for OSI
DP 8907	Information processing systems – database languages – network database language
DP 9007	Information processing systems – concepts and terminology for the conceptual schema and the information base
DP 9040	Information processing – Open Systems Interconnection – OSI virtual terminal service
DP 9041	Information processing – Open Systems Interconnection – OSI virtual terminal protocol
DP 9063/1	Information processing – text preparation and interchange equipment – text charts and text patterns – Part 1: facsimile equipment
DP 9063/2	Information processing – text preparation and interchange equipment – text charts and text patterns – Part 2: teletex equipment
DP 9064/1	Information processing – text and office systems – minimum information to be included in specification sheets – Part 1: facsimile equipment

DP 9064/2   Information processing – text and office systems – minimum informa-
             tion to be included in specification sheets – Part 2: character coded text
             and office systems including equipment suitable for participating in the
             CCITT telex and teletex services

DP 9075   Information processing systems – programming languages – relational
             database language

Appendix D
Glossary of Acronyms

The use of acronyms in the Information Technology industry is a widespread reality. The papers presented in this book are no exception: in most cases the authors explain the acronyms they use the first time they use them, but not subsequently. The following is a list of the more widely applicable acronyms used.

ACE	Automatic Cross-connection Equipment
ACF/VTAM	Advanced Communication Facility (VTAM)
ACSE	Association Service Control Element
Alvey	(Name) See note at end of section 24
AFNOR	French Standards Institute
ANA	Article Numbering Association
ANSI	American National Standards Institute
APPC	Advanced Program to Program Communication
ARP	Address Resolution Protocol
ARPANET	Advanced Research Projects Agency Network
ASN.1	Abstract Syntax Notation One
ATM	Automatic Teller Machine
AT&T	American Telephone & Telegraph Company
BIGFON	Experimental German videophone service
BFICC	British Facsimile Industry Consultative Committee
BSC	Binary Synchronous Communication/Control
BSGL	Branch Systems General License
BSI	British Standards Institution
BT	British Telecom
CAD	Computer Aided/Assisted Design
CAM	Computer Aided/Assisted Manufacturing
CASE	Common Application Service Element
CBMS	Computer Based Message System
CBX	Computerised Branch Exchange
CCCCP	Committee on Computer-Computer Communication Protocols
CCITT	International Telegraph & Telephone Consultative Committee
CCIR	International Radio Consultative Committee

CCR	Commitment, Concurrency & Recovery
CEC	Committee of European Communities
CENLEC	European Committee for Electrotechnological Standardisation ('normalisation')
CEPT	Conference of European Postal & Telecommunications Administrations
CERN	European Nuclear Research Centre
CFR	Cambridge Fast Ring
CHIEF	Customs Handling of Import & Export Freight
CICS	Customer Information Control System
CIM	Computer Integrated Manufacturing
CL/CO	Connectless/Connection-Oriented
CLIST	Command List
CMC	Communications Management Configuration
CMP	Communications Management Processor
CNM	Communications Network Manager/Management
Codec	Coder/decoder (analogue/digital)
CO-LAN	Central Office-Local Area Network
COS	Corporation for Open Systems (USA)
CO/TP	Connection-Oriented Transaction Protocol
CPE	Customer Premises Equipment
CRT	Cathode Ray Tube
CSDN	Circuit Switched Data Network
CSMA/CD	Carrier Sense Multiple Access with Collision Detect
CSPDN	Circuit Switched Public Data Network
DACS	Digital Access & Cross-connect System
DARPA	Defense Advanced Research Projects Agency (USA)
DASS	Digital Access Signalling System
DATEX-L	German digital circuit switched service
DATEX-P	German packet switched service
DBP	Deutsche Bundespost, the German PTT
DCA	Document Content, Architecture
DCE	Data Circuit Terminating Equipment
DDN	Defense Data Network (USA)
DE	Data Element
DEC	Digital Equipment Corporation
DEPS	Departmental Entry Processing System
DIA	Document Interchange Architecture
DIN	German Standards Institute

DIS	Draft International Standard
DISH	Data Interchange for Shipping (UK)
DISOSS	Distributed Office Support System
DNA	DEC Network Architecture
DoD	Department of Defense (USA)
DP	Draft Proposal (standard)
DPNSS	Digital Private Network Signalling System
DSA	Directory Service Agent
DSE	Data Switching Equipment
DTE	Data Terminal Equipment
DTI	Department of Trade & Industry (UK)
DU	Data Unit
EAN	Electronic Article Numbering
ECMA	European Computer Manufacturers Association
ECU	European Currency Unit
EDI	Electronic Data Interchange
EDP	Electronic Data Processing
EEC	European Economic Community
EMS	Electronic Message Systems
EMUG	European MAP Users Group
ENA	Extended Network Addressing
EP	Emulator Package
ESPRIT	European Strategic Pre-competitive Research Programme for Information Technology
FADU	File Access Data Unit
FAX	Facsimile transmission
FDDI	Fibre Distributed Data Interface
FDM	Frequency Division Multiplexing
FTAM	File Transfer, Access & Management
FTP	File Transfer Protocol
GOSIP	Government OSI Profile
GRIN	Graded Index (optical fibre)
GTMOSI	General Teleprocessing Monitor for OSI
GUS	Guide to the Use of Standards
HDLC	High-level Data-Link Control
HM	Her Majesty's (UK), eg HM Customs
IBC	Integrated Broadband Communications
IBCN	Integrated Broadband Communication Network

IBM	International Business Machines
ICA	Integrated Communications Adaptor
ICL	International Computers Ltd
ID	Identity/Identifier
IDA	Integrated Digital Access pilot project
IEEE	Institute of Electrical & Electronic Engineers
IFIP	International Federation for Information Processing
IKBS	Intelligent Knowledge Based Systems
IMS	Information Management System
IPM	Interpersonal Messaging Service
IS	International Standard
ISDN	Integrated Services Digital Network
ISO	International Standards Organisation
ITI	Industrial Technology Institute
ITU	International Telecommunications Union
IVDT	Integrated Voice/Data Terminal
JEDI	Joint Electronic Data Interchange
KDD	Kokusai Denshin Denwa Co Ltd (Japanese international carrier)
LAN	Local Area Network
LAPB	Link Access Procedure/Protocol B (X.25)
LAPD	Link Access Procedure/Protocol D (ISDN)
LCN	Logical Channel Number
LEN	Low Entry Networking
LLC	Logical Link Control
LU	Logical Unit
MAN	Metropolitan Area Network
MAP	Manufacturing Automation Protocol
MDN	Managed Data Network
Megastream	British Telecom 2.048 Mbits/s offering
MHS	Message Handling System
Minitel	French videotex based service/terminal
MMFS	Manufacturing Message Format System
MMI	Man-Machine Interface
MMS	Manufacturing Message Service
Modem	Modulator/demodulator (digital/analogue)
MOTIS	Message Oriented Text Interchange System
MSAU	Multi Station Access Unit
MTA	Message Transfer Agent

MTL	Message Transfer Layer
MTS	Message Transfer Service
MVS	Multiple Virtual Storage (operating system)
NBS	National Bureau of Standards (USA)
NCP	Network Control Program
NetBios	Network Basic Input/Output System
NetView	IBM's Network Management concept/products
NMA	Network Management Architecture
NPSI	NCP Packet Switching Interface
NTE	Network Terminating Equipment
NTO	Network Terminal Option/Operator
OA	Office Automation
O&M	Organisation & Methods
ODA	Office Document Architecture
ODETTE	European Motor Industry EDI Project
ODIF	Office Document Interchange Format
OFTEL	Office of Telecommunications (UK)
OR	Operations Research
OSI	Open Systems Interconnection
OSI-RM	OSI Reference Model
OSI-TP	OSI Transaction Processing
OSNS	Open Systems Network Support
PABX	Private Automated Branch Exchange
PAD	Packet Assembler/Dissembler
PAR	Positive Acknowledgement + Retransmission
PBX	Private Branch Exchange
PCM	Pulse Code Modulation
Pel	Picture Element
POTS	Plain Old Telephone Service
PSDN	Packet Switched Data Network
PSPDN	Packet Switched Public Data Network
PSTN	Public Switched Telephone Network
PTT/PT&T	Postal, Telegraph, & Telephone Administration
PC	Personal Computer
PS/2	Personal System/2
PU	Physical Unit
RACE	Research into Advanced Communications Technologies in Europe
RENAN	French ISDN pilot project – French philospher

RFS	Real File Store/System
RJE	Remote Job Entry
R/S/T	Reference Points in ISDN
SAP	Service Access Point
SASE	Specific Application Service Element
SC	Subcommittee
SCCP	Systems Services Control Point
SDLC	Synchronous Data Link Control
SE	Software Engineering, Systems Engineer
SITPRO	Simplification of International Trade Procedures
SLA	Service Level Agreement
SLR	Service Level Reporter
SMTP	Simple Mail Transfer Protocol
SNA	IBM's Systems Network Architecture
SNADS	SNA Distribution Services
SNI	SNA Network Interconnect
SPAG	Standards Promotion & Application Group (Europe)
SSRT	Sub-Second Response Time
S/T	Reference points in ISDN
TA	Terminal Adaptor
TC	Technical Committee
TCP/IP	Transmission Control Protocol/Internet Protocol
TDI	Trade Data Interchange
TDM	Time Division Multiplexer
TDMA	Time Division Multiple Access
Telnet	Specification within TCP/IP
TOP	Technical & Office Protocol
TP	Transaction Processing, Teleprocessing
TRADACOMS	Trading Data Communications
TRANSPAC	French packet switched network
TRMS	Transmission Resource Management System
TTX	Teletex
TTY	Teletype, Teleprinter
UA	User Agent
UAL	User Agent Layer
UDP	User Datagram Protocol
UNTDI	United Nations Trade Data Interchange
VADS	Value Added & Data Services

VAN(S)	Value Added Network (Services)
VAT	Value Added Tax
VDU	Visual Display Unit
VFS	Virtual File Store/System
VLSI	Very Large Scale Integration
VSAT	Very Small Apperture (satellite) Terminal
VTAM	Virtual Telecommunications Access Method
VTX	Videotex
WAN	Wide Area Network
WDM	Wavelength Division Multiplexing
WG	Working Group
XNS	Xerox Network System